*Slavery in
the United States*

Slavery in the United States

Four Views

JAMES C. MORGAN

McFarland & Company, Inc., Publishers
Jefferson, North Carolina, and London

My thanks to the publishers of the four books extensively discussed herein, for permission to reprint various passages. Specifically, to Little, Brown, for *Time on the Cross*, by Robert William Fogel and Stanley L. Engerman, ©1974 by Little, Brown and Company, Inc.; to Stanley M. Elkins and the University of Chicago Press, for Elkins' *Slavery: A Problem in American Institutional and Intellectual Life*, ©1968 by the University of Chicago Press; to Random House, for *The Peculiar Institution*, ©1956 by Kenneth M. Stampp; and to E.P. Dutton, for *American Negro Slavery*, by Ulrich B. Phillips, ©1918 by D. Appleton Co., Inc., ©renewal 1946 by Lucie M. Phillips.

Library of Congress Cataloguing-in-Publication Data

Morgan, James C., 1933–
  Slavery in the United States.

  Bibliography: p.
  Includes index.
  1. Slavery—United States—Historiography.
I. Title.
E441.M76   1985   973'.04960072   84-43220

ISBN 0-89950-162-1 (alk. paper)

Printed in the United States of America

McFarland   Box 611   Jefferson NC 28640

In memory of Bertram L. Mott, Jr.,
a much loved friend and Christian brother

Table of Contents

Acknowledgments

While studying at Princeton Theological Seminary, my mentor, Dr. D. Campbell Wyckoff, advised me to pursue graduate study at New York University. I am deeply indebted to him for his insight, encouragement, and patience in helping me to develop an interest in research. It was under his tutelage that the first seeds for this research were sown, and consequently reaped.

Dr. John Westerhoff, II, while teaching a course at Princeton Theological Seminary, enabled me to see the relativity of Christian principles to the daily routine which further increased the urgency for this research. I am grateful for the many telephone conversations and for his reading of the initial research proposal. His critique was most helpful in determining research parameters.

My friend and confidant, Dr. Bert Mott, spent many long hours reading and re-reading the many drafts which made the editing and revising much easier. He not only shared his time and expertise but allowed his home to become a favorite place for discussion and re-thinking. My gratitude cannot balance his unselfish giving and concern.

After coming to New York University and studying under Dr. Lee Belford, I was able, with his guidance, to develop the framework for this research. I am grateful for his quiet Southern charm and sensitivity to the ethnic situation embraced by this research.

I am grateful to God for a truly exceptional committee at New York University; the keen editorial eye of Dr. Roger Phillips; the ethnic sensitivity of Dr. Edward Ponder and the unrelenting drive of Dr. Norma Thompson for scholarly perfection, without which this research would have been meaningless. Dr. Thompson has been more than just a chairperson to me. She has been an unending spring of encouragement and enthusiasm, especially when the work became most difficult. More important than her scholarly guidance was her ability to always criticize without killing. If my appreciation could be measured to gold, she would be rich beyond comprehension.

It is impossible to acknowledge every person who aided this research. However, I would be very remiss if I did not thank the many librarians who spent countless hours locating hard-to-find books and manuscripts. I am especially grateful to Sandra Davis who on many occasions braved the elements in retrieving a book or material. I am also indebted to Claudia Taylor, my friend and typist, who spent many long hours away from her family typing the first draft of this research.

My children, even though pursuing an education away from home, supported this research in such a manner that my gratitude cannot equal.

My wife, Ada, while not fully understanding the urgency that drove me to "read just one more chapter," accepted the many hours I spent away from her and gave much needed support and joy to the whole family, never complaining. Thank you wife; thank you children; thank you friends.

Chapter I
Introduction

After returning to school in 1973 to complete my undergraduate work, I was amazed to find that most of my younger classmates had a very limited understanding of slavery and its effect on contemporary American thought.

Being brought up in the South, not far from where Nat Turner had his revolt, I had a deep-seated belief in the American way of life and especially the democratic form of government. All my life I had been taught to believe that "right will always prevail." I learned all that my limited and controlled environment would allow. Needless to say, I was not prepared for the many shocks that would follow my leaving the safety of my little community in Franklin, Virginia.

Upon entering a Northern college the first shock encountered was the confusion surrounding the identity of those American citizens of African descent born in the United States. Their history seemed to have been swallowed up in integrationist ideology. Blacks knew so little of their historical selves that the loss made almost no difference to their struggle upward.

Another shock came with the discovery of my own ignorance of American history. I was astounded to find libraries larger than one room; with microfilm; reference departments, and more than one person to help find material.

My education began with American history from the ground level. I soon found that I was most interested in the history of the slave and his community. I read everything I could find on North American slavery, which led me to investigate not only the institution itself but also the facts of culture that led to its establishment.

Format for the Investigation

Since the early 1860's, the United States government has made formal commitments to equal rights and freedom for all persons. The Confiscation Act of August 6, 1861, provided that any property used with the owner's consent and knowledge in aiding or abetting insurrection was lawfully subject to prize and capture. If the property consisted of slaves, they were to be forever free. Southern slaveholders were all of course considered insurrectionists. Many historians have believed however that because of the peculiar way in which Negroes gained their citizenship, they were not, in reality, able to enjoy the full benefit of this and subsequent human rights legislation.[1]*

Reading about the Confiscation Act, I at first found it difficult to understand how or why the African was enslaved. I did discover that the matter was far more complicated than I had thought. Robert Bone reports that when the Africans were brought to the New World, "they were quickly denuded of their native culture, tribal organization, language, family structure, religion—all were systematically extirpated."[2] What I and most blacks had been seeing in the movies and television about the African and his culture was restricted. Through my college reading, I was quickly forced to realize that the action of the slaveholders had caused the Africans' culture to approach a "zero" state. As one consequence, in the minds of most Americans, blacks included, the Africans became homeless as well as cultureless; thereby, their ability was limited to make constructive moral choices.

I began to look back to the part of my history that was cloudy. I began to wonder why so many Negroes did not want to discuss their history. Then, upon reading Novak's scheme for understanding a person's moral choices—which, simply put, states that for clarity, one should not only go back two generations but also go forward two generations—it became clear to me what faces most blacks who gaze backward over two generations. Elderly blacks would even find themselves in the institution of slavery. Here is the hotbed of feelings. Slavery, to most contemporary blacks, represents such a dark and ugly experience that they would disavow it. They pretend it has no relevance to their present situation. Novak wrote:

> To see the pattern of life adopted by a person's grandchildren is to discern more clearly the organic implications of the choices and efforts launched two generations earlier. Emotions, instincts, memory, imagination, passion, and ways of perceiving are passed on to us in ways we do not choose, and ways so rich with life that they lie far beyond the power of consciousness. We are ineffably ethnic in our values and our actions.[3]

Novak suggests (1) that a people's history determines its present as well as its future, (2) a people's history is neither negative nor positive, it its facts as they occurred, and (3) a people's history identifies them ethnically in the present as well as the future.

See Chapter Notes, beginning on page 159.

Armed with this little gem of enlightenment, I read David B. Davis' "Slavery and the Post-World War Historians." In this article Davis suggested that there are four primary views of slavery as it occurred in the United States: the (1) Progressive, (2) Racial Enlightenment, (3) Counter-Progressive, and (4) Cliometric Revolutional.[4]

The question that formed in my mind was, how could four different authors inspect the same sources and arrive at diverse conclusions? There had to be some overlooked data in the material, or each author brought to the research differing perceptions. The next question was, would either of these conditions—some missed information, or an outlook of one's own—allow slavery to be seen in such diverse ways? At this point in my research I found certain underlying social considerations that merited investigation.

Power is clearly the real "mover" in the Americanization process. Much concern for power exists among all citizens of the United States. There is womanpower, manpower, power for peace, armed power, green power, ethnic power, black power, and many more. Black power is one of the designations least understood. Some would believe that black power is the tool for liberating the black masses; others would believe that it propels the quest by Negroes for black domination.

According to Martin Luther King, Jr.,

> Black power, in its broad and positive meaning, is a call for black people to amass the political and economical strength to achieve their legitimate goals ... power is not desirable but necessary in order to implement the demands of love and justice. What is needed is a realization that power without love is reckless and abusive and love without power is sentimental and anemic. Power at its best is love implementing the demands of justice. Justice at its best is love correcting everything that stands against love.[5]

Negro Americans, as slaves, were denied access to the culture of their masters no doubt mostly, ultimately, because of a lack of power. Even today, as free Americans, blacks are not often seen as fully participating in the society at large. This is not to say that all Negro Americans were denied this access because there always have been individuals in every subculture who were able to be assimilated into the dominant culture. Black Americans are no exception economically. However, as Robert Coles so succinctly stated, "the Negro has his skin color to help him establish the nature of his problem and his belief, while white people must grapple for other mainstays of self-awareness or faith."[6] Thus it would seem that lack of power is one of the central elements of the "Negro problem."

In investigating the relationship between power and social roles I found that while America is a land of opportunity, it is also a land where racism predetermines the scope and nature of the ethnic's role. Black Americans, being farthest down on the ethnic ladder, usually receive first the effects of "racist views sharpened for the occasion." Accordingly Novak wrote:

> America is a land in which heterogeneous groups can find a toehold, a land changeable enough so that elites in power accurately feel threatened when rules of economic life and vectors of power change. But in part the ethnics were stamped 'inferior' because of racist views sharpened for the occasion. America is a land in which pride in English heritage gradually became pride in the Anglo-Saxon–Teutonic heritage, and the latter was all too near to pride in Nordic Race [Novak, pp. 80–81].

Therefore, since slavery was eliminated, economic and power sectors were changed with a resulting menace to the powerful. The degree and magnitude of this so called "threat" usually manifests itself by drastic change in governmental policy. And since the United States government is committed to universal human rights, this commitment seems to cause an increased demand on the natural and human resources which are shared by all people in the United States, blacks (ethnics) included. The Korean War, Vietnam, and World Wars I and II have added to this demand. Black Americans, while not enjoying "full citizenship," did endure the same hardships that were imposed upon those United States citizens who were able to enjoy full citizenship, and should be afforded the same consideration as any other citizen of the United States.

The seriousness of this denial of full citizenship to the Negro American is reflected by Franklin who stated that the National Negro Congress, late in 1946, filed a petition with the Economic and Social Council of the United Nations, seeking aid in the struggle to eliminate political, economic, and social discrimination in the United States. The fact that a people in the United States, created in and by people in the United States, should have to appeal to an international body, speaks very poorly for the democratic process.

In the democratic form of government, those forces controlling attitudes and policies towards human rights, domestic and foreign, are significant, both to the people who initiate the policy and those who are affected by the policy. An example of this significance is reflected in the military intervention in the integration of southern colleges and universities, beginning in 1956 with the Autherine Lucy/University of Alabama case. Even though federal troops were not used in settling the case, it marked the first major instance of federal/state clash over desegregation in the United States.[7]

This visible commitment of the United States government to ensure the civil rights of the Negro American was ambiguous in nature. On the one hand, it granted a limited amount of freedom to a few Negroes, while on the other hand, it created an atmosphere of "all is right with the world." Needless to say, the masses of Negroes remained and still remain in segregated school systems throughout the United

States. Admittedly, there are no signs over the doors, no governors to block door ways, and no visible restrictions in employment practices. If one would look closely, however, one would find few blacks in administration and teaching with very little change in the ideological structure of the school system. It remains a "white" structure, by whites and for whites.

Obviously "all was not right with the world," and by the time of the civil rights upheaval in 1956, when many people were expressing their views on the "Negro problem," very little thought was given to those attitudes and policies that had permitted slavery, caused a democratic constitution to be written, and set the United States government up as "the ideal model" for propagating a system of universal human rights. This dualism, nominal liberty and justice for all, and the actual liberty and justice for all had its roots in early English writings. Novak reports that David Hume, a noted English scholar, was able to write as early as 1748, "I am apt to suspect the Negroes, and in general all other species of men (for there are four or five kinds) to be naturally inferior to whites" (Novak, p. 83). While Hume was ethnocentric, he nevertheless expressed the dominant opinion held by Englishmen of his time. Thomas Jefferson, on the other hand, who was a proponent of human rights, owned slaves and even while he was espousing liberty and justice for all, his coffers were being lined with the profits from "black gold." According to Novak:

> Jefferson himself, restless about his attitudes, turns to a metaphor which is much used as the nineteenth century wears on, "the circumstance of superior beauty, is thought worthy attention in the propagation of our horses, dogs, and other domestic animals; why not in that of man?" [Novak, p. 84].

This statement by Jefferson, not only supports the notion of slave breeding but also posits support for the theory that the African while being human was no better than horses, dogs and other domestic animals. It is this ambivalence, where in one instance the slave is projected as a human while at the same instance he is compared with domestic animals, to which this discussion is directed with the intention of exploring the attitudes that would generate and support this type of ethnocentrism. It should be noted here that my purpose is not to explain the inhumanity found in the institution of slavery as that institution is recorded in history. My concern is with the attitudes that sponsored these inhumane conditions as they are related to the four models for interpreting slavery in the United States.

The issue that was most troublesome during this research was the ability of white Americans to "love" liberty and justice for themselves and their kind while at the same time depriving anyone believed to be of African descent of the right to liberty and justice. This dual attitude was seen clearly during the early era of civil rights movements. While the black American was struggling, in the streets of America, for humane treatment, many white Americans were struggling against them in the name of preserving "the American way of life." As soon as black Americans made sizeable gains, however, these same white Americans quickly adapted the methodology of the civil rights movements to gain more and better for themselves. Teachers, firemen, doctors, nurses, policemen, and the like all followed the movement pattern. It would seem that there is some equation between the blacks' struggle for equality and the struggle for equality by any minority; blacks cannot continue to be seen as apart. Gunnar Myrdal wrote, "the Negro problem is an integral part of, or special phase of, the whole complex of problems in the larger American civilization. It cannot be treated in isolation."[8] President Lyndon B. Johnson alluded to this:

> If we are to have peace at home, if we are to speak with one honest voice in the world — indeed, if our country is to live with its conscience — we must affect every dimension of the Negro's life for the better.[9]

Obviously, if the black is to have a "better" life, it will not result from legislation; one cannot legislate morality. It cannot come through using the tired methods of historiography nor can it arise outside the black community. It must come through new and unbiased methods of gathering data and new ways of interpreting them and via using new historiographers.

History teaches that each ethnic group in the United States has been able to survive as a group because it has been able to hold on to its particular traditions. Andrew Greeley quotes former Mayor Lindsay of New York City as saying:

> It is often stated that this city is a melting pot. That is not true. It is rather a series of small towns and neighborhoods. The strength of our city is in the addition of many separate cultures and traditions. The most stable of all our neighborhoods in New York City are those neighborhoods that have preserved traditions of language, traditions of dress, traditions of style of food, of look. Every person in our city came from somewhere.[10]

Accordingly, the stability of the black community depends upon its ability to preserve its culture. Therefore it is suggested that, since the contemporary black American's ancestors were Africans, who, according to Kardiner and Ovesey, had their African culture stripped from them, the contemporary black American's culture had its beginning in the institution of North American slavery. And according to Kardiner and Ovesey, the stripping away of a culture entails three conditions:

> (1) that the old types of organizations were rendered useless; (2) that the minimal conditions for maintaining a culture, or for developing a new one, were lacking and (3) that his adoption of American culture was, by the same token was limited. Hence the term acculturation cannot be applied to the Negro, at least not during slavery.[11]

Herein rests the core of the so-called Negro problem: since the slaves could not adopt the lost culture of their African forebears, they could not preserve the traditional language, dress, style of food, or religion; consequently, their offspring, the contemporary black American, does not have the support that historical continuity would bring. Black America long had no national holidays, no national symbols, and a negative national identity. In turn, the omission of these social constructs supports the premise that contemporary black Americans are often embarrassed by what would be their traditional foods, appearance and customs. This inability, on the part of contemporary blacks, to develop a sense of historical continuity and self-esteem hinders every aspect of Negro development including education. As a consequence, many educators suggest that if education is to be meaningful to blacks, they must first know their roots and have a pride in their beginnings. One of this country's leading educators, Martin Deutsch of New York University, wrote:

> Solution to the problem of children, particularly minority group children, involves the creation of social forms that can assist the youngster to achieve respect, identity, motivation to achieve, and intellectual purpose consistent with the changing necessities of our social system.[12]

This statement by Deutsch inadvertently suggests that a new understanding of culture must be reached before even education can become meaningful to all Americans, especially minority group Americans. Subsequently, this new understanding must mandate the necessary interpretive elements for examining the minority group's history and culture to the end that their history and culture will be afforded its pragmatic essence. Needless to say, in the case of blacks, slavery must be reexamined without passion and with the determination to firmly establish it as the milieu out of which came America's version of negritude.

Coles seemed to support this type of determination when he suggested that, while education is one tool for mainstreaming a minority group, the cultural bases of that educative process are the significant elements in the mainstreaming process (Coles, pp. 258-59). Since education and culture are so interrelated, it is of primary importance to the minority groups and especially the Negroes, to not only have their culture authenticated and documented, but also to have this information available for those around them so that the effects of social deprivation normally associated with blacks may be viewed with a broader understanding. Accordingly, Deutsch wrote:

> In many respects, the awareness of the retarding effects of social deprivation associated with ethnic group and social class membership offers an opportunity to develop procedures for all children who function below their intellectual capability [Deutsch, p. 3].

Here again is indication that new procedures are needed in the attempt to mainstream the minority group. And while this is a general statement, blacks should be considered first. For example, when a Frenchman

migrates to America, he is highly respected if he maintains a large degree
of his French ethnicity. On the other hand, Negroes born in America
who maintain a pragmatic sense of their culture are usually ostracized
by their own group and severely criticized by the dominant group. This
neither "in" nor "out" configuration tends to stagnate the development
of the Negro group. They are locked in a social bind that forces them
to attempt to be "something that they are not"; they either become "super
ethnics" with a WASP mentality or they are labeled anti–American.

With respect to those attitudes which foster the assumption that
black Americans are "culturally deprived" and therefore unable to determine the proper course of action for themselves to develop fully as
Americans, Coles wrote:

> I have come to see that children who grow up and experience the Negro's
> lot in our society, no matter how various its experience achieve at least
> some measure of self-determination [p. 259].

The strength of Coles' statement can only be explicated through a proper experience in negritude. And this proper experience must not be contaminated by the influence of WASP pressures. In a word, Coles was
alluding to one of the "mystic" elements within the social relationship
between the oppressor and the oppressed. For example, the slave hated
his slavery yet he could develop an attachment for his enslaver; likewise,
he realized that he was powerless yet he developed a scheme for succeeding
as a free person. Coles noted that those Negro children who "experience
the Negro's lot" tend to have a better sense of who they are and how
to get the best out of life. This could indicate that a better way for
mainstreaming the negroid masses may well lie in the development of
an educational system where minority cultures become an equal part of
the curriculum. Furthermore, it could also be suggested that cultural
assimilation is not necessarily the means for mainstreaming blacks.

Since one of the aims of this investigation was to determine the effect
of North American slavery upon the developing Negro culture, the four
models selected, Progressive, Racial Enlightenment, Counter-Progressive,
and Cliometric Revolutional, represent different conceptions of the Negro
American's culture. Accordingly, these four views of slavery in the United
States provide four different frameworks for analyzing the so-called "Negro
problem," generate new ways for interpreting the institution and effects
of slavery by supplying raw data needed for comparing the contrasting
the four different views, provide the elements needed to formulate a
"new" base for aiding blacks to better understand and accept themselves,
and provide a means for helping other ethnics to better understand the
black American with the aim of developing better ethnic relations in the
United States.

It was necessary for me to determine what data should be used among
the various primary sources and the wealth of secondary material. I
selected *American Negro Slavery* by U.B. Phillips because it represents

the earliest, most widely accepted historical interpretation of slavery in the United States. David B. Davis said of this work, "It helped to rehabilitate the South's progressive image by picturing slavery as a system of racial adjustments which had arisen in response to environmental pressures and human needs" (Davis, p. 2).

The book was written in 1918, at which time historians were divided on their views of slavery. Some regarded it as morally right; others found it indefensible. And for the next decade this book was considered by historians to be the only comprehensive scholarly work on slavery in the United States.

The author, U.B. Phillips, was a Southerner who believed in the moral structure of the South; he found it difficult to believe that a social order built on such high moral values could rest on such a corrupt foundation as slavery. Therefore, Phillips disregarded all other material, such as legal codes and traveler's accounts, and relied exclusively on the data furnished by actual plantation records. *American Negro Slavery*, according to Elkins, is, therefore, "a sympathetic account of the old plantation regime."[13]

It would seem that Phillips does not display a deep-seated hatred for Negroes. He understands them to be as children: cheerful and content with their relation to their masters. To Phillips, slavery was good for all parties concerned and good for every aspect of human development.[14] While the basic assumption in *American Negro Slavery* is that of the innate and inherited racial inferiority of the Negro, its value to this investigation rests in its scholarly treatment of the data, its role as the forerunner of progressivism and its ability to posit an aspect of slavery that only the proslavery mind could perceive. This book represents, to many historians, the challenge that fostered many more investigations of North American slavery. Thus it provides, to this investigation, a basis developing and judging the other three views expressed here.

In *The Peculiar Institution*, Kenneth Stampp is credited with the dethroning of Phillips as the authority on slavery in the U.S. Davis says, "Stampp has resolved the tension between progressive historiography and post–World War enlightenment" (Davis, p. 2). Therefore, this view of slavery is, first, the antithesis of Phillips' ideology; second, it represents the first Northern scholarly interpretation of slavery that was not polemical since Phillips, and third, it moved the interpretation of slavery from a moral position to one based on scientific investigation.

Stampp considered himself to have a better understanding of negritude: "One must know," he wrote, "what slavery meant to the Negro and how he reacted to it before one can comprehend his more recent tribulation."[15] Stampp "shifted the interpreted image of the Negro from a child-like, carefree simpleton to a less involved white child in a black skin. Innately, Negroes are, after all, only white men with black skins, nothing more, nothing less" (Stampp, pp. vii–viii). This statement allowed Davis to say about Stampp, "Stampp has come to symbolize the unwitting arrogance of white integrationists" (Davis, p. 2). Regardless of Stampp's "white integrationist's ideology," his book supplied a new conceptual framework for viewing slavery.

Slavery, by Stanley M. Elkins, represents the ideology of the counter-progressive historians. He was recognized by this group as their chief theoretician on slavery. Elkins structured his theory around the premise that slavery in Latin America was more open and flexible than in North America, and that this brought about a negative change in its victims. He suggested that North American slavery was similar to the Nazi concentration camps. He compared the behavior of these camp inmates with that of the Negro slave. Elkins believed that "slavery as we know it was created in America by Englishmen" (Elkins, p. 38). Elkins' method of developing conceptual categories and his answers to the questions evolving out of them, along with the debate that followed, were of paramount significance because they provide a useful means for interpreting the relationship between cultural heritage and economic pressure and between Negro accommodation and resistance to major cultural influences.

While Elkins' *Slavery* brought to this investigation a new and different view of slavery, it also complemented the two previous views in that it used Phillips' view as a model. Fogel and Engerman, however, in their *Time on the Cross*, provided the genesis for the cliometric revolutional view. This view embraces the ideology that slavery was a highly profitable investment; it was beneficial to the South's economy because the yield from slavery was comparable to investments in northern manufacturing. Slavery when seen from this point of view acquires a profitability status and as such tends to support the abolitions' ideology.

These authors structured their theory around four significant points: (1) slaves were highly efficient and productive workers, (2) slave agriculture was 35 per cent more efficient than the Northern system of family farming, (3) slave labor was successfully adapted to urban and industrial conditions, and (4) slave owners provided their workers with a material standard of life that compared favorably with that of free industrial workers.[16] Subsequently, by departing from the traditional interpretation of slavery, Fogel and Engerman provided a scientific means for cross-examining the previously cited views of slavery in the United States. Needless to say, this departure brought to the historical debate new ideas that previously might not have been accepted by most historians. These authors clearly posited slavery as a social institution that, even while restricting its victims, still allowed them the opportunity to develop as productive human beings.

The problem then became one of cause and effect. First, what were the attitudes of colonial Americans that would allow slavery to be developed? And second, how were these attitudes reflected in the developing group?

Attitudes Which Influenced Views of Slavery

Today, with many social problems escalating to disastrous dimensions, it is believed by many historians that the plight of the black American is lost in the concern for national survival and the urge to "keep busy" looking for solutions to the many national problems. Gunnar Myrdal warned many years ago, "America can no longer wait and see; she must do something big, and do it soon." Charles E. Silberman:

> But do what? — that's the rub. The prescription to do something appeals to the pragmatic bent of most Americans. But sheer busy-ness is not enough. Solving the problem of race is not only the most urgent piece of public business facing the United States today; it is the most difficult.[17]

Consequently, this problem, for which millions of dollars have been spent generating programs which would "give" black Americans such things as an integrated education, free medical care, fair employment practices, open housing, and help for dependent children, still remains, causing much anxiety and soul searching. In these troublesome times, to broach the institution of Negro American slavery as a means of understanding the culture of the black American is, to say the least, exasperating to some and simplistic to others. However, regardless of the trauma caused by such an approach and the money spent to alleviate the situation, the problem remains unsolved. The consequent anxiety, according to Martin Luther King, Jr., was spawned by guilt on the part of white America and self-hatred internalized by black America (King, pp. 33–36).

Rightfully, many Americans, black and white, will say that there are far too many books and articles already in circulation that deal with slavery. But regardless of the proliferation of slave literature, black Americans are still forced to prove their humanity every day; they are still considered to be outsiders. For America to continue to accept the black American's situation as something peripheral to normal American existence is tantamount to accepting the role of the institutional church as nonpolitical, saving souls while bodies die.[18]

While the Negro's situation is unique, the generating forces that produced the problem were, and are still, ingrained in the Americanization process.[19]* The transition from a free African to an African slave only occurred in the evolution of the original thirteen colonies from several independent provinces to statehood. Thus, if black America is to "arrive," every vestige of slavery must be probed until all of America is able to remove its effects from conscious thought; until there is no need for any America to be ashamed of history.

Hereafter in this chapter, references to page numbers only are to Jordan's White Over Black.

Obviously, this time has not yet come because modern blacks are still caught up in those attitudes that in the beginning allowed America to become a slave state. The question then becomes, what criteria were used in selecting people who were transported to become slaves in the United States?

Winthrop Jordan believed that when the Englishman first came into contact with the African, there were certain physical and social anomalies present which helped to determine the criteria for selecting the Africans as suitable candidates for slavery (pp. 3–4). While allowing Jordan's premise to formulate a basic explanation of the Englishman's first encounter with the African, many other authors will be cited as examining this premise.

Jordan believed that the most arresting element in this first encounter was the African's skin color (p. 4).[20] However, the African's darker skin was not the first complexion difference that Englishmen had encountered; they had been meeting people of color for many generations. It would seem that Englishmen were not as much concerned with the availability of a slave candidate as they were with delineating a threatening physical and social difference. Their method of delineation is best described by Jordan, "Englishmen could go a long way toward expressing their sense of being different from Negroes merely by calling them black" (p. 21). Once this difference was identified and clearly systematized, it was just a matter of "natural progression" to transfer their own ethnocentric values of black and blackness to the African (p. 11). (Is it not "peculiar" that many contemporary Negroes demand a black identity?) Inadvertently, the sudden shock of coming face to face with a historical and mythological figure of the black man forced Englishmen not only to explain the color difference, but to explore that difference for any and all similarities (pp. 44–46).

Causes for blackness

The Englishmen sought to find some scientific rationale for the conclusion they had reached concerning the dilemma that the African's skin color presented. This search started in Greek mythology, with "Phaeton driving the chariot sun wildly through the heavens," and ended somewhere between the "curse of Ham" and the "cliometrical conditions" theory (pp. 35–40). In either case, there is little or no evidence that would support or sustain the conclusions which the early English reached in determining the cause or causes for the African's skin color (pp. 11–20).[21]

Religious differences

Clifford Geertz believed that religion is the means through which a people's "ethos" comes to be reasonable and real:

> In religious belief and practice a group's ethos is rendered intellectually reasonable by being shown to be respectful of a way of life ideally adapted to the actual state of affairs the world view describes....[22]

Parsons, on the other hand, saw an ideology as a special sort of symbol system. He describes it as:

> A system of beliefs held in common by members of a collectivity ... which is oriented to the evaluative integration of the collectivity, by the process by which it develops to its given state, the goals to which its members are collectively oriented, and their relation to the future course of events.[23]

These statements by Geertz and Parsons seem to indicate that if the early English had attempted to understand the African's religious structure, they would have inevitably seen it as primitive and heathenistic because it was not oriented to the collective values of their own. The logical sequence of events, then, would have been for the English to either convert the Africans to their form of religion or assign them to a place outside their "real world." The English chose the latter because, according to Geertz, the "in religious group," saw religion as having two purposes:

> On the one hand, it objectivizes moral and aesthetic preferences by depicting them as the imposed conditions of life implicit in a world with a particular structure, as mere common sense given the unalterable shape of reality. On the other hand, it supports these received beliefs about the world's body by envoking deeply felt moral and aesthetic sentiments as experiential evidence for their truth [Geertz, p. 91].

Accordingly, the English believed the conversion of all non–Christians to be their sacred duty; therefore the heathenism of the African presented to them an opportunity to not only convert but to also relieve themselves of a dark mirror society. Jordan stated, "For Englishmen, then, the heathenism of Negroes was at once a counter-image of their own religion and a summons to eradicate an important distinction between the two people (p. 21). And for all intent and purposes, this conversion was absolutely necessary if the African and the American Indian were to measure up to "proper standards."

Since the English were a "Christian" people, they embraced the principle that all mankind sprang from one blood. However, they believed the blood of the Africans was "tainted" with heathenism as evidenced by their skin color. This allowed the English, first, to delay attempts to convert the African. Second, they mentally reduced the humanness of the African to a level below all other humans by asserting that the African's heathenism was a sinful condition which set them apart from the Christian God (p. 156).

Geertz, however, was of the opinion that a proper understanding of religious meanings embraced the principle that the symbols which constitute the religion proper must be understood in context and, further, each religious system must be accepted or rejected on the merits of its own continuity.

Therefore, this writer suggests that the role of ancestor worship, sacrificial feast, initiation rites, spirit worship, divinations, and any such elements that comprise a religious system cannot be measured by elements of a different religious system; therefore, when the English observed the African's religious system, they placed a negative value on it because it was so different from their own. The cultural bias of the English would not allow them to see these differences as anything except heathenistic practices and, as a consequence, the Africans were perceived as heathens (p. 24).[25]

Savage behavior

The English thought that the African's general behavior was so different from their own that they could not accept him as fully human. Jordan wrote:

> The conditions of savagery—the failure to be civilized—set Negroes apart from Englishmen in an ill-defined but social fashion. Africans were different from Englishmen in so many ways: in their clothing, huts, farming, warfare, language, government, morals, and table manners [p. 253].

These obvious differences not only stigmatized the Africans, but also categorized them. They allowed physical differences to be the criterion for determining human worth. Although present, the cultural differences caused by locational influences were overlooked, thereby allowing all Africans to be grouped according to skin color. Jordan stated, "the Negro's blackness lay at the root of the eventual European predilection for dividing the world's population into white men and colored" (p. 25). Have white men changed their own minds or have they caused the Negro to agree with them?

This struggle by Englishmen to relativize their role in the New World created within them a kind of ethnocentrism which allowed the Africans to become, at least to English minds, the type of base beings which their behavior exemplified.

In other words, when viewed through the peculiar lens of English culture, Africanisms, whether cultural, artistic, or behavioral, were a clear representation of evil and godlessness. Jordan stated:

> The necessity of continuously measuring African practices with an English yardstick of course tended to emphasize the differences between the two groups, but it also made for heightened sensitivity to instances of similarity [pp. 28–29].[26]

These "heightened instances of similarity" also caused the English to look for concrete ways to show that these differences outweighed the similarities.

Likeness to apes

The notion that the early English considered the African akin to apes is somewhat difficult for contemporary minds to accept; however, as was noted earlier, even Thomas Jefferson thought it worthy to view the slave as a lower animal. Jordan stated, "if Negroes were likened to beast, there was in Africa a beast which was likened to men" (pp. 28–29).

This observation, as simplistic as it may seem, formed the bases for many negative conceptions of the African which, even late in the 20th century, hold a great influence in Western thought as evidenced by such studies as Edward Topsell's *History of the Four-footed Beast*, Robert and Ada Yorkes' *The Great Apes: A Study of Anthropoid Life*, and H.W. Johnson's *Apes and Ape Lore in the Middle Ages and Renaissance*. All give detailed accounts of some of the types of supposedly ape/man relationships.

While it is true that not all Englishmen viewed the Africans as "natural" to slavery, most seemed to believe that slavery was a means of removing Africans from their heathenistic surroundings. The general attitude seems to have been one of concern and indifference – concern in that the Christian notions of the non–African world demanded that even savages should be afforded the opportunity of Christian conversion; indifference in the sense that the Africans' physical and social differences allowed the English to prejudge all Africans as savage and heathens. Therefore the selection of Africans as candidates for slavery was not just a matter of supply and demand; it forced the creation of a new system of slave labor that stretched the laws of property rights to the point of revulsion. North American slavery was a system based on man owning man.

Support for the Views

The original settlers of America were of European ancestry who in the process of building a nation became an ethnic amalgam of many peoples; and regardless of the amount of assimilation, each of these ethnic groups could then, as well as now, trace their ancestry back to their original roots. Africans, on the other hand, came by force, having all ancestral ties (except skin color) severed, and after some three hundred years or more of exposure to the American cultural system, cannot even trace their ancestry back to their last slave residence (Kardiner and Ovesey, pp. 38–44).[55] Negro American culture had its beginning in slavery and, therefore, should be considered a product of it.

Heretofore, Negro American culture has not been afforded an identity apart from its roots. It has always been viewed as an African culture struggling to become Americanized. As a consequence, this "struggling African culture" has always been accepted as a lower or primitive culture whose participants must be reflective of the demands of primitivism. This situation, in turn, forces the Negro American to be perceived as an outsider, doomed to the disgrace of having had slave status and of being a constant reminder to the slaveholders' progeny of the immorality of their ancestors.[28]

Since the Negro American's culture had its beginning in slavery, it stands to reason that the controlling mechanisms employed by the slaveholders would not only control the slaves but go a long way in determining the social outlook of the slaves. Alphonso Pinkney believed that this social outlook began with such things as the assigning of work details and work classification among the slaves. He stated, "slaveholders and their families, who usually preferred mulatto house servants, encouraged the division between house slaves and field slaves as a means of maintaining control over them."[29]

This method of control is reflected in all four views under discussion. Therefore, let it suffice to say here that one of the aims of North American slavery was to render the slave powerless. King believed that the black situation was one of powerlessness due to the lack of power on the part of the Negro and the immoral use of power by white America.[30] While this is true to the extent of the one culture clarifying the other, it does not address the issue of the powerlessness that is due to the Negro's inability to recognize and embrace the concept of negritude, a concept which defines and affirms the independent validity of Negro culture.

This inability allows the Negro the security that "false generosity" brings.[31] This pseudosecurity, in turn, gives the Negro a pseudofreedom which is dependent upon the benevolence of the greater society.

The false generosity premise, developed by Freire, is that an oppressed people become oppressed, first, by becoming victims of distortion. This distortion usually takes the form of perceiving oneself as less than human. The result is dissociation from history and the becoming of new persons created by the oppressor (Freire, p. 28).

The African, because of this distortion, received the status of slave which, to most white Americans, remains the most identifiable (except for skin color) of black Americans' attributes. Pinkney wrote:

> From 1877 to 1954 virtually all events pertaining to black people in the United States adversely affected their status. This period of more than seven decades saw profound changes in the society as a whole, but the Negro's status remains relatively fixed [Pinkney, p. 27].

Therefore, it seems very likely that once a people receive a given status rating, especially in a class and caste system, it is nearly impossible for them to lose it. Geertz, writing on status and status systems,

> The status system is a pure prestige system. From a man's title you know, given your title, exactly what demeanor you ought to display towards him and he towards you in practically every context of public life, irrespectively of whatever you may happen to think of him as a man [Geertz, p. 380].

As Geertz's words suggest, in accepting the African as a "savage and loathsome beast," the citizens of what was later to become the United States not only accepted a status system which titled the Africans and their progeny "slave," but also imposed the title "master" on and in the minds of white America for generations to come. It is important to note that this system was not arbitrarily conceived nor, for the most part, randomly accepted. It was born out of the conviction that the African is racially inferior to all other ethnic groups.[32]

Slavery, the Civil War, and Reconstruction all tended to harden the Southern planters into a "blame the Negro syndrome." The destruction of the South in the war was so devastating that many people traveling through it could not believe what they observed.[33]

As a consequence of this destruction, the South retaliated against Negroes, using such things as the Black Codes, Jim Crow Laws, and murder to force the newly freed blacks to succumb to a form of life just short of that which they had known in slavery.[34]

Needless to say, the climate became one of heated passion and distortion. There were lynchings, rapes, and murders. The Negro once again became the victim of circumstance and out of desperation many Negro leaders urged the masses to take up arms for their own protection.[35] The 80 or 85 year period after the fall of the Confederacy has been thoroughly examined. It would not serve the purpose of this book to review the many volumes written on the subject. Let it suffice to say here that many authors

saw this period in American history (1865–1950) as a troublesome time
for black America (Tannenbaum, p. 52).[36]

The hostile attitudes of white America towards black America had
their beginnings in the circumstances that arose in response to the early
Englishman's struggle for a sustaining autonomy. The question then
becomes, what was the mental attitude of white Americans, as reflected
in their behavior, that would allow the acceptance of slavery in the United
States? In the preface of his book, *White Over Black*, Jordan wrote the
following:

> A comprehension of the past seems to have two opposite advantages
> in the present: It makes us aware of how different people have been in
> other ages and accordingly enlarge our awareness of the possibilities of
> human experience, and at the same time it impresses upon us those
> tendencies in human beings which have not changed and which accord-
> ingly are unlikely to at least in the immediate future [p. ix].

If Jordan's understanding of history is correct, the logical place to start
in search for an understanding of black culture and negative white attitudes towards blacks is with that portion of American and European
history which deals with the institution of slavery. Anyone examining
this history will learn that African culture has been explored from all
angles but one. It has not been systematically examined from the point
of view of the slaves, and as a result, these previous examinations attempted to fit the African and black American culture into the traditional prescription. (Rawick's massive work is the exception.)

St. Clair Drake believes that Americans of other than northern and
western European ethnic background are beginning to demand participation in writing their own history.[37] One educator, in addressing the
problem of Negro historiography stated that black historians have a
responsibility that extends beyond what is normally required of white
historians: "the black historian, if he is to serve his generation, must not
hesitate to declare what he thinks the results of his studies mean."[38]

Granting that Chancellor Williams' and Drake's positions are valid,
then Jordan's position on the value of history towards a proper understanding of the present is all the more a guide to understanding Negro
American slavery and black American culture.

While using many authors' views, I have not in the chapters that
follow "hesitated to declare what I think the results of my study mean."
This approach to historiography may offend some and seem simplistic
to others, it, nevertheless, is necessary if black America is to find a "proper place in American history" (Drake, p. 7).[39]

In attempting to develop an unbiased understanding of the attitudes
and behaviors that permitted slavery to be accepted in the United States,
I discovered many ambiguous relationships.

A *fear/jealousy complex*

This complex caused many white males to fear the imputed sexual competency of the male slave, based partially on his own sexual ineptitude and mythical belief in the large size of the male slave's penis.[40] This fear of the Negro male's sexual ability was demonstrated by the many acts of castration performed against him during and immediately following slavery.

Every facet of human development in the contemporary black American, especially the male, is affected by this complex, resulting in black males' not being able to have leading roles opposite white females in the theater, in motion pictures. Furthermore, in most instances, administrative positions in places where large numbers of white females are employed have been denied the black male. Fear and jealousy on the part of the white male forces the black male to be "tied to his woman's apron string," which affects every generation of black male children. This position will be examined more fully in the final chapter.

Paradoxical relationship

This relationship between whites and blacks offered love and hatred simultaneously. For example, the white male could keep the black female slave in a subhuman environment, expose her to every imaginable degradation, and yet force her to be his companion in love making. The slave could hate slavery and yet do "acts of kindness" for his master. The master could whip a slave to the brink of death, and grieve at the death of that slave or members of that slave's family. Frederick Douglass suffered from this kind of paradoxical relationship. He wrote:

> I was again seized with a feeling of great insecurity and loneliness. I was yet liable to be taken back, and subject to all of the tortures of slavery ... but the loneliness overcame me. There I was in the midst of thousands, and yet a perfect stranger; without home and without friends, in the midst of thousands of my own brethern—children of a common father, and yet I dared not to unfold to anyone of them my sad condition.[41]

It should be noted that Douglass married a white woman. This points to another side of the complex: when some blacks gain a measure of success, they marry whites. This cannot be explained within the framework of WASP mentality, nor can it be understood outside of negritude. It is an outgrowth of slavery and the Americanization process and until this process is redefined, blacks and whites will continue to be locked in this paradoxical relationship.

Human/beast complex

This relationship produced a situation where the Negro was neither
human nor beast. And baptism could not "save" his soul nor could Christianity "wash him whiter than snow." But to deny blacks access to the
Christian way was to deny a central ethic. Therefore, as with their labor,
Negroes were "allowed" a limited return for their efforts. They could use
the master's system of "control theology" as a religious base. They could
serve the Euro-American god as long as he was subjected to the god of
the slave masters, and they could "shout" and "feel" the Holy Ghost as
long as it did not "teach" them truth. Joseph R. Washington, a prominent theologian at Albion College, wrote:

> It is our contention that the dominant white's color prejudice against
> Negroes is rooted in irrationalism that should be seen as the preconscious
> religion of white folk ... to be European was to be white and a master,
> to be African was to be colored and the slave of the white European
> master.... [It] was simply assumed from the beginning that colored peo-
> ple were destined (damned) to be slaves, and slaves were destined
> (damned) to be colored people without religious heritance.[42]

History suggests that not only were the Africans forced to come to
America, they were forced to give up their cultural heritage as well as
their traditions (Kardiner and Ovesey, p. 40).[43]

Granting that these were the conditions under which the African
enslavement began in America, the question becomes, could the Africans
sustain their culture under the strains of slavery? Kardiner and Ovesey
believed that the minimal conditions for the continuation of culture are
that (1) its constituents must be able to survive in sufficient numbers
to be able to perpetuate themselves, (2) its institutions must have
a functional relevance to the problems that confront the group, (3)
the relationships between the various statuses in the society—age, sex,
and social roles—must be able to continue in such a way that mutual
aggression and antagonisms do not disrupt essential cooperation, (4)
minimal instinctual satisfaction must be permitted each constituent to
preserve a workable balance between frustration and gratification, (5) each
constituent must be permitted at least minimal access to the whole
culture, and (6) emotional reciprocal interaction must be permitted the
various constituents (Kardiner and Ovesey, pp. 40–41).[44]

The African's culture was not afforded these conditions to the extent that they could survive in measurable numbers, and as a consequence,
the African's culture ceased to exist in contemporary American (Frazier,
p. 1).[45]

In reading the many accounts of slavery I have found the voice of
the slaves ignored. It seems that classical Western thought decided that

because of the conditions of slavery, the slave was rendered incapable of meaningful self-expression. Phillip Curtin seemed to think that this was due to the biased nature of western historiography:

> Two traditions formerly dominant in western historiography discouraged an earlier concern about Africa. One was a deep ethnocentric bias; history in France, and American history in the United States. Africa was simply beside the point, and history was also elitist concerned with those who governed countries, won battles, invented, discovered, and innovated. It was not much interested in ordinary people of Europe and America, much less of Africa.[46]

Subsequently, these restrictions on serious historical research set up limits which allowed scientific racism and xenophobic prejudice to control the type of research as well as the level and degree to which a "peripheral" culture would be examined. Robert Cruden offered a reason for this failure in historiography:

> Until we have devised some means whereby the historian may isolate his judgments as historian from the influences of his own past and his own cultural milieu; perhaps more importantly, some means whereby the community of historical scholars may abstract its critical judgments from the unexamined assumptions which it makes about the nature of knowledge, of man, of society, it seems premature to talk of history as a genuinely scientific discipline. Until that happy day, the historian will have to continue to beware of the lies of honest men—including his own.[47]

Cruden and Curtin seem to be agreeing with Williams, and if their premise is correct, it would explain why the African's culture is still being viewed as comparative to European culture. Further, this condition allows serious historical research to be restricted and the Third World to have little or no control over the interpretation of its own history and culture. As stated earlier, when a young man, I only knew the African to be a savage, afraid of Tarzan, desiring the love of white people and needing white dominance in order to survive. I was taught by history, for example, that Nat Turner was an ungrateful brute who was deluded by Satan to kill "innocent" white women and children. I was made ashamed of my African heritage and made to believe that "black must get back" while to be "white was all right." While Cruden and Curtin and Williams espouse a means of liberating the minds of all oppressed people, their voices go unheard.

The result has been that the Americanized African became a transplated African, forced to give up his heritage and become homeless. Having no viable means of acquiring the power necessary to make him acceptable as fully American, the African and his descendents became an unwanted and despised people who could not go back to Africa nor be accepted as equal Americans.

Xenophobic prejudice has been a common feature of past societies where differences in physical appearances ran parallel to differences in culture and social class. The African had been socially defined by Western thought long before the Englishman arrived in Africa. Accordingly, prejudice and racism had preempted their arrival. Joseph R. Washington stated:

> Racial prejudice cannot be understood without facing this mysterious element of color prejudice from which it springs. Even more, color prejudice cannot be understood rationally whether viewed from the history of intergroup antagonisms or modern reason based on science. Color prejudice is not rational but a demonic distortion of the irrational [Washington, p. 18].

Benedict, on the other hand, saw racism as "the dogma that one ethnic group is condemned by nature to congenital inferiority and another group is destined to congenital superiority."[48] Whether history accepts Washington's color prejudice theory and/or Benedict's dogma of racism, most free thinking Americans see both as evil and readily admit that a little of either is too much. The point to be made here is that without these two evils, the African probably would never have been forced from his homeland and America would be very different from what it is now. However, they were forced from their homeland to the New World and America is responsible for the Americanization of them.

The struggle of white Americans to advance requires that they develop systems of values out of facing the realities involved; however, if these realities do not include the African presence they are not reality. Accordingly, the manner in which white America defines its struggle must be divorced of all hostile and antagonistic language. Thus the manner in which Negro Americans perceive themselves, and the manner in which they and white America define them, must be positive.

Curtin stated, "words that begin with ethnic meaning frequently gain a cultural or social meaning through time, and, in some instances, the original ethnic meaning drops away altogether (Curtin, p. 18). An indication of the seriousness of this premise rests in the fact that contemporary black Americans have accepted a black definition of themselves in a society where black is the antithesis of white. One question, then, arises: is the acceptance of a black identity by Negro America a positive move forward or is it the final surrender of the Negro to the effects of a prolonged battle with racism? It seems to this writer that one of the goals of North American slavery was to force the African to see himself as his master saw him. Jordan stated that Englishmen could go a long way in establishing the differences between themselves and Africans simply by calling them black. The question this writer asks is, have blacks now internalized the negative values of their white brothers?

The English, through a system of social definition, contrived a system of subordination for the African that allowed prejudice and racism to become the rationale for their complete enslavement of the African—which could not have taken place unless "scientific" racism had been firmly established throughout the non–African world (Curtin, p. 20).

People like U.B. Phillips, and those who accepted his ideology, were able to generate a paternalistic interpretation of slavery that controlled Western historiography for many years, ending in much hate literature.[49]

The "believed natural inferiority" of the Negro eventually allowed the adoption of such things as the "Black Codes" of the South, the insurgence of the Ku Klux Klan and courts of law whose only purpose, as far as the Negroes were concerned, was to further entrench racism as the norm.[50]

White Americans deluded themselves into believing that they felt as they did about Negroes because the Negro's nature was inferior. Therefore, blacks should understand and not expect to be treated as whites. Samuel DuBois Cook stated it in this manner:

> Evil has been pursued for the sake of an alleged good. That is why so much injustice has been inflicted upon the Negro, not only with an easy conscience but with a sense of pride and moral duty.[51]

Cook may have pointed out a condition that explains the how and why of white America's attitude towards black America. If he is correct in that white America truly believes that black America should not expect to be treated the same as white people, then the solution to the so-called Negro problem rests not with alleviating the effects of the problem but with changing its causes.

Negroes found themselves in the late 1800's caught between a pseudofreedom and the urge to survive. The many legal means used against them to ensure that they could not leave the South or make a better life for themselves while remaining in the South, led to closed doors. Their former masters did not want them because they had "tasted" freedom, the federal government did not want them because they were an unpopular political responsibility, and the abolitionists did not want them because they represented a finished cause. The solution to this dilemma, for white America, was found in the Black Codes and exclusionary legislation.

While there has been a vast amount of literature generated concerning the significance of these codes and other anti-Negro legislation, the real significance of these acts and their effects on both the North and the South was lost in this country's inability to perceive the Negro as a viable part of the greater society. Theodore B. Wilson explained it in this manner:

> One of the reasons for the great difference in opinion between the North and the South as to what the Black Codes were and what they intended to accomplish was that neither of the sections realized that the Negro race

had become, during the development of slavery, a part of a new and unrecognized institution.[52]

While this "new unrecognized institution" was struggling to gain a foothold in America's emerging reform posture, America was being swept by a new and persuasive ideology, progressivism.

The Progressive Era

Arthur Mann believed that the America of the early 1900s was an amalgam of different interest groups struggling for power. Almost overshadowing both the Republican and the Democratic parties were the Progressives, who, for the most part, believed that out of experience came progress.[53]

Henry F. May described the Progressive era as "the time when people wanted to make a number of sharp changes because they were confident in the basic rightness of things as they were."[54]

Many historians believed the Progressives to be an offshoot of populists, who strongly believed that the power to govern belonged to the people, and that the function of government was to supply whatever means was necessary to accomplish the ends desired by the people. Poor people must not be exploited by the opportunists (Mann, p. 6). The Negro of the South as well as the North was caught in a political squeeze: they had achieved physical freedom, but were still denied active participation in the political process. New laws and new restrictions prevented them from using their vote for their own betterment. Hicks explained:

> The Tilman machine in South Carolina continued to function smoothly for years as the agency through which the poorer [white] classes sought to dominate the government of the state.[55]

The political situation was one of change and exchange. And the politicians of the South, especially the Democrats, came to power by way of the back door. They used the Compromise of 1877 to promise President Hayes their support for withdrawing federal troops from the South (Mann, p. 6). Consequently, "Jim Crow" and "white supremacy" became the controlling mechanisms for the newly freed Negroes. Franklin stated, "the South was back in the Union, and with a leadership strikingly like that of the South which had seceded in 1860."[56]

While the South was busy rebuilding "an underground plantation system, the rest of the country was busy rooting out corruption in "high places" and the Negro fell once again between the cracks. And when Chamberlain posited the notion that the poor people of the eighteenth and nineteenth centuries were caught between unemployment and inadequate employment, he did not necessarily include Negroes because they were still classified as property and the value of property was in its utility. Concerning this, Mann said that if property is the master force in every society, one cannot understand American institutional development until one has come to understand the part property played in shaping the fundamental law. This implies that the slave was the master force in the American economy for many years, and that if we are to understand America's institutional development, we must understand slavery's role therein. Needless to say, understanding the African presence is the "key" to solving the effects of slavery and American institutional development.

Progressivism, then, was kin to the ideology upon which the Emancipation Proclamation was forged, and because of its nature, it was expected by many Americans that a solution to the "Negro problem" was close at hand. This kind of forward thinking would seem to indicate that the progressives were good for a struggling America. Conversely, they were very selective in their application of ideas. Slavery and the Negro were, however, far removed from this "great upward" movement. May wrote:

> Obviously, Negroes were not among those for whom opportunity must be preserved; their road was blocked not by corrupted interest but by a caste system. Most progressives brought themselves, not without some twinges of conscience, to acquiesce in this system and put the greatest American injustice out of their minds; it did not fit their pattern of thought ... there was no lack of demonstration that Negro equality was impossible. Only a small minority of progressives, many of them heirs of the abolitionist tradition, worried much about the man farthest down [May, p. 27].

Thus it seems that the so-called "Negro problem" is a mixture of social notions ranging from dehumanizing passions to heartrending despotism. Only the black man or the black woman can effect the necessary change; society does not have time. Because of the nature of their Americanization, their history and culture are so entwined with the institution of slavery that the suffering of their forebears usually proves too painful for a dispassionate examination.

This writer submits that the four views of slavery presented here should be viewed synoptically; they should be considered as separate stages of Negro development while still representing a composite. The intention is that through such a process, black America will be afforded a fresh and positive place in American historiography. Obviously, there is no great gnostic truth where slavery and the Negro is concerned; however, if black Americans are ever to have an equal place within America's amalgamated family, attitudes and beliefs must be changed. And while some Americans will continue to hold some or many of the beliefs that allowed the African to become a slave property, most Americans will probably readily accept the validity of the questions raised in this book.

> How would you have us, as we are?
>   Or singing 'neath the load we bear,
> Our eyes fixed forward on a star,
>   Or gazing empty at despair?
>
> Raising or falling? Men or things?
>   With dragging pace of footsteps fleet?
> Strong, willing sinews in your wings,
>   Or tightening chains about your feet?

James Weldon Johnson

Chapter II
The Progressive Model

This model is based on the book, *American Negro Slavery*, by Ulrich B. Phillips. Phillips was born in La Grange, Georgia, November 4, 1877. He began early to show interest in the institution of slavery. According to Stanley M. Elkins, his work was "an intensive study of slavery that should not only challenge the deepest assumptions of Rhodes and Hart but would also make drastic alterations in the views held on the subject by thousands and thousands of American readers."[1] Phillips was a scholar of the highest rank; even though he was the first Southerner to produce a widely accepted scholarly work on slavery, his credentials demanded his acceptance as a scholar.[2]

Background Data

The beginning of the Civil War found some quarter of a million free Negroes in America. They were free in the sense that they could own property, use a restricted vote, and move about more easily than the slave population.[3]

Theodore B. Wilson believed that the significance of this group rested in the fact that "the Negro race had become unrecognized—a social institution in America."

A further point of significance is that this free Negro class later became the Negro middle class.[4] While there is no concrete way of determining the actual class composition of this group, most historians concede that in spite of the many social restrictions placed on these people, they made the greatest strides in assimilating European culture. Frazier stated:

> The free Negro constituted, in fact, the element in the Negro population that had made the greatest progress in acquiring European culture. The pattern of life of the well-to-do free Negroes in the plantation South was the same as the patriarchal family pattern of the slave holding whites. Moreover, their outlook on life and their values were the same as the white model [Frazier, p. 19].

The free Negro class came into being because of the physical and social structure of plantation life. Furthermore, plantation labor was divided into two distinct work groups: the field hands and the house servants. The latter, by nature of their servitude, had a closer association with their masters and inevitably this led to the internalization of the racial prejudices held by their masters. This process eventually caused the free Negroes and the house servants to see themselves as "better" than the Negro masses (Frazier, p. 17).[5]

This elitist attitude of the free Negroes was based to a large extent on such factors as: (1) they could read and write the master's language, (2) they had a limited understanding of the master's religion, (3) they, for the most part, were lighter in complexion, (4) they owned property, and (5) they had acquired a limited degree of economic security (Frazier, pp. 23–24).[6]

This class and caste division of the early Negro population was to have damning effects on the future social structure of the Negro community. However, let it suffice to say here that many of the internal problems of contemporary Negro American life had their beginnings during the plantation system's reign.

Wilson portrayed the early colonials as believing that in the beginning slavery was not identified solely with Africans because they were not the first slaves. The Indians were the first slaves and their slavery was justifiable because they were infidels and they were captured in battle. The Negroes, like the Indians, were enslaved because they were captured in battle and they, too, were infidels. This argument broke down when "the circumstances of the slave trade became widely known and the Negroes could remove themselves from the category of infidel by merely accepting Christianity." The final justification for Negroes' enslavement rested with their "so called 'natural infirmity'"(Wilson, p. 18). The idea of the inferior black who was suited to the condition of slavery justified its institution. Wilson summarized this situation in this manner:

> One of the most effective means of controlling slaves was the fostering among the slaves themselves of the belief of the great inferiority of their race. The slave who thoroughly internalized the idea of Negro stupidity and animality disregarded his own aspirations for better things and discredited the Negro rebel who suggested that he do otherwise. He was conditioned to obey.... Quite plainly the free Negro could not escape contamination from the concept of racial inferiority. The Negro servant's descent into slavery was paralleled by the free Negro's loss of social and political status. When the black race came to be identified with slavery, the fortunes of the Negro became indissolubly linked with the fortunes of the slave. When the Negro slave came to be regarded as some sort of sub-human, the concept applied with equal force to the Negroes who were free [Wilson, pp. 18–19].[7]

This situational statement by Wilson indicates that the Negroes, free or bond, were caught up in a situation over which they had no control. They were forced to accept a social definition of themselves that had no relevance to their actuality. It would seem that the dominant thought of that time was concerned more with validating slavery than helping the free Negro to fit into America's vast melting pot.

This was a time in which the moral code for America was being defined. It was also a time in which all Negroes were beginning to establish the social constructs which would govern their behavior for times to come. Since history suggests the notion that the female of the group transmits the culture of that group,[8] the treatment of the Negro female was a determining factor in the shaping of the Negro personality. Consequently, during these formative years when the sexual abuse of the Negro female was prevalent, there was also an ardent dislike for miscegenation. This dichotomized situation allowed the Negro female opportunity to receive the best of two worlds. On the one hand, she enjoyed the privileges of having the physical attraction of white males, while on the other hand, she was a stabilizing force which allowed her male counterpart to have some semblance of identity. This dual role caused much anxiety on the part of both the Negro male and female slaves.[9]

The exploitation of the female slave and the harshness of the institution of slavery had to produce within the slave community some degree of hostility toward the slave holders. To many historians this hostility took the form of rebellion, runaways and open defiance.

Slave revolts

The significance of the slave revolts to the forming of attitudes towards the Negro American is not so much in the reality of their occurrence but in the fear that they might occur (Greene, p. 31).

While there may have been many instances of slave rebellion, there were only four of major consequence: (1) the revolt at Stono, South Carolina, in 1738; (2) Gabriel's Revolt, Richmond, Virginia, in 1800; (3) Denmark Vessey's Plot at Charleston, South Carolina, in 1822; and (4) Nat Turner's Insurrection near Southhampton, Virginia, in 1831. History shows that while these attempts at freedom by the slaves did not gain them their freedom, they did fortify the white community against them. This fortification took the form of many new laws and regulations which further denied human rights to the slaves as well as the opportunity of the free Negroes to pursue life, liberty and a reasonable degree of happiness (Greene, pp. 32–39).[10]

Southern attitudes in 1865-1866

Many Americans seemed to believe that the Emancipation Proclamation was conceived overnight and that most Southerners yielded to its pressure because of fear. While this may be true to a certain degree, authors like Wilson and Genovese, to name two, were of the opinion that the majority of the slave holding class sincerely believed that their slaves were better off in the institution than they would be if left to their own devices. Concerning this Wilson cited many incidents that showed that the Southerners could not understand why "their" slaves would want freedom, especially since most of them had never known anything about it (Greene, pp. 43-52). It would seem that the Southerners had, in trying to justify their institution of slavery, only succeeded in deluding themselves. As it will be shown in a later chapter, the slaves had many opportunities to learn about freedom; they learned it from the free Negroes, from their masters, from newly acquired slaves, and as some slaves later confessed, they learned it from "being dumb."[11] Many entries in diaries, newspapers, and oral reports suggest that the situation was such that the Negroes were confused as to the meaning of freedom. In many instances they believed that the government was going to give them "forty acres and a mule." The white South, on the other hand, did not want this to happen and set about to reestablish the old Southern way of life. These times proved to be very trying for the newly freed Negro (Greene, pp. 52-55).[12]

The resulting situation then became one of power and powerlessness, and since the ex-slave holder controlled the lawmaking machinery, he used the law to restore the freedmen to their "proper place." Wilson wrote:

> Some of the more discriminatory regulations ordered the arrest of Negro "vagrants," forbade freemen to travel without passes, provided for the registration of former slaves, prohibited their leaving the plantations of their erstwhile owners, and compelled them to enter into labor contracts [Greene, p. 59].[13]

An understanding of the plight of the freedmen is significant because by measuring their progress, especially in the economic area, one can better understand the attitudes of white America towards all Negroes.

Even after freedom, Negroes were still looked upon as inferiors and as such, even during Reconstruction, they found very little to do that would afford them the opportunity of moving up the economic ladder. Consequently, the sixteenth, seventeenth, and eighteenth centuries found the South believing more and more in the progressive's ideology. The need to move the South from a slave holding society to a more industrialized community, according to Davis, allowed the historians of that time to consign the study of slavery to a marginal place in the curriculum:

A course on the history of religion in America never touched on the slave's religion or on the religious controversies over slavery. We simply took note of the dates when the major Protestant denominations had divided along sectional lines. At best, slavery could be perceived as a variant on the history of immigration and ethnic conflict.[14]

This so-called oversight was the outcome of the South's and America's struggle for many years, to decide the slavery question without actually acknowledging that Negroes had something to contribute. Davis said, "After preparing for my Ph.D. orals in 1954, I remained totally ignorant of the works of such black historians as W.E.B. DuBois, Carter G. Woodson, Charles H. Westly, Benjamin Quarles, Eric Williams, C.L.R. James, and John Hope Franklin" (Davis, p. 2). This statement by Davis not only alludes to an oversight by most historians but also illuminates Phillips' reason for using exclusively plantation records as a primary source for his book, *American Negro Slavery*.

Elements of the Progressive Model

Phillips began to develop his theory of the innate racial inferiority of the Negro by depicting his homeland as a hostile and savage land. He saw the African as having the crudest form of religion and the most beastly dietary habits. Concerning this he wrote:

> The proper course for common place persons at ordinary times was to follow routine fetish observances; but when beset by witch-work the only escape lay in the services of witch-doctors or priests. Sacrifices were called for, and on the greatest occasions nothing short of human sacrifice was acceptable.... As to diet, vegetable food was generally abundant.... In the jungle game animals were scarce, and everywhere the men were ill equipped for hunting. In lieu of better they often fain to satisfy their craving for flesh by eating locust.... In such conditions cannibalism was fairly common.[15]*

According to Phillips, the family structure of the African was primitive and void of any semblance of civility. The wife was little more than a slave to her husband who "had bought her at the time of their marriage." Polygamy was a common practice, and most African women gladly accepted it because through it their daily load was lessened (p. 6).

Phillips believed that the African was well conditioned to slavery and that the form of slavery to which he subjected his own kind was often cruel and usually ended in the death of the slave (p. 6). To Phillips, American Negro slavery was good for all parties concerned and especially good for every aspect of the slave's human development (p. 343).[16]

Hereafter in this chapter references to page numbers only are to this book.

In support of this premise, Phillips cited many incidents whose
design was to depict the human development of the slave as a normal
part of the slave holder's daily routine. Included in this daily routine
were such activities as:

1. The exchange of slaves

> Thompson Phillips who was about to sail for Jamaica exchanged a half
> interest in his one-legged Negro man for a similar share in Isaac Lathrop's
> Negro boy who was to sail with Phillips and be sold on the voyage [p. 187].

2. Considering slaves were common merchandise

> A man from Knoxville, Tennessee, in December, 1775, sent notice to
> a correspondent in Kentucky that he was about to set out with slaves for
> delivery as agreed upon, and would carry additional ones on speculation;
> he concluded by saying, "I intend carrying on the business extensively"
> [p. 188].

3. In some cases allowing slaves to seek their masters

> In the city of Washington in 1864, a woman whose husband had been
> sold South, was furnished with the following document: "The bearer,
> Mary Jane, and her two daughters, are for sale. They are sold for no earth-
> ly fault whatever" [p. 191].

Phillips believed that certain social and technical developments influenced the attitudes and behaviors of the slave holders towards the
slaves. A composite overview of some of these elements follows.

The domestic slave trade

Phillips believed that with the demise of the Atlantic slave trade
domestic slave trading became a viable business. Concerning this, he
wrote:

> As soon as the African slave trade was closed, the interstate traffic began
> to assume the aspect of a regular business though for some years it not
> only continued to be of a small scale but was oftentimes merely inciden-
> tal in character [p. 189].

The magnitude of this domestic trading seems to be of primary concern to the four authors in developing the models under examination.
Phillips, the first of these authors to be examined, seemed to believe this
was not a serious situation, and it arose as an incident to the normal hand-
ling of property—in this case, the slave. The underlying assumption made
by Phillips was that slaves were property and since their status was determined prior to their arrival in this country, the slave holder had no choice
but to make the best of a troubled situation. Davis wrote of Phillips,
"Nor was it accidental that Phillips helped to rehabilitate the South's
progressive image by picturing slavery as a system of racial adjustment
which had risen in response to environmental pressures and human needs"
(Davis, p. 3).[17]

The cotton regime

The fact that the increased need for cotton caused a greater need for slave labor does not need to be expounded here. However, it is necessary to note that this particular facet of the supply and demand cycle must be examined to the end that it influenced the attitudes of the slave holders toward the Negro slaves. Furthermore, because of the nature of cotton growing, the slave became the primary factor in determining the profit or loss margin. As a consequence, the slave holders realized that their very existence depended upon how well they used their slaves; therefore, slave management became the central issue during the cotton regime (pp. 205-10). Concerning this, Phillips wrote:

> The leadership of the American cotton belt could not be impaired, for its facilities were unequaled. Its long growing season, hot in summer by day and night, was perfectly congenial to the plant; its dry autumns permitted the reaping of full havest, and its frosty winters decimated the incest pests. Its soil was abundant. Its skilled managers were in full supply, its culture was well systematized, and its labor adequate for the demand. To these facilities were added in the southern thought of time, as essential for the permanence of the cotton belt's primacy, the plantation system and the institution of slavery [p. 228].

Plantation life

The type and size of plantation that slaves found themselves belonging to depended to a large measure on the type of crop grown, the lay of the land, the character of the master, and local tradition. The utilization of the slave usually fell into one of the two methods: gang or task systems. Both were designed to get the maximum production from the slave (p. 228). The significance of both methods, to this research project, rests in the fact that each determined a particular relationship between the slave and the master. The relevance of this is that the more intimate the slave's relation to the master, the more easily they were able to assimilate the master's culture. Concerning this Frazier wrote:

> While all of the slaves were under the surveillance of the whites, the house servants lived constantly in close association with their masters. Very often these house servants had associated from childhood with their masters. Consequently, they acquired early the speech of their masters, a fact which set them off from the more isolated field hands, who spoke a dialect. Living in close association with whites, the house servants were subjected to a type discipline which caused them to identify themselves with their masters. This discipline included both moral and religious instruction [Frazier, p. 17].

Management

Phillips thought that the well-being of the plantation as a whole depended on the best use of equipment and "humane" treatment of the slave. He cited these incidents:

1. P.C. Weston of South Carolina wrote in 1856

   The proprietor, in the first place, wishes the overseer most distinctly to understand that his first object is to be, under all circumstances, concerned with the care and well being of the Negroes [p. 262].

2. J.W. Fowler's preamble to his rules, 1857

   The health, happiness, good discipline and obedience, good, sufficient and comfortable clothing, sufficiency of good, wholesome and nutritious food for both man and beast being indispensably necessary to successful planting, as well as for reasonable dividends for the amount of capital invested, without saying anything about the master's duty to his dependents, to himself, and his God, I do hereby establish the following rules and regulation for the management of my Prairie Plantation [p. 262].

3. J.H. Hammond's plantation manual contained these words

   A good crop means one that is good taking into consideration everything: Negroes, land, mules, stock, fences, ditches, farming utensils, etc., all of which must be kept up and improve in value. The effort must therefore not be merely to make so many cotton bales or such an amount of other produce, but as much as can be made without interrupting the steady increase in value of the rest of the property.... There should be an increase in number and improvement in condition of Negroes [pp. 262–63].

4. For the care of the sick

   Acklen, Maniqualt and Weston provided that mild cases be prescribed for by the overseer in the master's absence, but for any serious illness a doctor be summoned. One of Telfair's women was a semi-professional midwife and general practitioner, permitted by her master to serve some blacks and whites in the neighborhood. For home needs Telfair wrote of her: Elsey is the doctress of the plantation. In case of extraordinary illness, when she thinks she can do no more for the sick, you will employ a physician [p. 263].

5. Religious instruction

   I therefore want all of my people encouraged to cultivate religious feeling and morality, and punished for inhumanity to their children or stock, for profanity, lying and stealing. And again, I would that every human being have the gospel preached to them in its original purity and simplicity. It therefore devolves upon me to have these dependents properly instructed in all that pertains to the salvation of their soul [p. 296].

6. The master's function

   A planter should have all his work laid out, days, weeks, months, seasons and years ahead, according to the nature of it. He must go from job to

job without losing a moment in turning round, and he must have all
the parts of his work so arranged that due proportion of attention may
be bestowed upon each at the proper time [p. 272].

7. The overseer's function

In the overseer all the virtues of a master were desired, with a deputy's
obedience added. Corbin enjoined his staff that they "attend their business
with deligence, keep the Negroes in good order, and enforce obedience
by the example of their own industry, which is a more effectual method
in every respect than hurry and severity [p. 273].

8. Care and control of slaves, John Taylor, 1809

The addition of comfort to mere necessaries is a price paid by the master
for the advantages he will derive from binding his slaves to his service
by a ligament stronger than chains, far beneath their value in a pecuniary
point of view; and he will moreover gain a stream of agreeable reflections
throughout life, which will cost him nothing [p. 275].

9. A Virginia planter's essay of 1884

Virginia Negroes are generally better tempered than any other people;
they are kindly, grateful, attached to persons and places, enduring and
patient in fatigue and hardship, content and cheerful. Their control should
be uniform and consistent, not an alteration of rigor and laxity. Punishment for real faults should be invariable but moderate. The best evidence
of the good management of slaves is the keeping up of good discipline
with little or no punishment [p. 276].

10. Food allowance

The allowance now given per week to each hand is five pounds of good
clean bacon and one quart of molasses, with as much good bread as they
require; and in the fall, or sickly season of the year, or on sickly places,
the addition of one pint of strong coffee, sweetened with sugar, every
morning before going to work. The slaves may well have gardens, but
the assignment of patches for market produce too greatly encourages a
traffic on their own account, and presents a temptation and opportunity,
during the process of gathering, for an unscrupulous fellow to mix a little of his master's produce with his own [p. 277].

11. Slave personality

It is obvious that Phillips believed that his observations were indicative of the true slave personality. To him the slave was a product of
the institution and whatever he was in his homeland, Africa, was lost
to the molding influences of the institution. Accordingly, he wrote:

While produced only in America, the plantation slave was a product of
old world forces. His nature was an African's profoundly modified but
hardly transformed by the requirements of European civilization. The
wrench from Africa and the subjection to the new discipline while
uprooting his ancient language and customs had little more effect upon
his temperament than upon his complexion. Ceasing to be Foulah, Cor-

omantee, Ebo or Anglola, he became instead the American Negro [p. 291].

This view of Negroes gives no indication that Phillips had a deep-seated hatred for them; conversely, it tends to reflect a side of American thought that usually affords white America a great deal of satisfaction. In viewing Negroes in this manner, slavery is seen as a needed instrument for the sound development of the Negro's personality. Frazier stated the premise in this manner:

> Perhaps the main reason for the bitter reaction on the part of some white Americans (some book stores refused to carry the book, *Black Bourgeoisie*, because it was so controversial) was that it destroyed or tended to destroy the image of Negroes which they wanted to present to the world at this time. The picture white Americans wanted to present to the world was that although Negroes had been enslaved and had suffered many disabilities since Emancipation, on the whole they were well off economically, had gained civil rights, and had improved their social status. Therefore, what had happened to them during slavery, which was after all a mild paternalistic system, should be forgotten along with the other injustices which they have suffered since. Moreover, their economic position was superior to that of other peoples of the world, especially the colored peoples [Frazier, p. 10].

Phillips wrote, "The planters had a saying, always of course with an implicit reservation as to limits, that a Negro was what a white man made him" (p. 291). Based on this Southern view of the Negro slave, he went on to say:

> The molding, however, was accomplished more by groups than by individuals. The purposes and policies of the masters were uniform, and in consequence the Negroes, though with many variants, became largely standardized into the predominant plantation type (p. 291).

According to this understanding, Phillips saw Negroes in a paradoxical configuration. On one hand, all of their negative qualities came from African ancestry, while on the other hand, all of their positive attributes came from white man. This "predominant plantation type," of which Phillips wrote, invariably became the standard by which all Negroes in white thought were symbolized. Phillips described the slave in this manner:

> The traits which prevailed were an eagerness for society, music and merriment, a fondness for display whether of person, dress, vocabulary or emotion, not flagrant sensuality, a receptiveness toward any religion whose exercises were exhilarating, a proneness to superstition, a courteous acceptance of subordination, an avidity for praise, a readiness for loyalty of a feudal sort, and a healthy human repugnance toward overwork [p. 291].

Phillips seemed to be concerned with six major areas of Negro life:

(1) food, (2) shelter, (3) work, (4) police regulations, (5) medical care, and (6) punishment.

Food

Phillips described the view of slaves held by Corbin, Acklen and Fowler, all large plantation owners:

> They ought to have their belly full ... see that their necessities be supplied, that their food and clothing be good and sufficient, their houses comfortable; and be kind and attentive to them in sickness and old age.... There will be stated hours for the Negro to breakfast and dine (in the field), and those hours must be regularly observed. The manager will frequently inspect the meals as they are brought by the cook — see that they have been properly prepared, and that vegetables be at all times served with meat and bread.... The allowance for every grown Negro, however old and good for nothing, and every young one that works in the field, is a peck of corn each week and a pint of salt, and a piece of meat, not exceeding fourteen pounds per month.... The suckling children, and all other small ones who do not work in the fields, draw a half allowance of corn and salt.... Feed everything plentifully, but waste nothing [p. 265].

According to Phillips' sources (plantation records) the slave received an ample supply of good food. It would seem that the plantation owners were very much concerned with the care and well-being of "all their property."

Shelter

Phillips wrote:

> Each family had a dry and airy house to itself, with a poultry house and a vegetable garden behind.... The houses were to be completely emptied and their contents sunned, the walls and floors were to be scrubbed, the mattresses to be emptied and stuffed with fresh hay or shucks, the yard swept and the ground under the house sprinkled with lime [p. 267].

Work

Reflected throughout Phillips' writings are these tendencies toward work as cited in certain plantation records:

> The Negroes to be tasked with the work allows it. I require a reasonable day's work, well done — the task to be regulated by the state of the ground and the strength of the Negro ... a task is as much work as the meanest full hand can do in nine hours, working industriously.... This task is never to be increased, and no work is to be done over task except under urgent

necessity.... No Negro is to be put into a task which he cannot finish with
tolerable ease [p. 267].

Police regulation

It was commonly understood and accepted that slavery could exist
only by force of positive legislation. Phillips disagreed with this position.
He wrote:

> This is not historically valid, for in virtually every American community
> where it existed at all, the institution was first established by custom alone
> and was merely recognized by statutes when these came to be enacted.
> Indeed the chief purpose of the law was to give sanction and assurance
> to the racial and industrial adjustments already operative [p. 489].

This meant that the plantation owner was free to do whatever he
deemed necessary in order to maintain his need-cost balance and that
the law would adjust itself to legalize his actions.

Medical care

A sample overseer's contract contained the following:

> Procure a book of medical instructions and a supply of the few requisite
> plantation medicines to be issued to the nurses with directions as need-
> ed.... In case of serious injury to a slave, however, the sufferer was to be
> laid upon a door and sent by the plantation boat to a doctor [p. 256].

It would appear, according to Phillips, that most of the plantation
owners were solicitous in the care of the sick slaves. They used semiprofes-
sional midwives, overseers and any such person that was convenient.

Punishment

Punishment for slaves included such things as whippings, deporta-
tion, death, branding and breaking on the wheel. It was a common practice for the owner to decide on the kind and amount of punishment that
the slave was to receive. Phillips cites several types and amounts as reflected
in actual plantation and court records.[18]

Negroes are depicted as childlike, lazy, morally loose, accommodating towards their masters and for the most part unfamiliar with
human attributes and tendencies. Furthermore, they were mentally un-
prepared to redefine their situations. As a consequence of this mental
lag, Phillips wrote concerning the controversy over Negro enlistment into
the colonial army:

> Had the Negroes in general possessed any means of concerted action, they

might conceivably have played off the British and American belligerents to their own advantage. In actuality, hower, they were passive elements whose fate was affected only as far as the master race determined [p. 117].

The progressive model further depicts Negro Americans as a people void of human attributes, torn from their homeland, disoriented and completely dominated by another cultural group. They were given no reason for their enslavement other than "God ordained it" and made to believe that their sole survival depended on the "good nature" of their masters.

Finally, Phillips saw the institution of slavery as a necessary element in the Americanization of the colonial wilderness. He believed that the "barbarous" African needed the advantages that slavery afforded. He wrote:

> In barbaric society slavery is a normal means of conquering the isolation of workers and assembling them in more productive coordination. Where population is scant and money little used it is almost a necessity in the conduct of large undertakings and therefore more or less essential for the advancement of civilization. It is a means of domesticating savage or barbarous men, analogous in kind and in consequence to the domestication of the beast of the field [p. 344].[19]

Coupling this understanding of slavery with the sociological effects of being raised in the deep South, it appears virtually impossible for Phillips to see the Negro slave in any other configuration except that formulated in his *American Negro Slavery*. Throughout his book Phillips displayed a deep love for his native South and an equal love and belief in the paternal aspects of the slave system. He saw Negro slaves as helpless children, spawned by circumstances over which they had no control. He wrote:

> The characteristic American slave, indeed, was not only a Negro, but a plantation workman; and for the present purpose a knowledge of the plans and requirements of plantation industry is no less vital than an understanding of human nature.... The Negroes themselves show the same easy going amiable, serio-comic obedience and the same sturdy lightheartedness and the same love of laughter and of rhythm, which distinguished their forebears [p. viii].

This, then, was Phillips' understanding of the Negro slave and the institution of slavery in the United States.

Summary of the Elements of the Model

In conclusion, this model is comprised of the following elements:

The Negro/slave was
1. Innately and by way of inheritance racially inferior to all other races

2. Chattel personal (humans held and treated as property)
3. Cheerful and happy
4. Content with his/her status
5. Childlike
6. Ordained of God to be a slave for life

The institution of slavery was
1. A school for training the slave in human attributes
2. A labor force
3. A very humane system

The institution provided
1. Adequate food, clothing, medical care, protection, shelter, fair working conditions and working hours
2. A means for the African to overcome his savagery

The final word on Phillips' *American Negro Slavery* rests with Phillips. He wrote:

> The government of slaves was for the ninety and nine by men, and only for the hundredth by laws. There were injustice, oppression, brutality and heartburning in the regime, — but where in the struggling world are these absent? There were also gentleness, kind-hearted friendship and mutual loyalty to a degree hard for him to believe who regards the system with a theorist's eye and a partisan squint. For him on the other hand who was known the considerate and cordial, courteous men and women, white and black, which that picturesque life in its best phases produced, it is impossible to agree that its basis and operation were wholly evil, the law and the prophets to the contrary notwithstanding [p. 514].

Chapter III
The Racial Enlightenment Model

The racial enlightenment model is based on Kenneth Stampp's book, *The Peculiar Institution: Slavery in the Ante-Bellum South*. This model views slavery as an inhumane institution whose scope and structure developed in the Negroes "a paralyzing fear of white men," to "impress upon them their innate inferiority," and to "instill in them a sense of complete dependency."[1]* While the racial enlightenment model followed the general outline of Phillips' progressive model, it made two distinct differences: one, the slaves hatred slavery; and two, the system was cruel and debilitating.

Stampp like Phillips was a scholar of the greatest magnitude, differing from Phillips only in that he was a Northerner. Professor Stampp was a teacher and outstanding historian, having taught at several institutions of higher learning, and holding such prestigious positions as the President Adams Fellowship in History and the John Simon Guggenheim Fellowship. For a more detailed description of Stampp's credentials, see the Appendix.

Background Data

Much had been said about the harshness of the plantation system of slavery. Nevertheless, there still remains a tremendous need to re-examine the institution because for too long it has been viewed as either morally right or morally wrong. As a consequence of this kind of thinking, Stampp believed that a new approach to the slavery question had to be devised that would deal with the slaves' reaction to slavery. Concerning this understanding, Stampp wrote:

> One can feel compassion for the antebellum southern white man; one can understand the moral dilemma in which he is trapped. But one must remember that the Negro, not the white man, was the slave, and the Negro gained the most from emancipation. When freedom came—even

Hereafter in this chapter references to page numbers only are to this book.

the quasi-freedom of "second class citizenship" the Negro, in literal truth, lost nothing but his chains [p. 340].[2]

The 1950's found America deeply involved in two lines of conflicting pressure. Of these, Davis wrote:

On the other hand, however parochial their discipline, historians had by then become aware of the sociological literature on racial prejudice and "the Negro problem."[3]

It is not surprising to find historians of that day so engaged, because they, for the most part, were still laboring under the progressive idea that "slavery had always been peripheral to the major forces and struggles that explained the rise of American civilization." Davis said:

The nineteenth century obsession with slavery had obscured the fundamental cleavages in American society: the cleavages between labor and business, between farmers and middle men, between self-seeking conservatives and liberal men of vision [Davis, p. 4].

This so-called obsession had caused a proliferation of scholarly works that tended to saturate the mind to the point of revulsion.

We have been offered new and often startling conclusions regarding the history of racial prejudice; the demographic patterns of the Atlantic slave trade and various slave populations; the nature of slave occupations and the adaptability of slave labor to skill or industrial employment; the relative efficiency of slave and free labor; the profitability of the institution and its relation to economic growth; the various forms of slave resistance, including insurrection; the place of slavery in American political and constitutional history; the nature of slave cultures; including religion, folklore, and various adapted forms of African culture; and above all, the similarities as well as the contrasts between the slave systems of the world [Davis, p. 3].[4]

It would seem that in spite of this preponderance of slave literature, the slave problem was not taken very seriously. The indication is that Negroes, even though they had been emancipated, were still expected to sit on the sidelines and leave the decision making to whites. George P. Rawick wrote:

The black slave has usually been portrayed as the victim who never enters his own history as its subject, but only as the object over which abstract forces and glorious armies fought. Historians have justified this absence of slave voices in the history of slavery and American people by insisting that, after all, the slave left no records, accomplished little that was "noteworthy," and therefore did not have much history ... while slavery has left an indelible mark on American life, the slaves themselves have rarely been heard telling their own stories. The masters not only ruled the past in fact, they rule its written history. Like the rest of the population which did not lead "notable" lives, the slaves appear usually only as faceless and nameless people, murmuring and mumbling off stage.

At best, only the loud and demanding voice of an exceptional slave, such as the great black abolitionist leader, Frederick Douglass, is heard, and then only above the din of the speeches of politicians, statesmen, and ideologists of all persuasions. The history of black Americans has been treated by most historians as a specialized, exotic subject, not as a central focus for the study of the development of the American people.[5]

Another possible explanation for this attitude toward the Negro may be found in the ideology that "freedom is obtained through conquest, not as a gift."[6] Still another possible reason may be found in the protest of contemporary Negro leadership. Davis wrote:

> The crisis, they insisted, was not one "in black and white" or in "race relations." White scholars who studied "the Negro problem" were simply the intellectual heirs of slave holders who had studied problems of slave management. Black history, when controlled by whites and when dominated by the psychological needs of whites, was simply another weapon to preserve the cultural hegemony of the dominant race.[7]

Regardless of the reasons why, the fifties found Negro Americans just where Phillips had left them, "at the feet of their kindly and paternal white father, singing and dancing without a care in the world."

Insofar as the Negro was concerned, America had not moved very far from where it was in the forties. That is to say, Negroes were just as frustrated and just as left out as they had ever been. The frustration, by this time, had spilled over into white America because by now middle class white Americans were getting less for their dollar and the country was moving towards another war. Probably the most significant condition during this period was that economic and social influences had once again developed that would allow America to look for a scape-goat (Washington, pp. 24–25). While the election of Negroes served this purpose, all was not gloom and despair because Negroes began to find their voice and spoke out firmly and judiciously.[8]

With the publication of Kenneth Stampp's *Peculiar Institution* in 1956, came a long awaited rebuttal to Phillips' *American Negro Slavery*. The climate was such that many historians believed that Stampp's book "ended the era of inhibition by insisting on the peculiar urgency of understanding the history of slavery as a key to understanding the present." This peculiar urgency "allowed Stampp to sanitize the subject and thereby place it on the profession's agenda"; Davis continued:

> Never again, presumably would it be necessary to debate the moral wrong of slavery or to rehearse the evidence concerning food, shelter, working hours, police regulations, medical care and punishment [Davis, p. 3].

What had happened between Phillips' reign as the great intellectual of slave history and the anxious acceptance of Stampp as a redeeming messiah? For one thing, Gunnar Myrdal had written *An American Dilemma*, in which he refocused the thrust of Phillips' interpretation of American slavery from an agrarian posture to a re-examination of themselves by white America. This is best evidenced when Myrdal wrote:

> To the great majority of white Americans the Negro problem has distinctly negative connotations. It suggests something difficult to settle and equally difficult to leave alone. It is embarrassing, it makes for moral uneasiness. The very presence of the Negro in America; his fate in this country through slavery, Civil War and Reconstruction; his recent career and his present status; his accommodation; his protest and his aspirations; in fact his entire biological, historical and social existence as a participant American represent to the ordinary white man in the North as well as in the South an anomaly in the very structure of American society. To many, this takes on the proportion of a menace — biological, economic, social, cultural and at times political. This anxiety may be mingled with a feeling of individual and collective guilt. A few see the problem as a challenge to statesmenship. To all it is trouble.[9]

Thus for the first time the slavery problem was viewed as a white American problem rather than as an isolated set of Negro attitudes and behaviors. Myrdal approached Phillips' position with the idea that valuations and beliefs determine behavior. As a consequence, who and what the Negro was depended, for the most part, on how well the white man's system of valuations and beliefs balanced. He wrote:

> The moral struggle goes on within people and not only between them. As a people's valuations are conflicting, behavior normally becomes a moral compromise. There are no homogeneous attitudes behind human behavior but a mesh of struggling inclinations, interests, and ideals, some held conscious and some suppressed for long intervals but all active in the bending of behavior in their direction [Myrdal, p. xliv].

To take this line of thought a little further, Myrdal wrote, "the unit of a culture consists in the fact that all valuations are mutually shared in some degree" (Myrdal, p. xliv). Negroes, whether of the progressive era or of the enlightenment era, would not fit into this ideology with a positive configuration, because they have always been perceived as peripheral to the common American system of valuations and beliefs. For example, a white person could place, a very high value on the principle," liberty, equality, and justice for all, and still hold dear to his heart deep-seated prejudice against the Negro. He could engage in those activities which would deprive that Negro of these same rights — believing in his heart that he had done the right and moral thing.[10]

It would seem that Myrdal laid the groundwork for Stampp and the racial enlightenment liberals to not only attack Phillips but to usher in a new kind of racism. Davis said of Stampp:

> Stampp has come to symbolize the unwitting arrogance of white integrationists who assumed "that innately Negroes are, after all, only white men with black skins, nothing more, nothing less" [Davis, p. 2].

What seemed to be happening in this historical age was that white America was beginning to realize that "the breaking" of Africans during their enslavement had produced side effects which had not been explained in the normal use and understanding of historical research. Therefore, when Myrdal posited the idea that Negroes had internalized many of the white prejudices directed at them from the "all-white" world, many white Americans began to look for a new interpretation of Negro American slavery. Myrdal wrote:

> Even the American Negroes share in this community of evaluations: they have eagerly imbibed the American creed and the revolutionary Christian teaching of common brotherhood; under close study, they usually reveal also that they hold something of the majority prejudice against their own kind and its characteristics [Myrdal, p. xliv].[11]

This new quest, when viewed along side America's recent victory over Nazism and the horrors of their death camps, refocused American thought to an age-old problem, Negroes. And when in 1944, Myrdal suggested that "the Negro's entire life, and consequently, also his opinions on the Negro problem, are, in the main, to be considered as secondary reactions to more primary pressures from the side of the dominant white majority" (Myrdal, p. xlvii), America shuddered in her intellectual boots. With an almost frantic effort she sought to remove "Uncle Tom" and "Black Sambo" from her textbooks and minds of her children. America began to refurbish the ideal, "America the beautiful, home of liberty and justice for all" (Davis, p. 1).

The final contribution of Myrdal to be considered at this point is his idea that the Negro problem cannot be, as has been done, studied in isolation. On this account Myrdal wrote:

> The Negro problem is an integral part of, or a special phase of, the whole complex of problems in the larger American civilization. It cannot be treated in isolation [Myrdal, p. xlix].

Here again, Myrdal moved from the normal to an extreme. Heretofore, the normal tendency of white America was to attempt to localize and demarcate the Negro problem to the segment of society where blacks lived. According to Myrdal, this served two main functions: first, it allowed white America to externalize the problem; and second, it assigned a "place" for the Negro. The comfort and security that came with being white began to erode to a feeling of guilt and shame. Myrdal was an instant "savior" whose moral approach to the slave/Negro problem would in a few short years allow Stampp to sail into modern history unchallenged.

This same historical age as seen through the eyes of John Hope Franklin, another historian, begins with the postwar years, especially 1946, in which the climate was being formed that would allow Stampp to dethrone Phillips. It was in this year that President Harry S Truman appointed a committee to inquire into the civil rights conditions. This committee's report, *To Secure These Rights*, according to John Hope Franklin, "strongly denounced the denial of civil rights to some Americans, and it called for a positive program to strengthen civil rights including the elimination of segregation based on race, color, creed, or national origin, from American life."[12] In that same year President Truman appointed another committee to study the racial problems of higher education. It, too, recommended needed progressive changes. Following this, in 1948, the President appointed still another committee to study the armed services' racial situation. Its report, *Freedom to Serve*, "was a blueprint of the steps by which integration was to be achieved." The Army was the first of the services to adopt a new policy and in 1949 it opened all jobs to qualified personnel. The Korean war presented a battlefield test of the Army's integration policy. Franklin wrote:

> When the North Korean forces began pressing the United Nations forces, especially the Ninth United States Infantry Regiment, the commanding officer began to use men from his all Negro Third Battalion. They were immediately acceptable to the whites "because at a time like that, misery loves company." After General Matthew Ridgway assumed command of all forces in the Far East, he asked permission from the Defense Department to integrate all Negroes throughout his command. Between May and August 1951 the extent of integration in Korea jumped from 9 percent to 30 percent of troops in the field. A special Army report declared that the integration of Negroes had resulted in an overall gain for the Army. At long last, black Americans had become a vital and integral part of the military manpower pool of the Nation [Franklin, p. 464].

While the authenticity of this statement is open to challenge, it serves a purpose in helping to determine the climate of the postwar years as seen through the eyes of a Negro historian.

The gains of the Negro American were many during these formative years. When the A.F. of L. merged with the C.I.O. in 1955, two Negroes, A. Phillip Randolph and Willard Townsend, were elected vice-presidents of the new organization. This was a notable gain for Negro America for it showed a dramatic change in white America's valuation and belief structure. Needless to say, the trauma caused by this move set into motion forces which in a few short years would influence the Supreme Court to make its most important decision as far as the Negro was directly concerned.

The Negro continued to make steady progress. In 1947 the larger hotels of Washington began to accept Negro guests; likewise the restaurants in 1953; and in 1955 the Interstate Commerce Commission decreed that all racial segregation on interstate trains and buses must end by January 10, 1956. In 1947 a federal district judge, J. Wates Waring, declared that Negroes could not be excluded from the Democratic Primary in South Carolina, and in 1954 Illinois sent Negro Democrat William Dawson to the House of Representatives of the United States Congress for his seventh consecutive term. The progress was steady and increasing. America, both white and Negro, was beginning to feel the need to move away from Phillips' model of Negro America, but because valuation and beliefs cannot be changed through legislation, white America remained caught up in Myrdal's *American Dilemma*.

Another reflection found in the same historical age is best described by E. Franklin Frazier:

> When, during a discussion of changes in Chicago, a member of the old family remarked to a member of another that "the old families are never in the newspapers" and received the sympathetic rejoinder that "these people are struggling to get where we were born," they were expressing their partly genuine and partly affected contempt for the new classes that were coming into prominence in the large Negro community. Although these old families had a similar contempt for the migrants who came during earlier periods, they had never felt their positions menaced as they did when the masses of ignorant, uncouth, and impoverished migrants flooded the city during the first World War and changed the whole structure of the Negro community. The earlier migrations had caused little change in the status of the Negro in the city; but, when the Negro community was overwhelmed by the black hordes from the southern plantations, new barriers were raised against the Negro. The old residents, especially those who had prided themselves upon their achievements and their culture, literally fled before the onrush of the migrants. Some of the mulatto families moved into the white neighborhoods. But, as we have seen, the vast majority of the older residents who formed the upper class moved to the periphery of the Negro community.[13]

This situation as described by Frazier was probably the first time a scholarly Negro writer dared to expose to the literary white world in America the deeply rooted class separation in the Negro community. What this means is that even though the Negro leadership was and is talking about progress, "progress" means a "maintaining of the status quo for them and their kind."[14]

This group, as depicted by Frazier, had arrived and did not want their "position" endangered by newcomers who did not want their "sophistication nor class." So while white America is struggling to find a way to undo the effects of prolonged slavery, the Negro "leadership" is busy trying to preserve blacks meager gains.

The 1950's and 60's ushered in an era of self-examination and a "need to know" mentality. Many Americans wanted to know why Negroes were not satisfied with their state; why they could not be like them and take advantage of their situation as they had done in the past; why should so much be given to them when they seemed to do so little with what they had?

The answer to these and similar questions may be found in an examination of Paulo Freire's ideology. Freire seems to think that the beginning of human betterment starts with the individual realizing that he/she is not at the point of development warranted at a particular time. In other words, he says, "concern for humanization leads at once to the recognition of dehumanization" (Freire, p. 31). This was the case of Negro Americans in this historical age. They were beginning to look about themselves and for the first time in their American existence, they had the power, however limited, to change the world. They began to get better jobs, education, housing, use of public utilities and the like. But in all their getting, they did not get freedom. Freire wrote:

> Freedom is acquired by conquest, not by gift. It must be pursued constantly and responsibly. Freedom is not an idea located outside of man; nor is it an idea which becomes myth. It is rather the indispensable condition for the quest for human completion [Freire, p. 31].

In other words the 50's and 60's allowed the Negro community to see themselves, for the first time, as still being dependent on the white world. This is not to say that Negroes should have rejected the many varied social plans, but that they should have had a plan of their own that would in the long run help to deal with their state in an effective manner. Freire wrote:

> The oppressors, who oppress, exploit, and rape by virtue of their power, cannot find in this power the strength to liberate either the oppressed or themselves. Only power that springs from the weakness of the oppressed will be sufficiently strong to free both. Any attempt to soften the power of the oppressor in deference to the weakness of the oppressed almost always manifests itself in the form of false generosity; indeed, the attempt never goes beyond this [Freire, p. 29].

It should be reasonably clear that while Negro Americans enjoy many aspects of freedom, they themselves are not free. Therefore, when Stampp came on the scene in 1954, he found the Negroes enjoying a false generosity; a family structure less matriarchal; and in general, humans void of the chains of slavery but heavily chained with new chains of progress. Davis wrote:

> Kenneth Stampp has been hailed for resolving the tension between progressive historiography and postwar racial enlightenment—for recognizing "that one must know what slavery meant to the Negro and how he reacted to it before one can comprehend his more recent tribulations" [Davis, p. 2].

Elements of the Model

The institution's beginning

Stampp believed that greed was the motivating factor that allowed the institution to have its beginning. He wrote:

> Slavery, then, cannot be attributed to some deadly atmospheric miasma or some irresistible force in the South's economic evolution. The use of slaves in southern agriculture was a deliberate choice (among several alternatives) made by men who sought greater returns than they could obtain from their own labor alone, and who found other types of labor more expensive. "For what purpose does the master hold the servant?" asked an ante-Bellum Southerner. "Is it not that by his labor he, the master, may accumulate wealth?" [p. 5].

It would seem that Stampp further believed that some historians held the idea that the primary reason for the existence of slavery's institution and development was peculiar climatic and environmental conditions. This Stampp strongly disallowed by declaring, "Southerners did not create the slave system all at once in 1619; rather, they built it little by little, step by step, choice by choice, over a period of many years" (p. 6). This position by Stampp allowed him to place the blame for slavery squarely on the shoulders of the Southerner, thereby answering one of the age-old debate questions, why had slavery thrived in South? Stampp took his indictment a step further when he quoted DeBow as saying:

> According to tradition, Negroes had to be brought to the South for labor that Europeans themselves could not perform. "The white man will never raise cane, never raise a cotton or sugar crop in the United States. In our swamps and under our sun the Negro thrives, but the white man dies." Without productive power of the African whom an "all wise Creator" had perfectly adapted to the labor needs of the South, its land would have remained "a howling wilderness" [p. 7].

Stampp considered this position a weak excuse by the Southerner for keeping slaves. He went on to write, "In the swamplands Negroes did not thrive any better than the white man. But Negro slaves, unlike free whites, could be forced to toil in the rice swamps regardless of the effect upon their health. That was the difference" (pp. 7-8).

Stampp postulated that there were three myths which kept the Negro in bondage for two centuries: (1) the all-wise Creator had designed the Negro for labor in the South; (2) that by intellect and temperament he was the natural slave of the white man; and (3) Africans were barbarians who therefore needed to be subjected to rigid discipline and severe controls (p. 11). This understanding allowed Stampp to depart from the traditional perception of the Negro slave and generate a different approach to the problem.

The slave labor system

One of the concerns of Stampp's model was labor and labor conditions. He felt that the working conditions were cruel and the hours were too long:

> On the sugar plantations, during the months of the harvest, slaves were worked to the point of complete exhaustion. They were, in the normal routine, worked from sixteen to eighteen hours a day, seven days a week [p. 85].

Because of the nature of the work and the inhuman treatment, Stampp believed that the slave used many methods to show his contempt for his master. From the breaking of equipment to pretending to be ill, the slave sought to establish some control of his life (pp. 87–88). It is this line of thinking that allowed Stampp to view the same resource material as Phillips and come to altogether different conclusions. It must be stated, however, that Stampp's sources included a wider range of material. For example, he used manuscripts from Alabama's State Department of Archives and History, Montgomery; University of California Library; Fayette County Court House, Lexington, Kentucky; University of Kentucky Library; Department of Archives, Louisiana State University; Maryland Hall of Records, Annapolis; Maryland Historical Society, Baltimore; National North Carolina Department of Archives and History, Raleigh; Southern Historical Collection, University of North Carolina; Virginia Historical Society, Richmond; Virginia State Library, Richmond; and the University of Virginia Library. These are listed simply to show the extent that Stampp went to avoid having his work too easily classified as a polemical reply to Phillips.

Stampp went on to write:

> Slavery was above all a labor system. Wherever in the South the Master lived, however many slaves he owned, it was his bondsmen's productive capacity that he generally valued most. And to the problem of organizing and exploiting their labor with maximum efficiency he devoted much of his attention [p. 34].

It would seem that where Phillips posited the idea that "slavery was good for all parties concerned," Stampp, on the other hand, thought slavery to be good for the masters and the slave holding group.

Slave breaking

Stampp believed that the well-being of the institution of slavery depended solely on the complete and absolute submission of the slave to his master's will. He wrote:

To achieve the "perfect" submission of his slaves, to utilize their labor profitably, each master devised a set of rules by which he governed [p. 143].

The process by which this was accomplished allowed Stampp to come to the conclusion that what most masters wanted by way of behavior was simply not an acquiescence on the part of the slave, but a genuine willingness to please. It is the opinion of Davis and others that the most reliable sources of information on this subject, and on the subject of slavery in general, will be found in the actual slave reports compiled by the W.P.A. writers (Davis, p. 7). Conflicting patterns of behavior did not seem to cause the slave holders any great concern because in the final analysis, the slave was property. Concerning the solving of this problem, Stampp wrote:

> Legislators and magistrates were caught in a dilemma whenever they found that the slave's status as property was incompatible with his status as a person. Individual masters struggled with this dilemma in different ways, some conceding much to the dictates of humanity, others demanding the utmost return from their investment [p. 143].

However, the final word remained with the master and in almost every instance the slave as chattel prevailed. As a consequence of this kind of logic, the prevailing question was, how did the masters gain this absolute control? Stampp outlined five steps for breaking new slaves:

1. First step: to establish and maintain strict discipline ... they must obey at all times, and under all circumstances, cheerfully and with alacrity.... It greatly impairs the happiness of a Negro to be allowed to cultivate an insubordinate temper. Unconditional submission is the only footing upon which slavery should be placed.

2. Second step: to implant in the bondsmen themselves a consciousness of personal inferiority. They had "to know and keep their place," to "feel the difference between master and slave," to understand that bondage was their natural status. They had to feel that African ancestry tainted them, that their color was a badge of degradation.

3. Third step: to awe them with a sense of their master's enormous power. "The only principle upon which slavery could be maintained was the principle of fear.... "We have to rely more and more on the power of fear.... We are determined to continue as masters, and to do so we have to draw the reign tighter and tighter day by day ... it was essential "to make them stand in fear."

4. Fourth step: to persuade the bondsman to take an interest in the master's enterprise and to accept his standards of good conduct.... The master should make it his business to show his slaves that the advancement of his individual interest is at the same time an advancement of theirs.

5. Fifth step: to impress Negroes with their helplessness, to create in them a "habit of perfect dependence" upon their masters [pp. 144–46].

Stampp stated that this goal was seldom reached and that the average slave remained a constant problem to his master. The data examined in this research project tend to indicate that "this breaking" had a more serious effect than Stampp could realize.

The slave and freedom

Phillips and the proslavery writers believed that the slave was void of any concept of freedom. They were eager to show that the slave's "nature" was inclined to readily accept domination. Stampp cited this instance:

> Bondsmen generally were cheerful and acquiescent ... because they were treated with kindness and relieved of all responsibilities; having known no other condition, they unthinkingly accepted bondage as their natural status. They found themselves first existing in this state, and passing through life without questioning the justice of their allotment, which, if they think at all, they suppose a natural one [p. 86].

This proslavery position allowed Stampp's approach to challenge Phillips and his supporters, and as Davis stated, "lay to rest the age old debate of the slave liking his slave status." Stampp took a position, which Davis agreed with, that since most historians had not personally experienced slavery, they could hardly expect to know exactly how the slave felt about slavery (p. 86).

Stampp noted that plantation records showed that at best the slave was a "troublesome property." He cited the following:

> A South Carolinian: "The white man does not know the Negro so well as he thinks he does." A Virginia master believed that "slaves had their faculties sharpened by constant exercise and their perceptions were extremely fine and acute." An overseer decided that a man who "put his confidence in a Negro was simply a damned fool." A Georgia planter concluded: "So deceitful is a Negro that as far as my experience extends I could never in a single instance decipher his character.... We planters could never get at the truth" [pp. 87–88].

It would seem that Stampp was closer to the truth than Phillips because the very institution itself brought the slave into contact with the freedman; it also, through contact with the master, allowed the slave to have at least a limited understanding of freedom. Stampp wrote concerning this:

> That they had no understanding of freedom and therefore accepted bondage as their natural condition is hard to believe. They had only to observe their masters and the other free men about them to obtain a very distinct idea of the meaning and advantages of freedom. All knew that some Negroes had been emancipated: they knew that freedom was a possible

condition for any of them. They continually have before their eyes, persons of the color, many of whom they have known in slavery ... freed from the control of masters, working where they pleased, going whither they pleased, and expending their money how they pleased [p. 88].

This departure by Stampp allowed him to view the slave in a non-traditional posture; it further allowed the first step to be taken in what Myrdal called "cumulative causation." Stampp not only broke away from the traditional view of the Negro slave, he cast a deep shadow over the white world's need to maintain their own form of racism.

That the slave preferred freedom to slavery is of little significance to understanding his early cultural development. But since Phillips and his supporters made an issue of this point, it fits the purpose of this research project to allow Stampp his rebuttal. He cited a South Carolina doctor saying:

> To offer to the race the nominal freedom which a free colored person possesses in our land, is a test by no means satisfactory, it is about as reasonable as it would be to put a muzzle on a pig's nose, and then invite him to the potato patch. Of course, he would prefer to remain in his pen, and drink the swill you might be pleased to give him [p. 93].

Runaway slaves

If, as Phillips stated, the slaves were cheerful and content, why did they run away? Stampp seemed to be of the opinion that they ran away for various reasons: they ran when they were angry with their masters; they ran when the need to be free overwhelmed them; they ran to avoid punishment; they just ran. Stampp wrote:

> The advertisements for runaways were filled with personal tragedies such as the following: "I think it quite probable that this fellow has succeeded in getting to his wife, who was carried away last Spring out of my neighborhood." Lawrence, age fourteen, was trying to make his way from Florida to Atlanta where "his mother is supposed to be." Mary "is no doubt lurking about in the vicinity of Goose Creek, where she had children." Will, aged fifty, "has recently been owned in Savannah, where he has a wife and children." Items such as these appeared regularly in southern papers [p. 112].

Slave as chattel personal

It would seem that while Stampp was very much concerned with the human element of slavery, he was unable to divorce himself from his own cultural influences, thereby greatly limiting his sensitivity to the main issue, the inalienable right of man to live "in the image of God." This is not to say that he was void of sympathetic feelings for the slave, conversely, he felt as much sympathy as it was possible for a white man to feel. The observation that is made here is that Stampp too, like Phillips, was attempting to cross cultural lines in his quest to do pure research (Williams, pp. 22–23). Stampp wrote:

> The unsentimental prose of legal codes and court records, of sheriff's notices and administrator's accounts, gave some indication of the dehumanizing effects of reducing people to "chattels personal." ... Slaves were bartered, deeded, devised, pledged, seized, and auctioned. They were awarded as prizes in lotteries and raffles; they were wagered at gaming tables and horse races. They were, in short, property in fact as well as in law [p. 201].

It is important that this concept of "chattels personal" be fully understood because it is the undergirding principle which allowed the whites to perceive the African as less than human and as a property endowed by God to be treated as such.[15] The question of why the African was chosen for slavery is still unanswered. Frederick L. Olmsted wrote:

> It is difficult to handle simply as property, a creature possessing human passions and human feelings ... while, on the other hand, the absolute necessity of dealing with property as a thing, greatly embarrasses a man in any attempt to treat it as a person.[16]

Stampp seemed to agree with this premise because throughout his book he saw the slave holders as a people caught in a dualism; they wanted to be known as great humanitarians, while at the same time they allowed themselves to become dependent upon the slaves and the high rate of return that an investment in them would bring. Therefore, it would seem that from the very beginning the African was doomed to become the slave of the white man.[17]

Stampp recognized that the slave, to many slave holders, had a threefold identity. First, he was chattel personal; second, he was real estate; and third, he was human, to a certain degree. According to Stampp, the antebellum slave codes clearly stated:

> The slaves were deemed, held, taken, reputed and adjudged in law to be chattel personal, in the hands of their owners and possessors and their executors, administrators and assigns, to all intents, constructions and purposes whatsoever. Slaves had the attributes of personal property everywhere, except in Louisiana (Kentucky before 1852) where they had the attributes of real estate.... In states where slaves were generally considered as personal property, they were treated as realty for purposes of inheritance. In Louisiana, where they were supposedly like real property, they retained many of the characteristics of "chattel personal" [pp. 196–97].

While Phillips saw the master as kind and paternal in his treatment of the slave, Stampp saw the master as an owner of property with absolute control of the same. He cited the master as:

Recognizing the slave as property "of a distinctive and peculiar character," he was a person who was legally at the disposal of his master, whose property was very nearly absolute. "The master," proclaimed the Louisiana code, may sell him, dispose of his person, his industry, and his labor; he can do nothing, possess nothing, nor acquire anything but what must belong to his master…. Legally a bondsman was unable to acquire title to property by purchase, gift, or devise; he could not be a party to a contract. No promise of freedom, oral or written, was binding upon his master [p. 197].

According to this understanding, the slave was not only a property in the minds of the slave holders, he was by law chattel personal–real estate. The efficacy of this system of ownership rested with the slave's ability or inability to resist it. Needless to say, in most instances, the slave was powerless and the system prevailed.[18]

Slavemongering

One question constantly surfaced during the examination of the resource data. Was slavemongering among the slave holders an accident of nature, or was it a premeditated adventure born of selfish greed? Of this Stampp wrote:

One of the early propagandists for Florida proclaimed: "The climate is peculiarly adapted and fitted to the constitution of the Negro. It is an excellent and cheap climate to breed and raise them. The offet of the Sugar House fattens them like young pigs." … Masters who prized prolific Negro women not only tolerated but sometimes came close to promoting sexual promiscuity among them…. Every child born to a slave woman became the master's property, and usually the child's ultimate capital value far exceeded the cost of raising him … seldom did female chattels disappoint their owner. After all, sexual promiscuity brought them rewards rather than penalties…. It is remarkable the number of slaves which may be raised from one woman in the course of forty or fifty years with the proper kind of attention [p. 281].

Stampp thus portrayed the slave holders, in general, as not only engaged in slavemongering, but they encouraged the slaves to "please" their masters by being prolific.

It would seem that trading in slaves was the natural outcome of economic development and land expansion. The great westward movement and the exhaustion of many local farming lands inadvertently created a greater need for slaves, especially since the Atlantic slave trade was very much restricted, if not closed altogether. Concerning this, Stampp wrote:

The Atlantic and border states, with Virginia constantly ranking first among them, were the exporters of slaves. In the three decades between 1830 and 1860, Virginia exported nearly three hundred thousand—almost the whole of her natural increase. Maryland and Kentucky each exported about seventy-five thousand, North Carolina about one hundred thousand, South Carolina about one hundred seventy thousand, and Missouri and Tennessee smaller numbers [p. 238].

These figures alone indicate that if a normal moral code were in use, the slave population, under normal circumstances, could not have supplied enough slaves to fill these requirements. In support of this,

A Virginia farmer boasted:

"My slave women were uncommonly good breeders; I do not suppose that there was a lot of women anywhere that bred faster than mine." Every infant, he exulted, was worth two hundred dollars at current prices the moment it was born [p. 246].

A Tennessee Court protected

The heirs of an estate by prohibiting the sale of a slave woman who had given birth to several children. To sell this slave, "so peculiarly valuable for her physical capacity of child-bearing," the court believed would have been an "enormous sacrifice" [p. 246].

A South Carolinian advertised:

Wish to sell fifty "prime orderly Negroes," ... They were purchased for stock and breeding Negroes, and to any Planter who particularly wanted them for that purpose, they are a very choice and desirable gang [pp. 246–47].

An unsuccessful Mississippi farmer was described as:

A small planter who was "an unsuccessful farmer, generally buying his corn and meat," but who "succeeded very well in raising young Negroes" [p. 247].

The degree and extent that slavemongering was permitted during the plantation regime is not significant to this research project; however, what is significant is the attitude of the masters that would permit any at all and the attitude of the slaves towards this inhuman adventure. Stampp cited:

Seldom did female chattels disappoint their owners. After all, sexual promiscuity brought them rewards rather than penalties; large families meant no increased responsibilities and, if anything, less toil rather than more (p. 248).

The point that Stampp unknowingly raised concerns the difference between what Fanny Kemble, a Georgia plantation owner's wife, observed and the present plight of the poor Negro female. She observed:

That she understood distinctly what it was that gave them [Negro female slaves] value as property. "This was perfectly evident to me from the meritorious air with which the women always made haste to inform me of the number of children they had borne, and the frequent occasions on which the older slaves would direct my attention to their children, exclaiming, "Look missis! little niggers for you and massa; plenty little niggers for you and little missis!" [p. 248].

It seems that slavemongering tended to have an effect on the female slave that went beyond mere sexual activity. It would appear that in the process of slavemongering, the female slave began to see herself as something less than morally human. Nevertheless, let it suffice to say here that the implication of slavemongering was dehumanizing.

Slave maintenance

While Stampp agreed with Phillips that slave maintenance was an important category, he differed with him in its administration. He believed that most slave holders were ignorant of sound nutritional principles. He wrote:

> In any case, the adequacy of the provisions furnished the slaves must be judged in the light of what ante-bellum Southerners knew about the principles of nutrition.... In 1859, Dr. John H. Wilson wrote: "It was common notion that fat bacon and pork are highly nutritious; but almost everything, even the lightest and most watery vegetables contain more nutritive muscle-building elements. Yet these fatty articles of diet are peculiarly appropriate on account of their heat-producing properties [p. 283].

Consequently, Stampp seemed to believe that the maintenance of the slave was more of a means for getting the most out of them rather than, as Phillips posited, a humane enterprise.

Paternalism

Stampp believed that the antebellum paternalism as posited by the slave holders was an unrealistic explanation of slave behavior, ignoring the forces that produced the need for such behavior. He wrote:

> The kernel of fact—the reality of ante-bellum paternalism—needs to be separated from its fanciful surroundings and critically analyzed. How much paternalism was there? Under what circumstances did it occur? What was its nature? [p. 322].

This would indicate that Stampp was not convinced that the so-called "good relationship" between slave and master was a real condition. He was of the opinion that much of the slave's accommodating manner was a result of prolonged and severe enslavement. There have been many occasions where the Negro, out of necessity, allowed himself to be debased in order to satisfy "that peculiar need" in his employer. This peculiar need of white people to completely dominate Negroes is a primary result of the American slave system. It was born out of the polemics of difference and nurtured in the selfish need to survive. Stampp wrote that, "When the Negro is definitely a slave, it would seem that the alleged natural antipathy of this white race to associate with him is lost" (p. 327). This statement appears to support the idea that what has been called "the white man's love for the Negro" is in actuality an outward show of his inwardly felt mastership. Stampp wrote:

> These were the facts "out of real life" from which grew the legend of racial harmony in the Old South.... "Meta has nursed sister's baby as well as her own for three days.... There was the "faithful and kind old nurse" who watched over her master in his infancy ... the "faithful and devoted" field hand who earned his regard "by implicit obedience to all his commands. These cases were not imaginary but arose out of real life" [p. 325].

Stampp best summarized the situation when he wrote:

> After a century, few remember that southern slavery was not so much a patriarchal institution as a practical labor system. Few recall that the slave holders were more often ambitious entrepreneurs than selfless philanthropist. And few ask what the slaves themselves thought of bondage.... The most generous master, so long as he was determined to be master, could be paternal only toward a fawning dependent.... The slave who had most completely lost his manhood, who had lost confidence in himself, who stood before his master with hat in hand, head slightly bent, was the one best suited to receive favors and affection of a patriarch. The system was in essence a process of infantilization — and the master used the most perfect products of the system to prove that Negroes were a childlike race, needing guidance and protection but inviting paternal love as well.... He made them the butt of his humor and fair game for a good natured practical joke. He tolerated their faults, sighed at their irresponsibility, and laughed at their pompous and ridiculous attempts to imitate the whites [p. 328].

It would seem from the evidence that what the average white person regarded as love was in actuality a type of fear. The slave, out of desperation, had to know his master's will and above all he had to understand that in all instances of conflict, he would receive the brunt of any action taken. Stampp saw this situation in this manner:

> But the predominant and overpowering emotion that whites aroused in the majority of slaves was neither love nor hate but fear. "We were always uneasy," an ex-slave recalled; when "a white man spoke to me, I would feel frightened," another confessed. In Alabama, a visitor who lost his pocketbook noted that the slave who found it "was afraid of being whipped for theft and had given it to the first white man he saw, and at first was afraid to pick it up" [p. 381].

Stampp went on to explain that this fear took many forms. The most demonstrative of these were often expressed by masters in their advertisements for runaway slaves. Stampp stated it in this manner:

> When they (masters) advertised for runaways, the owners frequently revealed a distressing relationship between the two races, a relationship that must have been for these slaves an emotional nightmare. In their advertisements no descriptive phrases were more common than these: "stutters very much when spoken to"; "speaks softly and has a downcast look"; "has uneasy appearance when spoken to"; "stammers very much so as to be scarcely understood." "I feel lighter,—the dread is gone," affirmed a Negro woman who had escaped to Canada. "It is a great heaviness on a person's mind to be a slave" [p. 381].

Labor, slave and free

Stampp wrote:

> Pro-slavery writers frequently contended that northern workers suffered greater privation than southern slaves. They demonstrated this by contrasting the hardships of the lowest paid, most heartlessly exploited factory hands with the comforts of the best treated bondsmen. They found abundant evidence of widespread poverty among new immigrants and among unskilled or semi-skilled workers in the industrial towns of the north-east, especially during periods of economic depression [p. 281].

This argument has been used by the elite since the inception of slavery to either excuse the dehumanization of slavery or to justify its existence. Phillips was of the latter opinion, while Stampp disagreed with both positions. He seemed to feel that there was no comparison between free labor and slave labor. While both Stampp and Phillips believed that they were clarifying a central tenent of slavery, labor and morality, Myrdal and others thought that a person's labor cannot be conscripted without first reducing that person to chattel personal. Once this is done, there is no humane ground for an open in-depth discussion of free and slave labor synoptically.

The profitability of slavery has been an age-old debate used by both pro- and antislavery proponents. Phillips represented the slave holding class while Stampp represented the antislavery class. The significance of this age-old debate to this research project rests with the attitudes of both groups rather than the morality of the debate itself. The research data compiled in this project indicates that the slave holders did not want to admit that slavery was profitable because of the moral implications involved in such an admittance. Stampp took the position that unless there was a profit to be found in slavery, why be so engaged? He put it this way:

> If the employment of slaves was unprofitable (or nearly so), it must somehow be explained why slaves brought high prices in the market and

why masters continued to use them. To say that no other form of labor
was available hardly answers the question, for slave labor could have been
converted into free labor by emancipation [p. 384].

Stampp's argument was that even though the slave holder may have been
able to find some other form of enterprise that would have given him
an equal return per investment, he was "emotionally and ideologically
committed to the agrarian way of life—to the Jeffersonian idea that those
who live on the land were more virtuous than those who engaged in commerce and industry" (p. 385). This "commitment to the agrarian way
of life" caused the slave holder to find sensible ways to justify his use
of slaves. He usually started by positing the notion "that Negroes were
unfit for freedom." He next used a fear tactic; the race problem would
be exacerbated—"because the presence of a horde of free Negroes would
pose an immense social danger and threaten southern civilization." And
finally, "slavery was, above all, a method of regulating race relations,
an instrument of social control" (p. 387).

Stampp believed that this was a weak position and for all intents
and purposes slavery existed because it was profitable for the slave holders.

Regardless of whether slavery was or was not profitable, the slave
holder kept his slaves until he was forced to release them. His reasons
may have been based on a nonprofit scale; however, his attitude was one
which saw the slave as property and as such he continued his slave status
until forced to do otherwise.

In summary, while Stampp used a wider range of source materials,
he followed the basic outline of Phillips. He was inevitably influenced
by the scholarship of Phillips and set out to develop a polemic that would
counterbalance this monumental work which had pervaded historical
thought for so many years.

This model of Negro culture as posited by Stampp is a sharp departure from Phillips' model in that Stampp saw the Negro slave as a human
caught in a milieu of untimely circumstances. He wrote concerning this:

> Today we are learning much from the natural and social sciences about
> the Negro's potentialities and about the basic irrelevance of race, and we
> are slowly discovering the roots and meaning of human behavior. All this
> is of immense value to the historian when, for example, he tries to grasp
> the significance of the Old South's "peculiar institution." I have assumed
> that the slaves were merely ordinary human beings, that innately Negroes
> are, after all, only white men with black skins, nothing more, nothing
> less. I did not, of course, assume that there have been, or are today, no
> cultural differences between black and white Americans. Nor do I regard
> it as flattery to call Negroes white men with black skins.... I have simply
> found no convincing evidence that there are any significant differences
> between the innate emotional traits and intellectual capacities of Negroes
> and whites [pp. vii–viii].

Summary of the Elements of the Model

In conclusion, this model is comprised of the following elements:

The Negro/slave was
1. A poor victim of circumstances—a white man in a black skin
2. Chattel personal
3. A slavery-hater
4. Poorly fed
5. Expected to work long and hard hours
6. Inhumanely treated
7. Mongrelized
8. Forced to accommodate
9. Constantly seeking freedom

The institution of slavery was
1. Not a school
2. A cruel labor force
3. Inhumane
4. Exploitive
5. Oppressive
6. A systematic dehumanizing process

The institution of slavery provided
1. Necessary staples
2. The means to keep "the slave standing in fear."

Chapter IV
The Counter-Progressive Model

The counter-progressive model is based on Stanley M. Elkins' book, *Slavery: A Problem in American Institutional and Intellectual Life*. Elkins, like Phillips and Stampp, was an exceptional scholar. While his critics are varied and many, his academic achievements were second to none. (For personal data concerning Elkins, see the Appendix.)

This model is concerned with that interpretation of slavery as posited by Elkins. Elkins believed that North American slavery was so dehumanizing that its victims underwent a drastic personality change. He developed his thesis around the premise that this personality change only took place in the North American system of slavery. While there were many historians who challenged this premise, all or at least most of them credited Elkins with bringing the models of Phillips and Stampp under new considerations. It is these new considerations that set the parameters for this portion of this research. However, before these new considerations can be examined, the relative position of the Negro needs to be analyzed in terms of economic and social progress.

Background Data

After the introduction of Phillips' *American Negro Slavery* and Stampp's *Peculiar Institution*, some major social changes took place in America. For the first time the Negro moved into the "mainstream of American life" in appreciable numbers.[1]

Accomplishments

1955. Mrs. Rosa Parks was arrested — seeds planted for Montgomery Bus Boycott.

1955. The Metcalf-Baker Law was passed forbidding discrimination in housing assisted by FHA or Veterans Administration funds.

1955. Robert Weaver was appointed state rent commissioner (New York).

1955. Marian Anderson became the first Negro American to sing on stage of the Metropolitan Opera House.

1957. Henry Aaron voted most valuable player in the National League and won his first home run title.

1959. Negroes were elected to local office in North Carolina.

Supreme Court action

1955. Ordered school boards to draw up desegregation procedures "with all deliberate speed."

1956. Rules bus segregation unconstitutional.

Presidential action

1957. President Eisenhower ordered paratroopers into Little Rock.

These are but a few of the gains that the Negro had made when Elkins released his book. In light of these many accomplishments, it would seem that the Negro had "arrived"; in fact, the masses were still where Phillips had left them and much to the surprise of many historians integration was failing even before it had begun.

In the middle and late 1950's the Negro Americans were caught between the reality of being whole persons and the participatory act of living as whole persons. They were still acting out the roles assigned to their forefathers with little hope of passing on to their children anything less than slave status. Concerning this theodicy, Peter Berger wrote:

> The individual finds his ancestors continuing mysteriously within himself, and in the same way he projects his own being into his children and later descendants. As a result, he acquires a (to him) quite concrete immortality, which drastically relativizes the mortality as well as the lesser misfortunes of his empirical biography. "I must die but my children and children's children will live on forever." ... The entire collectivity, bound together by ties of blood, thus becomes (to its own self understanding) quite concretely immortal, for it carries with it through time the same fundamental life that is incarnate in each of its members. To destroy this immortality, an enemy must eradicate every last living soul belonging to the collectivity.[3]

In the late 1950's and the early 1960's when many Americans were either preparing for or engaged in the civil rights movement, many legislators still found a necessity for new civil legislation in order to aid Negro Americans in their quest for a reasonable degree of self-fulfillment. For example, in 1959, California abolished its antimiscegenation act and passed a law forbidding discrimination in public housing (Ploski and Marr, pp. 27–31). This "need to legislate" mentality was and is a definite indication that the majority of Negroes had not "arrived."

These times found the liberal white American and the newly migrated Negro enjoying a pseudo-democratic relationship. These white liberals believed that Negroes were as Stampp had projected them, a white man in a black skin; a victim of peculiar circumstances. While the Northern Negroes saw themselves under ever constant pressure to define and defend their existence, the Negroes of the South were caught up in the South's struggle to re-establish a stable economy. Consequently, since the majority of Negroes resided in the South, the Negro masses had little opportunity to either define or defend themselves.[3]

In 1944, when Myrdal published his monumental work, he was able to uncover several attitudes towards Negro Americans that had lain hidden for many years. He believed that the "convenience of ignorance" allowed the Southerners to believe that they knew "just how to handle the Negro." He wrote:

> The insistence on the part of the Southern whites that they have reliable and intimate knowledge about the Negro problem is one of the most pathetic stereotypes in the South. In fact, the average Southerner "knows" the Negro and the interracial problem as the patient "knows" the toothache — in the sense that he feels concern — not as the diagnosing dentist knows his own patient's trouble. He further knows the Negro in the sense that he is brought up to use a technique in dealing with Negroes by which he is able to get them into submissive patterns of behavior. This technique is simple; I have often observed that merely speaking the Southern dialect works the trick [Myrdal, p. 31].[4]

Myrdal went on to explain that the Northerner differs from the Southerner only in that he judges all Negroes by the ones with whom he has had the most dealings. All Negroes are like his cook or his housekeeper or some other favorite servant. This type of mentality usually developed a "super Negro analyst" who spends much time going to community meetings where they "can come to know each other." The significant point to be noted here is that this attitude is very similar to the old paternal Southern attitude. In support of this premise, Myrdal stated, "They often confess how vastly their knowledge of the Negro has increased because they, in these meetings, had a chance to talk to Reverend So-and-so, or Doctor So-and-so" (Myrdal, p. 41).

It would seem that even though Stampp had uncovered another facet of Negro personality, white America was still unable to see Negroes as they are. Myrdal wrote:

> The ignorance about the Negro is not, it must be stressed, just a random lack of interest and knowledge. It is a tense and highstrung restriction and distortion of knowledge, and it indicates much deeper dislocation within the minds of the Southern whites [Myrdal, p. 42].[5]

Myrdal's treatment of this "distortion of knowledge" is rather unique. He used the following quotations from prominent Negroes to help support his case:

> *Booker T. Washington*: Whites are moved by a bad conscience. If they really believe there is danger from the Negro it must be because they do not intend to give him justice. Injustice always breeds fear.
>
> *James Weldon Johnson*: ... the main difficulty of the race question does not lie so much in the actual condition of the blacks as it does in the mental attitudes of the whites.... The race question involves the saving of black America's body and white America's soul.
>
> *Ray Atannard Baker*: It keeps coming to me that this is more a white man's problem than it is a Negro.... Yes, we Southerners need a freedom from suspicion, fear, anxiety, doubt, unrest, hate, contempt, disgust, and all the rest of the race-feeling-begotten brood of viperous emotions [Myrdal, p. 4].

Myrdal goes on to state that "the Negroes base their fundamental strategy for improving their status on this insight":

> The careful observer will discover another characteristic of Negro psychology—his quick perception of physical disadvantage and his equally quick adjustment to secure the moral advantage. In all the agitation concerning the Negro's status in America, the moral advantage has always been on his side, and with that as a lever he has steadily effected progress in spite of material disadvantage [Myrdal, p. 42].

This statement by Myrdal indicates that there may be some credence to the Negroes' claim that they do have some gnostic truth about how to deal with the white world. The point seems to be that because Negroes were the ones enslaved, they therefore had to study their masters in order to please them. As a consequence, white America had not found any disadvantage in their convenience of ignorance theory, thereby perceiving themselves as masters.

Negroes, even though free, were still troublesome members of white society, and in 1959 when Stanley Elkins' *Slavery* was introduced to the American public it was a welcome relief to Stampp's "white man in a black skin" model because in spite of all efforts, the Negroes had not been able to "wash away" their black skins.

While Stampp's *Peculiar Institution* had replaced Phillips' *American Negro Slavery*, Elkins was hailed as the answer to the Negro problem. Davis was able to write that to many historians Elkins' book "dictated the framework of much of the ensuing debate over slavery."[6] Elkins' interpretation of slavery then became the latest tool for an in-depth analysis of slavery in the Western Hemisphere.

Elements of the Model

State of institution

Elkins enlarged this debate by first viewing the state of the institution of slavery. He posited the idea that the institution had lost its relevance to societal needs as early as 1830 and that the seeds of destruction for slavery followed shortly thereafter; however, America refused to see the problem of slavery as anything but a moral issue. Accordingly, he wrote:

> Every phase of the movement combined to produce in our abolitionist that peculiar quality of abstraction which was, and has remained, uniquely American. For them, the question was all moral; it must be contemplated in terms untouched by expediency, untarnished by society itself. It was a problem of conscience which by mid-century would fasten itself in one form or another, and varying degrees, upon men's feelings everywhere.[7]*

He saw the demise of the institutional church as the beginning of the end for all long-established institutions. This understanding permitted Elkins to view slavery not so much as a system of labor but a system necessary to the institution of slavery. Quoting him, "slavery might have been approached not as a problem in pure morality but as a question of institutional arrangements" (p. 28). This premise led Elkins to ask:

> How had slavery in the United States come into being? There is nothing natural about it.... It had nothing to do with characteristics which might have made the Negro peculiarly suited either to slavery or to the labor of tobacco culture.... Nor was it a matter of common law.... In certain altogether crucial respects slavery as we know it was not imported from elsewhere but was created in America—fashioned on the spot by Englishmen in whose tradition such an institution had no part [pp. 37–38].

While this position was not unique in itself, it did allow Elkins the opportunity to attempt to separate his thesis from his most influential prototype, Tannenbaum, who earlier in his *Slave and Citizen* had laid the foundation for just such a position. Elkins went on to posit the idea that "motive of gain" coupled with the dynamics of a new system of capitalism fostered the growth and acceptance of slavery in the New World.

*Hereafter in this chapter references to page numbers only are to this book.

The institution of slavery, as seen by Elkins, was above all a social instrument borne out of the times. It was more than a moral or amoral occurrence. Slavery was a manmade enterprise with good and bad elements, and if mankind was to overcome its evil implications man must see it as it actually existed. He went on to write:

> Neither antagonist, in short—burning with guilt or moral righteousness, as the case may have been—could quite conceive of slavery as a social institution, functioning, for better or worse, by laws and logic like other institutions, mutable like others, a product of human custom, fashioned by the culture in which it flourished, and capable of infinite variation from one culture to another [p. 37].

Capitalism and slavery

To Elkins the uniqueness of North American slavery could not be explained away using the old methods of historical research because "American slavery was unique, in the sense that, for symmetry and precision of outline, nothing like it had ever previously been seen" (p. 38). He believed that North American slavery was a new form of servitude in that it created new laws to explain as well as sanction its existence (pp. 38–42).[8] It would seem that Oscar and Mary Handlin greatly influenced Elkins in coming to this conclusion.[9]

Elkins thought that the very struggle and the hardships encountered by the early settlers of America allowed them the impetus to use capitalism as a means of surviving handsomely. He wrote:

> Was it the "Motive of gain"? Yes, but with a difference.... Here, even in its embryonic stages, it is possible to see the process whereby capitalism would emerge as the principal dynamic force in American society. The New World had been discovered and exploited by a European civilization which had always, in contrast with other cultures, placed a particularly high premium on personal achievement, and it was to be the special genius of Englishmen, from Elizabeth's time onward, to transform this career concept from its earlier chivalric form into one of economic fulfilment—from "glory" to "success" [p. 43].

Elkins began to look at what he called four major legal categories which defined the status of the American Negro slave. They were, "term of servitude," "marriage and the family," "police and disciplinary powers over the slave," and "property and other civil rights." These categories are different from those of Phillips. These categories inadvertently led Elkins to virtually the same conclusion as Stampp. "The basic fact was, of course, that the slave himself was property. He and his fellow bondsmen had long since become chattel personal ... to all intents, constitutions and purposes whatsoever."[10] He explained the four major legal categories so:

Term of servitude: Had in effect been established during the latter half of the seventeenth century; a slave was a slave for the duration of his life, and slavery was a status which he transmitted by inheritance to his children and his children's children [p. 52].

Marriage and family: That most ancient and intimate of institutional arrangements, marriage and the family, had long since been destroyed by the law, and the law never showed any inclination to rehabilitate it [p. 53].[11]

Police and discipline: The slave was the property of his master and the police and the law was one of the means for ensuring that all concerned abided within [pp. 56–58].

Civil rights: The rights of property, and all civil and legal "rights" were everywhere denied the slave with a clarity that left no doubt of his utter dependency upon his master [p. 59].

To Elkins slavery represented a paradox. On the one hand there was the "warm sentiments of the good master for his blacks" while on the other hand these same "good masters" held that "all slaves were black; slaves are degraded and contemptible and should be kept in a state of slavery" (p. 61). Elkins saw this Southern attitude as descriptive of Southern mentality wherein capitalism was concerned:

That very strength and bulwark of American society, capitalism, unimpeded by prior arrangements and institutions, had stamped the status of slave upon the black with a clarity which elsewhere could never have been so profound, and had further defined the institution of slavery with such nicety that the slave was, in fact, degraded. That the black, as a species, was thus contemptible seemed to follow by observation [p. 61].

The open system of slavery

To Elkins the Latin American system of slavery differed greatly from the North American system by viewing the slave as a human entity thereby allowing the main constructs of his social order to remain intact. Under this system of slavery the slave was allowed enough social space (open system) to develop as a human being. Elkins described it this way:

In Latin America, the very tension and balance among three kinds of organizational concerns — church, crown, and plantation agriculture — prevented slavery from being carried by the planting class to its ultimate logic. For the slave, in terms of the space thus allowed for the development of men and women as moral beings, the results were an "open system" (p. 81).

This departure by Elkins from the traditional way of viewing slavery allowed him the opportunity to build a base that would later establish his conception of slave personality.

The closed system of slavery

In the North American system of slavery the slave was projected as property having no legal or social rights other than those granted by the master. This system was so restrictive that even the church could not positively impact upon its degrading effects. Elkins put it this way:

> The North American system had developed virtually unchecked by institutions having anything like the power of their Latin American counterparts; the legal structure which supported it, shaped only by the demands of a staple-raising capitalism, had defined with such nicety the slave's character as chattel that his character as a moral individual was left in the vaguest of legal obscurity. In this sense American slavery operated as a "closed system" [p. 81].

Elkins believed that such a "closed system" should have "produced noticeable effects upon the slave's very personality" (p. 82).

Sambo

The "Sambo Thesis" was not a new one because Samuel E. Morison and H.S. Commager had caused quite a stir at Queen's College in the early 50's by their use of the term. (For a detailed account of this early use, see their book, *The Growth of the American Republic*.) Elkins believed that the "Sambo Thesis" came primarily from Southern lore. He wrote:

> Sambo, the typical plantation slave, was docile but irresponsible, loyal but lazy, humble but chronically given to lying and stealing; his behavior was full of infantile silliness and his talk inflated with childish exaggerations. His relationship with his master was one of utter dependence and childlike attachment: it was indeed this childlike quality that was the very key to his being [p. 82].

He asked, "Was he real? What order of existence, what rank of legitimacy, should be accorded him? Is there a scientific way to talk about this problem?" (p. 82). These "simplest of questions" afforded to Elkins' Sambo Thesis the legitimacy that it needed if he was to interpret slavery void of its moral implications. In all fairness, Elkins showed both sides of this position, the open and the closed system, and he tried to keep morality out of his considerations. Accordingly, he stated, "Northern reformers ... in ante-bellum times, thought that nothing could actually be said about the Negro's true nature because that nature was veiled by the institution of slavery." This Elkins saw as a weak excuse for not facing the issue. He believed that the "Sambo" type did exist and he even conceded that this side of the slave's personality may have been just "role play" on the part of the slave. However, even after drawing from Stampp's model that "there were plenty of opportunists among the Negroes who played the roles assigned them" (p. 83), he still believed that there had to be a significant personality change in order for the slave to even convincingly engage in the role play. He wrote:

> And if Sambo is uniquely an American product, then his existence and the reasons for his character, must be recognized in order to appreciate the very scope of our slave problem and its aftermath. The absoluteness with which such a personality (real or unreal) had been stamped upon the plantation slave does much to make plausible the ante-bellum Southerner's difficulty in imagining that blacks anywhere could be anything but a degraded race [p. 85].

It would seem that after examining these two types of slave systems, Elkins came to the conclusion that the Sambo personality was a direct product of the "closed system." Concerning this, Elkins wrote:

> It will be assumed that there were elements in the very structure of the plantation system — its "closed" character — that could sustain infantilism as a normal feature of behavior. These elements, having less to do with "cruelty" per se than simply with the sanctions of authority, were effective and pervasive enough to require that such infantilism be characterized as something much more basic than mere "accommodation." It will be assumed that the sanctions of the system were in themselves sufficient to produce a recognizable personality type [p. 86].

The African cultural argument

The research data examined thus far regarding the counter-progressive model shows Negroes to be racially inferior, Sambo-like, primitive, etc. Elkins believed that these concepts of the personalities of Negroes are not inherent to their nature (p. 89). Actually, they were spawned through a series of social developments (p. 90). In Phillips' model, Negro character is based on race which to all intents and purposes has been discredited. The most enduring model of Negro character is based on the "primitive nature of African tribal culture" (p. 91). This premise too is viewed by Elkins as somewhat less than desirable. He believed that the early anthropologists built their induction into the New World slave system. Elkins wrote of this:

> We can suppose that the pseudo-anthropologists of the early 1900's must have begun, in their reasoning, not with Africa but with the depressed state of Negro existence in this country. They were thus prepared a priori, in their efforts to make connections, to find something comparable in the original tribal state [p. 82].

While this is not an outright accusation of an attempt to misinterpret data, it would seem that Elkins is implying that the African was doomed to be perceived as he was made to be by the institution of slavery. This assumption by Elkins is significant because it helps to establish the Negro American's personality as being strictly American-made. Elkins broke abruptly with Herskovits on his African transferrals and posited the cultural development of the Negro American inside the North American plantation regime. He stated:

> The present writer is accepting without question the findings and generalizations put forth in the above work (Melville J. Herskovits, *The Myth of the Negro Past*), insofar as they relate to the Negro in Africa. Quite another matter, however, is the effort made by Professor Herskovits to exhibit a wealth of African cultural survivals as having been retained in American Negro life.... On the contrary, few ethnic groups seem to have been so thoroughly and effectively detached from their prior cultural connections as was the case in the Negro's transit from Africa to North America [pp. 93–94].

While this assumption by Elkins received wide criticism, it would seem that R.S. Rattay agreed with at least a portion of this assumption.[12]

Elkins went on to further strengthen his case by writing:

> No true picture, cursory or extended, of African culture seems to throw any light at all on the origins of what would emerge, in American plantation society, as the stereotyped "Sambo" personality. The typical West African tribesman was a distinct warlike individual; he had a profound sense of family and family authority; he took hard work for granted; and he was accustomed to live by a highly formalized set of rules which he himself often helped to administer.... He was the product, in any case, of cultural traditions essentially heroic in nature.... Something very profound, therefore, would have had to intervene in order to obliterate all this and to produce, on the American plantation, a society of helpless dependents [p. 98].

Shock and detachment

Elkins was concerned with examining those experiences that would irrevocably change the African from a proud warrior to a helpless dependent. He cited five stages of shock which he believed accomplished this end:

1. Shock of capture
   It is an effort to remember that while enslavement occurred in Africa every day, to the individual it occurred once.
2. Long walk to the sea
   Under the blaring sun, through the streaming jungle, they were driven along like beasts tied together by their necks.

3. Sale to the slavers

> After being crowded into pens and kept for days, the slaves were brought out for examination. Those rejected would be abandoned to starvation; those who were bought — were branded, given numbers inscribed on leaden tags, and herded on shipboard.

4. Middle passage

> The holds, packed with squirming and suffocating humanity, became stinking infernos of filth and pestilence ... disease and death followed.

5. Sales in West Indies

> The seasoning process completed the series of steps whereby the African Negro became a slave [pp.98–100].[13]

The Africans, as depicted by Elkins, lost all connection to the old values, sanctions, and standards which normally would have helped them to adjust to their new life. They were then faced with "where were they to look for new standards, new cues — who would furnish them?" Elkins wrote:

> He could now look to none but his master, the one man to whom the system had committed his entire being: the man upon whose will depended his food, his shelter, his sexual connections, whatever moral instruction he might be offered, whatever "success" was possible within the system, his very security — in short, everything [p. 102].

This complete domination of the slave by the North American system caused Elkins to conclude that in the final analysis, the slave became fully enslaved (p. 102).

The holocaust and slavery

Elkins continued to develop his thesis by comparing slavery with the holocaust. He posited the notion that there were many items of relevance which slavery and the holocaust held in common. Needless to say his critics found no saneness in his discourse; nevertheless, Elkins raised more questions which needed to be dealt with in a sane and unbiased manner. For example, he wrote:

> The experience (American slavery and the holocaust) showed, in any event, that infantile personality features could be induced in a relatively short time among large numbers of adult human beings coming from very diverse backgrounds.... It forced a reappraisal and new appreciation of how completely and effectively prior cultural sanctions for behavior and personality could be detached to make way for new and different sanctions, and of how adjustments could be made by individuals to a species of authority vastly different from any previously known [p. 88].

This understanding permits an investigation of slavery to depart from the old debate of morality and ask such questions as: What effects does a prolonged enslavement have on humans? Are there any traces of the slave mentality in contemporary Negro America? How much of the slave owner's racism is still internalized by Negro America? And is contemporary white America much different from its antebellum counterpart? Elkins tried to set the stage for an exploration and expansion of these types of questions and even though some of his critics seem to think that he failed, he, nevertheless, caused and is still causing historians to take note of his discourse. And while most historians cannot agree with him, most accept his thesis as a well documented discourse on slavery.

Elkins readily admitted that the concentration camps were not like the plantation system of slavery; however, he believed that there were enough similarities to merit at least a limited comparison. The arrest, transporting and the entrance into the death camps resembled the capture, long trek to the sea, and the introduction into the seasoning camps of Brazil of the African slave (pp. 103–106). It would serve no practical purpose for this research to compare and contrast every element of the death camps with the institution of Negro slavery; consequently, only those main elements will be considered.

Elkins believed that in the death camps the inmates developed a type of split personality. On the one hand, they felt that the cruelties were not happening to their personal self but to an objective self. This, according to Elkins, allowed them to view their "limitless future in the camp," their constant hunger, and personal deprivation as a "real break" with the outside world and in time the "real life" would become the life in the camp (pp. 107–108).

Elkins cited several accounts by survivors of these death camps as to what it meant to survive:

> *Mrs. Lingens-Reiner*: Will you survive, or shall I?
>
> *Dr. Cohen*: I think it is of primary importance to take into account that the superego acquires new values in a concentration camp, so much at variance with those which the prisoner bore with him into camp that the latter faded.
>
> *Old prisoners to new prisoners*: If you survive the first three months you will survive the next three years.... Be inconspicuous.... To be inconspicuous required a special kind of alertness—almost an animal instinct—against the apathy which tended to follow the initial shock [p. 110].

Elkins went on to cite several more incidents of behavior that seem to be very similar to the plantation slave's behavior:

> The most immediate aspect of the old inmates' behavior was its childlike quality.... Some of these behaviors developed slowly, others were immediately imposed on the prisoners and developed only in intensity

as time went on.... The inmates' sexual impotence brought about a disappearance of sexuality in their talk; instead, excretory functions occupied them endlessly. They lost many of their customary inhibitions as to soiling their beds and their person. Their humor was shot with silliness and they giggled like children when one of them would expel wind [p. 111].

It would seem that the slave of Phillips' model was very similar to the inmates of the death camps. Elkins believed that this childlike behavior provided the genesis for a complete identification with the SS guards or masters. He quoted Bruno Bettelheim as follows:

A prisoner had reached the final stage of adjustment to the camp situation when he had changed his personality so as to accept as his own the values of the Gestapo.... The old prisoners came to share the attitudes of the SS toward the "unfit" prisoners; new comers who behaved badly in the labor groups or who could not withstand the strain became a liability for the others, who were often instrumental in getting rid of them. Many old prisoners actually imitated the SS; they would sew and mend their uniforms in such a way as to make them look like those of the SS [p. 112].

Elkins went on to posit the notion that in a prolonged enslavement where absolute power is exercised over the inmates, the inmates can very easily identify with the captors as father figures. Concerning this he wrote:

To all these men, reduced to complete and childish dependence upon their masters, the SS actually became a father-symbol. The SS man was all-powerful in the camp, he was lord and master of the prisoner's life. As a cruel father he could, without fear of punishment, even kill the prisoner and as a gentle father he could scatter largesse and afford the prisoner his protection.... The closed system, in short, had become a kind of grotesque patriarchy [p. 113].

Based on his analysis of the death camps, Elkins came to the conclusion that the literature itself provides three basic tests of the "profundity of the thoroughness of the changes which had been brought about in them" (p. 114). He listed these tests as follows:

The absence of resistance: Even upon liberation, when revenge against their tormentors at last became possible, mass uprisings very rarely occurred. Even when the whole system was overthrown by allies, nothing happened [p. 114].

Scarcity of suicide: Though there were suicides, they tended to occur during the first days of internment, and only one mass suicide is known.... For the majority of the prisoners the simplicity of the urge to survive made suicide, a complex matter of personal initiative and decision, out of the question [p. 114].

Absence of hatred: This is probably the hardest of all to understand. Yet the burning spirit of rebellion which many of their liberators expected to find would have had to be supported by fierce and smoldering emotions; such emotions were not there [p. 115].[14]

Slave personality

Elkins believed that the change in the personality of the slave had to be complete in the sense that new forms and support structures had to replace those eliminated by the institution.

This personality change, according to Elkins, was not just a change per se but a change that went beyond itself; "change that does not go beyond itself, is productive of nothing: it leaves only destruction, shock, and howling bedlam behind it unless some future basis of stability and order lies waiting to guarantee it and give it reality" (pp. 89–102). The proper understanding of this change should help to clarify the Negro problem in that the constituents of the problem could be viewed in a new configuration which could possibly eliminate all other presupposed conclusions. Elkins more so than any of the other historians seemed to have a better grasp of this type of change. He thought that the other side of this change had to do with stability; "the process of adjustment to a standard of social normality" (p. 116).

Elkins' "Sambo" and "personality change thesis" passed all of the practical scientific explanations of such a change. They left nothing to chance or to probability and are best described by Elkins in these words:

> The Negro was to be a child forever. "The Negro ... in his true nature, is always a boy, let him be ever so old...." "He is ... a dependent upon the white race; dependent for guidance and direction and even to the procurement of his most indispensable necessaries...." "Apart from this protection he has the helplessness of a child—without foresight, without faculty of contrivance, without thrift of any kind" [p. 132].

These were the terms that the white race demanded of the Negro as payment for their "love" for him.

Elkins believed that there are three theories for explaining personality: Freudian, Sullivan, and role play; the latter being the most relevant to the personality development of the death camp inmates and the Negro American. Elkins thought that the roles assigned to both groups were so implicitly clear that the end result could not only be predicted but also controlled. He explained roles in this manner:

> The social and psychological sanctions of role playing may in the last analysis prove to be the most satisfactory of the several approaches to Sambo, for, without doubt, of all the roles in American life that of Sambo was by far the most pervasive.... The sanctions against over-stepping it were bleak enough, but the rewards—the sweet applause, as it were, for performing it with sincerity and feelings—were something to be appreciated on quite another level. The law, untuned to the deeper harmonies, could command the player to be present for the occasion, and the whip might even warn against his missing the grosser cues [p. 131]....

Elkins went on to explain that once the roles had been assigned the master took great delight in watching his players perform; after all, "they were actually viewing their own masterpieces" (p. 131). He continued:

> Much labor had been lavished upon this chef d'oeuvre, the most genial resources of the Southern society had been available for the work; touch after touch had been applied throughout the years, and the result—embodied not in the unfeeling law but in the richest layers of Southern lore—had been the product of an exquisitely rounded collective creation [p. 131].

Accordingly, Elkins felt that this whole performance was not just a forced activity but that the masters actually believed that the slaves enjoyed the performance as much as they did. He quoted Edward Pollard as saying:

> I love to look upon his countenance shining with content and grease; I love to study his affectionate heart; I love to mark that peculiarity in him, which beneath all his buffoonery exhibits as a creature of the tenderest sensibilities, mingling his joy and his sorrows with those of his master's house. Love, even on those terms, was surely no inconsequential reward [pp. 131-2].

It would seem that the "Sambo" personality type to which Elkins alludes is to him a direct product of the social constructs of the North American plantation regime. Elkins further believed that these slave owners built into their system the means for not only producing a seasoned product but made allowances for the maturation of that process. Elkins quoted John Dollard as saying:

> Accommodation involves the renunciation of protest or aggression against undesirable conditions of life and the organization of the character so that protest does not appear but acceptance does [p. 132].[15]

Up to this point in his thesis Elkins had compared Latin American slavery with North American slavery; the German concentration camps with North American slavery; explored the "Sambo" thesis and examined the demise of the primary American institutions.

Now he turned his attention to the place of intellectualism and the problem of slavery. This discourse has received far too little attention; any future model for examining Negro culture must explore the many facets of the intellect as posited by Elkins. For example, he wrote:

> It could be said that institutions define a society's culture, that they provide the stable channels, for better or worse, within which the intellectual must have his business—if, that is, his work is to have real consequences for society and if he himself is to have a positive function there. Institutions with power produce the "thing" not only upon which one leans but also against which one pushes; they provide the standards whereby, for men of sensibility, one part of society may be judged and treated against another. The lack of them, moreover, removes the thinker not only from the places where power resides but also from the very idea of power and how it is used [p. 143].[16]

   The place of the intellectual in interpreting history seems, according
to Elkins, to be a place of power. And if, as it was posited earlier, power
misused can destroy, then if the Negro is to have a share in interpreting
his own history he must be allowed to gain intellectual status—and power.

   Elkins tried to divorce himself from the moral debate over slavery;
however, he could not ignore the significance of the consequence of sin,
guilt, innocence, and reform because they were an intricate part of all
dialogue concerning the slavery issue. At one point he said, "Reform
movements in the United States appear to have been given a unique
character by reason of the special part played in them by guilt" (p. 158).
This indicates that he believed that the manner in which America handled
its deep felt guilt over slavery was and is the underlying principle for
shaping America's present day policy toward Negro America. For example, why is it necessary for America to sponsor and support so many pieces
of legislation for the protection of the Negro's human and civil rights?
Why, in spite of these many laws, does the Negro still lag far behind
other immigrants who have come to this country? Why, especially since
Negro Americans are a product of the Americanization process, are they
still treated as something less than fully American?

   In the discussion that followed, Elkins raised the question of who
should shoulder the responsibility for slavery. Consequently, he wrote:

   Subordinating everything to its rightness or wrongness was the theme of
   all transcendentalists' sermons; slavery became not really a social problem
   but a moral abstraction. And once they came to the decision that it was
   wrong, which they all did, the burden of guilt for its continued existence
   became theirs and that of their hearers [p. 170].

He went further in his examination by taking a quote from William
E. Channing, the gentle perceptor of the transcendentalist.

   It [slavery] had stripped him [the Negro] of self-respect, that amid its
   arrangements he had been "trained to cowardice and low voices," and
   that where "adult morality was not demanded of him he was prey to every
   kind of licentiousness, intemperance, dishonesty, and theft...." That while
   slavery was "radically, essentially evil," the fixing of guilt was by no means
   its most pressing urgency. "Because a great injury is done to another, it
   does not follow that he who does it is a depraved man" [p. 171].

   It would seem at this point that Elkins had won his argument because
on the one hand the intellectuals were saying that slavery was wrong and
evil, while on the other hand some were saying, yes, it was wrong and
evil, but the slave owners cannot be blamed for its evil. The question
is, then, who should be blamed for its evil except those who founded,
established, and maintained it? Should the African be blamed because
he was weak and simple? Or should God be tasked because He did not
prevent it? Was Elkins right in stating that slavery was not a living thing
but a social ill that man made?

What makes this model counter-progressive? First, it was designed not as a history of American Negro slavery but as a proposal. Elkins' model proposes that certain kinds of questions be asked in future studies of the subject that had not been asked in previous ones (p. 224). Next it used a different type of source material, thereby enabling it to be concerned with a different type of problem.

For example, most of the other models (Phillips and Stampp) were concerned with health and maintenance; therefore, they consulted manuscripts and plantation records. Elkins was concerned with infantilization and personality development, the sequence of "shock and detachment," the implications about "human nature," and the differences between Latin American slavery and North American slavery. His thesis was diametrically opposed to those of Phillips and Stampp, as evidenced in his comparison of the German concentration camps and American Negro slavery. This model attempts to view the Negro not as radically inferior but as a victim of social disorder.

For instance, what, then of the reality of Sambo? Did the "Sambo role" really become part of the slave's "true" personality? Regardless of how unpleasant these questions may be, future studies of the Negro problem must deal with them. For example, Negro personality must be to a degree schizophrenic because of the manner in which it was and is being developed. However, this does not mean that the Negro operates in an "on/off" configuration. The Negro personality is a young one and for all intents and purposes, must be viewed as such.[17] Elkins wrote:

> We could, if we wished, propose a theory of personality in which the self is divided into two parts, a "true" part and a "false" part, and then say that the false part is mutable and adaptable, and the true part rigid and unchanging [p. 228].

Here it appears that he opened the door for serious investigation of the "self" and especially the Negro "self."

In defense of his "shock detachment" Elkins wrote:

> The difficulty might be stated as follows: (a) The shock of enslavement must have been experienced with equal acuteness by Negroes in Latin America, and by those going to North America; why then should a "Sambo" type emerge in the latter and not in the former? (b) How in any case is this infantilization to be accounted for in later generations of slaves, who did not experience such a shock? (c) For that matter, how much do we really know about the incidence of "Sambo" in the first generation? [p. 229].

Profitability

Elkins' next difference was his treatment of profitability of slavery. He thought that there was not enough evidence to draw any reasonable and sound conclusions. Therefore, he left that part of the debate to his predecessors. However, he did allow himself a brief discourse on the matter in these words:

> Any inquiry [into the profitability of slavery] must begin with Southern culture and its long-standing commitment to Negro slavery. It must assume all the arrangements of Southern life that somehow depended on and radiated from this commitment: not only a deep rooted labor system, but a body of law, a system of race relations, a style of life. It might be objected that such items are not economic. But actually they are: any conceivable venture in large scale agriculture had to proceed from there; any criterion of "profitability" would have to take all this as given; these arrangements made competition on any other basis out of the question" [p. 232].

Plantation mentality

Finally, Elkins saw the problem of slavery as a construct of the Southern mind. (It should be noted that the Southern mind was not limited to the South.) Nevertheless, this problem is expressed by Elkins in the following manner:

> The crux of the matter was that the South simply could not picture the Negro as an adult, and it was this aspect of slavery that no amendment to the Constitution, even when ratified in good faith by the Southern conventions themselves, could do very much to alter. The South's incapacity to imagine the Negro in any role but that of the helpless dependent would influence, for years every effort of the white community to establish a new and stable relationship with its former slaves [p. 240].

Therefore, as a consequence, the slave had to be brought to the understanding that "he could do, be, or feel" anything except that which his master forbade. This was accomplished, according to Elkins, through social and legal systems designed expressly for this purpose. He wrote:

> Both the traditional legal structure of American slavery and the social character of ante-bellum plantation life did tend to produce slaves who were in fact helpless, dependent, and lacking in initiative. As isolating mechanisms, law and customs, precisely in their most genial form, functioned with an efficiency so thorough that perhaps no one could have foretold or understood the entire web of consequences [p. 240].

He went on to say "but one feature of American slavery is clear; the slave's welfare depended entirely on the good will of the master, and whatever rights and privileges he had could be withdrawn at a moment's notice" (p. 241).

This model does much to direct attention to contemporary thought on American slavery because it allows the liberal mind to reevaluate the effects of a prolonged state of enslavement. For example, the Iranian hostage situation caused most Americans to stand in awe of the conditions of the 52 Americans who were held. According to newspaper and television accounts, most Americans are horrified at the possible long-term effects that this prolonged enslavement may have on these 52 Americans after being held for over 400 days. Elkins' treatment of slavery tends to parallel the hostage situation in that he saw slavery to be an agent for changing human personality. The point to be made here is that while many historians readily criticized Elkins for his personality change thesis, ironically, they are forced to view this prolonged hostage situation in the light that a definite personality change occurred.

Elkins' treatment of the slavery question has received much attention. Almost every facet of his thesis has undergone careful scrutiny; therefore, the purpose of this research limited portions of this criticism or debate will be included for the sake of clarity.

Elkins' Critics

Ann J. Lane said of Elkins, "whatever the limitations of the book, ... it has without doubt extended to examination of slavery in the United States in permanent and profound ways." She goes on to say, "Asking in effect the barest and simplest questions one could ask about slavery — what did slavery do to the slave? — he forced the discussion of the slave system in this country to be examined within the larger view of slavery in the Caribbean and Latin America."[18]

This seemingly positive endorsement by Lane did not delay the cries of Elkins' critics. David B. Davis examined Elkins' comparison of Latin American slavery with the slavery system of North America in this manner:

> It seemes to me that this comparison of Latin and Anglo-American slavery suffers from three basic weaknesses. First, he assumes that North American law, unlike that of Latin American refused to recognize the slave as a moral personality.... Second, he ignores the fact that the "classical" view of slavery, as embodied in Latin culture, drew as much from Plato and Aristotle as Cicero and Seneca.... Third, Tannenbaum seems to think of Negro slavery in Latin America as a relatively unchanging institution, and assumes that certain humane laws of the eighteenth and nineteenth centuries were typical of bondage in all Latin America throughout its long history. Even more questionable is his assumption that the admirable laws of European governments were obeyed by colonial slaveholders.[19]

Next to follow Davis was Earl E. Thorpe, who disagreed with Elkins' every point. He started with Elkins' very approach to the book. "Thus Professor Elkins clearly indicates that he is going to beware of the heavy hand of prejudice which he feels has done damage to previous writings about the Negro."[20]

Thorpe wrote:

> Because his own biases blurred his vision, and of the too loose fashion in which Elkins handles his analogy, we must conclude that the challenge laid down for historical scholars in 1944 by Professor Hofstadter has not yet been met. Professor Elkins should have been more impressed with the words of Herbert J. Aptheker, written in 1943, which states: "The dominant historiography in the United States either omits the Negro people or presents them as a people without a past, as a people who have been docile, passive, parasitic, imitative".... Elkins should have been more impressed with the words of a planter who wrote in 1837: "The most general defect in the character of the Negro is hypocrisy, and this hypocrisy frequently makes him pretend to more ignorance than he possesses; and if his master treats him as a fool, he will be sure to act the fool's part." Finally, Professor Elkins should have been more impressed with the work of the Association for the Study of Negro Life and History, which has devoted almost a half century of labor directed towards disproving the Sambo and similar stereotypes [Thorpe, pp. 41–42].[21]

Thus it would seem that Thorpe not only felt that Elkins fell prey to his own criticism of his predecessors, but that he did not consult the leading scholars on Negro culture and Negro history.

The next criticism to be considered is that of Eugene D. Genovese, who was willing to see some merit in Elkins' efforts. He wrote:

> Despite the hostile reception given by historians to Elkins' *Slavery*, it has established itself as one of the most influential historical essays of our generation. Although Elkins ranges widely, we may restrict ourselves to his most important contribution, the theory of slave personality, and bypass other questions, such as his dubious theory of uncontrolled capitalism in the South.[22]

Genovese further stated:

> Elkins' book has raised the study of Southern slavery to a far higher level than ever before.... It has demonstrated forcefully the remarkable uses to which psychology can be put in historical inquiry. It has brought to the surface the relationship between the slave past and a wide range of current problems flowing from that past.... We cannot simply replace his psychological model with a better one; we must recognize that all psychological models may be only used suggestively for flashes of insight ... if we are to profit from Elkins' boldness, we shall have to retreat from it and try to solve the problems he raises by the more orthodox procedures of historical research [Genovese, pp. 73–74].

Roy Simon Bryce-Laporte wrote:

> To put it succinctly our criticisms of Elkins are directed not to his history but rather to his sociology — to its overly deterministic and prematurely

comparative features. Despite our criticisms, Elkins' treatment of slavery has profound significance to those social scientists and historians interested in the behavior of captive men—past, present, and future. It represents the most provocative and successful effort yet to reopen the study of slavery, an event of the past, on terms amendable to behavioral analysis.[23]

Thus it would seem, from the amount of criticism that he received, that Elkins must have struck a vital cord among America's major historians. Nevertheless, Elkins' thesis stands, and it is very probable that before too many years, many American scholars will see the need for such comparative studies as Elkins made when he compared Latin American slavery with North American slavery, and the German concentration camp inmates with the American Negro slaves.

Summary of the Elements of the Model

This model is comprised of the following main elements:

The Negro/slave was
1. A poor victim of circumstance
2. Undergoing a personality change which allowed him to become docile but irresponsible, loyal but lazy, humble but chronically given to lying and stealing, full of infantile silliness, reflective of childish exaggerations in speech
3. More deprived than his Latin American counterparts
4. Sharing a common experience with the death camp Jews

North American slavery was
1. Void of positive models for the slave
2. The instrument that destroyed the African's social system
3. Created in America by Americans
4. A social entity spawned out of the demise of formal American institutions

Chapter V
The Cliometric Revolutional Model

The cliometric revolutional model for interpreting slavery in the United States is based on the ideology that applied mathematics and statistics provide a better tool for interpreting slavery than the traditional method of conjecture and nonmeasurable sources. The cliometricians were able to divorce themselves from the moral debate and concentrate on many facts that heretofore could not be dealt with effectively because mathematics and statistics had not been developed to their present level of sophistication.

William Fogel and Stanley Engerman have acknowledged that Alfred H. Conrad and John R. Meyer were the first cliometricians to make sizeable accomplishments using this methodology and they conceded that their work inspired them to some degree. While this model is based primarily on the book, *Time on the Cross*, by Fogel and Engerman, the insights of Conrad and Meyer are used when applicable. Fogel and Engerman are scholars of the highest rank and as such are accepted completely by the academic world. (For biographical information, see the Appendix.)

Background Data

By the time of the publishing of Fogel and Engerman's book, *Time on the Cross*, the Negro American had made many further gains in the area of social advancement. The following is a limited list of those advancements[1]:

Civil rights

1960 — "Sit-Ins" era began.
1961 — Several bus loads of Freedom Riders organized by CORE set out on a ride through the South to test compliance of bus stations with Interstate Commerce Commission desegregation order.

1963 — Two hundred thousand Americans of all races marched on Washington, D.C.

1964 — One person was killed, 140 injured and 500 arrested in Harlem riot.

1965 — Martin L. King, Jr., announced plan for an economic boycott of Alabama.

1965 — Grand jury in Selma, Alabama indicted three white men for murder of the Rev. James J. Reed.

1965 — Senate passed Voting Rights Bill.

Accomplishments

1961 — Adam Clayton Powell, Jr., became chairman of House Education and Labor Commission.

1961 — Robert Weaver appointed Administrator of Federal Housing and Home Finance Administration.

1961 — James B. Parsons appointed Federal District Judge.

1964 — Martin L. King, Jr., won Nobel Peace Prize.

1964 — Malcolm X resigned from the Black Muslims and formed the Organization for Afro-American Unity.

1964 — Arthur Ashe was the first black to win American Singles Tennis Championship.

1965 — Vivian Malone was the first black to graduate from the University of Alabama.

1965 — Pope Paul VI named John P. Cody Archbishop of Chicago.

1965 — Thurgood Marshall was nominated Solicitor General.

1966 — Constance B. Motley was the first black woman to be named to a federal judgeship.

Presidential actions

1962 — President Kennedy ordered banning segregation in Southern paper mills and federally financed housing.

1962 — James Meredith was admitted to University of Mississippi — 12,000 troops were sent to maintain order.

1963 — President Kennedy was the first president to declare segregation morally wrong.

1967 — President Johnson appointed a blue ribbon panel to "investigate the origins of the disorder in our cities."

1967 — President Johnson nominated Walter E. Washington to head municipal government of Washington, D.C.

1968 — Civil Rights Bill was passed.

Negro martyrs

1963 — Medger Evers was assassinated.

1963 — Four Negro children were killed in bombing of 16th Street Baptist Church, Birmingham, Alabama.

1964 — James Chaney and Andrew Goodman were murdered for voter registration.

1965 — Malcolm X was shot to death.

1968 — Martin L. King, Jr. was assassinated.

While this list does not contain all the events which happened to the Negro American during the 60's and 70's, it does point to some of the significant ones.[2]

Fogel and Engerman believed that the most direct and accurate way to do historiography on Negro American slavery was through the methodology of the cliometricians. Concerning this method, they wrote.:

> Cliometricians have amassed a more complete body of information on the operation of the slave system than has been available to anyone interested in the subject either. during the ante-bellum era or since.[3]*

Normally this should give some authenticity to their work. However, because of the different conclusions that they reach, their work has not received the wide acclaim that a work of this magnitude would be expected to receive. Therefore, because of the different conclusions reached by Fogel and Engerman, their findings form a major tool for comparing and contrasting the four models in the final chapter. Accordingly, it is important to note what Fogel and Engerman had to say about their book:

> This will be a disturbing book. It required forbearance.... For the findings we discuss not only expose many myths that have served to corrode and poison relations between the races, but also help to put into a new perspective some of the most urgent issues of our day [p. 8].

Accordingly, they laid out ten principal corrections of the traditional characterizations of the slave economy:

1. Slavery was not a system irrationally kept in existence by plantation owners.
2. The slave system was not economically moribund on the eve of the Civil War
3. Slave owners were not becoming pessimistic about the future of their slave system during the decade that preceded the Civil War
4. Slave agriculture was not inefficient when compared with free agriculture

Hereafter in this chapter references to page numbers only are to Fogel and Engerman's Time on the Cross.

5. The typical slave fieldhand was not lazy, inept, and unproductive
6. The course of slavery in the cities does not prove that slavery was incompatible with an industrial system regime
7. The belief that slave breeding, sexual exploitation, and promiscuity destroyed the black family is a myth
8. The material (not psychological) conditions of the lives of slaves compared favorably with those of free industrial workers
9. Slaves were exploited in the sense that part of their income which they produced was expropriated by their owners
10. Far from stagnating, the economy of the ante-bellum South grew rapidly. Between 1840 and 1860, per capita income increased more rapidly in the South than in the rest of the nation [pp.5–6].[4]

Another declaration, made by these authors was:

> While the cliometricians have been able to construct reasonably reliable indexes of the material level at which blacks lived under slavery, it has been impossible, thus far, to devise a meaningful index of the effect of slavery on the personality or the psychology of blacks [p. 9].[5]

Fogel and Engerman realized the seriousness of their sharp departure from the normal mode of interpreting historical data when they wrote:

> There is no such thing as errorless data. The questions with which cliometricians must always grapple are the nature of the errors contained in the various bodies of data that they employ and the biases that such errors will produce in estimates based on data containing them. When evaluated from this standpoint, evidence falls not into just two categories (good and bad), but into a complex hierarchy in which there are many categories of evidence and varying degrees of reliability [p. 10].

Support for the Model

Sugar and Slavery

The question that touches all four of these models for interpreting slavery in the United States is: What caused slavery to spread so quickly throughout the southern half of this country? Fogel and Engerman believed that it was not the expansion of the cotton and tobacco crops, as Phillips had posited, that adversely effected the Atlantic slave trade; it was the European's craving for sugar. Concerning this, they wrote:

> To those who identify slavery with tobacco and cotton, the small U.S. share in the slave trade may seem unbelievable. Consideration of the temporal pattern of slave imports, however, clearly reveals that the course

of the Atlantic slave trade cannot be explained by the demand for these crops.... It was Europe's sweet tooth, rather than its addiction to tobacco or its infatuation with cotton cloth, that determined the extent of the Atlantic slave trade. Sugar was the greatest of the slave crops. Between 60 and 70 percent of all Africans who survived the Atlantic voyages ended up in one or the other of Europe's sugar colonies [pp. 15–6].[6]

This is not to imply that Fogel and Engerman believed that the demand for sugar caused an increase in slave imports in the colonies; conversely, they believed that by the time the colonies had developed a reasonable sugar producing system, the Atlantic slave trade had all but been eliminated (pp. 20–2).[7] They seemed to believe that the reason the slave population in the colonies increased over the population of the Latin American system was primarily "natural increase." They wrote:

> While the imports of Africans certainly contributed to the growth in the slave populations of the United States colonies, they were of secondary importance in explaining that growth after 1720. Natural increase was by far the more significant factor during the eighteenth and nineteenth centuries [p. 24].

Natural increase may well have been the reason for this population increase; however, unless there was a concerted effort in stimulating the slaves to engage in procreation (slave breeding), illness and disease must have had some influence on these population figures.[8] These authors intimated that there was a drastic difference between the Latin American system of slavery and the North American system of slavery, the latter affording a more fertile environment for procreation. While this view may be ethnocentric, the previous models, progressive, counter-progressive, and racial enlightenment, especially the counter-progressive, do not support it.

This departure from the traditional understanding of slave population allowed Fogel and Engerman to posit the notion that there were many differences between the Latin American system of slavery and the North American counterpart. First, they believed that there was a higher death rate in Latin America. Second, they believed that poor food and intense work schedules made the Latin slave more vulnerable to the diseases of that locale. And third, the average Latin American slave had not developed the immunities needed to resist diseases that were prevalent in their environment (pp. 25–6). When this premise is weighed against the fact that there were fewer African women in Latin America, the logical question becomes, Were these local Creole women able to produce more surviving infants than their African counterparts? Fogel and Engerman stated it this way:

> Even if African-born women had been as fertile as Creole women, the imbalance in the sex ratio among Africans would have resulted in a relatively low birthrate. But the fertility of African women was substantially below

that of Creoles. Thus while the Creole population was not only able to reproduce itself but to grow at moderate rates, the African population could not. The combination of an unbalanced sex ratio with low fertility made the African birth rate much too low to offset the very high African death rate.... Emotional shock, generally poor health, venereal disease, abortion, infanticide, and the distortion of family life created by the unbalanced sex ratio have all been cited as possible causes [pp.28–9].

These facts are significant because they not only challenge the positions of the authors of the other models, but they imply the notion of a whole new approach to establishing the Negro's culture as American made. This conclusion is based on the following statement by Fogel and Engerman:

> U.S. slaves were not only in closer contact with European culture, they were also more removed from their African origins than were slaves in the Caribbean ... the great majority of the slave populations of the British and French Caribbean Islands were born in Africa ... the great majority of the slave populations of Jamaica, Barbados, Martinique consisted of Africans who had arrived in the New World within the previous decade. On the other hand, native born blacks made up the majority of the slave population in the U.S. colonies as early as 1680 ... by 1860 all but one percent of U.S. slaves were native born, and most of them were second, third, fourth, or fifth generation Americans. These Americans not only had no personal experience with Africa but were generally cut off from contact with persons who had such direct experience [pp.23–4].

This statement by Fogel and Engerman intimates that not only were the Africans stripped of their native culture but that by 1860, 99 percent of the Negro slaves were more authentically American than their white rulers. Fogel and Engerman said, "There were, of course, many ways in which the culture of whites and blacks differed in 1860. One was that a larger proportion of blacks were native born" (p. 24). This seems to be a clear indication that, at least from 1860 on, the Negro American was a definite by-product of the Americanization process. The significance of this premise, to white American thought and behavior, rests with those racist notions that depict Negro Americans as outsiders who have not in the past or present contributed to the growth of America, and who should be satisfied with their state, accepting a second class citizenship.

Who is actually the lesser citizen? Were those slaves who were born in America knowing no other culture, history, and tradition than that which was spawned with them, or those immigrants who were born in other countries, having several hundreds of years of cultural enrichment, to be classified as the most authentic American? While Fogel and Engerman did not pursue this line of thought, they did set the tempo and direction for future American historiography.

Emancipation

Fogel and Engerman believed that the enslavement of man by man is an age-old concept. They suggested that even Christian theologians "accepted" slavery as a necessary element in the nature and order of things. Concerning this, they wrote:

> In the spiritual realm "all men were brothers in union with God," but in the temporal realm slavery was "a necessary part of the world of sin." Thus, "the bondsman was inwardly free and spiritually equal to his master, but in things external he was a mere chattel" [p. 30].

Fogel and Engerman believed that most of the framers and promoters of "liberty and justice for all" accepted slavery (pp. 30-1). The "Church," John Locke, Thomas More, Pope Gregory XI and even St. Paul the Apostle accepted the dictum that "masters and slaves must accept their present station, for the earthly kingdom could not survive unless some men were free and some were slaves" (p. 31).[9]

Fogel and Engerman thought that while slavery was universally accepted, all men did not condone it, and as early as 1772, many groups and formal organizations began to sow the seeds that would eventually pull down "a system which stood above criticism for three thousand years" (p. 32). They sketched this movement in their chronology of Emancipation, 1772-1888 (pp. 33-4).[10] This is not to play down Elkins' account of these antislavery activities but to simply state that Fogel and Engerman not only cited these activities but they supported them with measurable evidence. The significance of these antislavery activities cannot be overstated because they caused the whole slavery question to be viewed from an altogether different vantage point.

Elements of the Model

Slave occupations

Fogel and Engerman exploded many old myths about slavery. First of these was the notion that most slaves were common laborers. They wrote:

> They were not only tillers of the soil but were fairly well represented in most of the skilled crafts.... In the city of Charleston, about 27 percent of the adult male slaves were skilled artisans.... Some bondsmen even ascended into such professions as architecture and engineering.... To a surprising extent, slaves held top managerial posts. Within the agricultural sector, about 7.0 percent of the men held managerial posts and 11.9

percent were skilled craftsmen (blacksmiths, carpenters, coopers, etc.). Another 7.4 percent were engaged in semi-skilled and domestic or quasi-domestic jobs: teamsters, coachmen, gardeners, stewards, and house servants [pp. 38-9].

These figures would indicate that the idea that all slaves were a liability to their masters is false and further that many slaves actually supported the master in a way that he could not do himself.

Next, Fogel and Engerman stated that most historians attempting to evaluate slavery saw it as an outdated system relying mostly on the whip to promote discipline and efficiency. This notion they disallowed and indicated that in spite of its limiting effect, slavery did offer positive incentives to the slave (p. 41).

It would appear that the assumption that the slave engaged only in agriculture is misleading because, according to Fogel and Engerman, the slave had to be proficient in all the support activities of the plantation system. They stated it this way:

> While the great majority of slaves were agricultural laborers, it is not true that these agriculturalists were engaged only in a very few, highly repetitive tasks that involved no accumulation of skills. With the exception of entrepreneurial decisions regarding the allocation of resources among alternative uses and the marketing of crops and livestock, slaves engaged in the full range of agricultural activities [p. 41].

The next erroneous assumption made by traditional historians, according to Fogel and Engerman, was that the majority of slaves spent most of their labor in raising and marketing cotton. This model suggests just the opposite. While cotton may have been the primary crop, the slave had to do other maintenance as well.

Fogel and Engerman were of the opinion that the plantation system was a highly efficient and productive method of agriculture. They relied on mathematics and statistics to verify their findings; therefore, this model is not laced with moral implications. Accordingly, these authors summarized slave labor distribution in this manner:

> Cotton, was of course, the single most important crop on large cotton plantations, requiring about 34 percent of the labor time of slaves ... the rearing of livestock took about 25 percent. The remaining 34 percent of the working time of slave hands was divided among land improvement, the construction of fences and buildings, the raising of other crops (oats, rye, wheat, potatoes, etc.).... Perhaps the most notable change in slave occupations between 1790 and 1860 was the redirection of the labor of field-hands.... Yet, great as was the redirection of labor from tobacco to cotton, its consequences for the development of slave skills should not be misconstrued. Whether they worked on tobacco or on cotton plantations, field hands spent most of their time raising livestock, grains, and other food crops [pp. 42-3].[11]

Interregional redistribution of slaves

Next, Fogel and Engerman examined the premise that the selling of slaves was a profitable enterprise and that the redistribution of slaves was a haphazard exercise caused by poor plantation management. This investigation led Fogel and Engerman to write:

> In 1690, Maryland and Virginia contained slightly over two thirds of the entire black population.... By 1820 the share of slaves in Virginia and Maryland had declined to 35 percent.... Two factors combined to bring about this rapid geographic redistribution of slaves. The spectacular rise in the world's demand for cotton and the improvement of transportation [pp. 44–6].

This redistribution of slaves caused Fogel and Engerman to ask the following questions: How were slaves moved from East to West? Were blacks in the interregional movement sold by owners in the East to slave traders who transported them to western markets where they were resold? Or did most slaves make the interregional journey with their owners as part of the movement in which whole plantations migrated to the West?

These were critical questions for Fogel and Engerman because they believed that "several of the main aspects of the traditional interpretation of the slave economy hinged on the answer" (p. 47). For example, if the "Old South" did mismanage the soil then slave trading would have been necessary and vital to the support of the agricultural community. This in turn supports the traditional interpretation of the economic structure of slavery. On the other hand, if what Fogel and Engerman stated is true, then their premise that "84 percent of the slaves engaged in the westward movement migrated with their owners" (p. 48) would disallow the previous interpretation and afford the cliometricians a sizeable gain in authenticity.

It would seem that Conrad and Meyer saw this redistribution in a different configuration. They wrote:

> Slavery was profitable to the whole South, the continuing demand for labor in the Cotton Belt ensuring returns to the breeding operation on the less productive land in the seaboard and border states. The breeding returns were necessary, however, to make the plantation operations on the poorer lands as profitable as alternative contemporary economic activities in the United States.[12]

The fact that certain states were known as breeding states and certain other states were buying states never entered this dialogue. For example, in the first decade the breeding states included Virginia, Maryland, Delaware, North Carolina, Kentucky, and the District of Columbia; the buying states were South Carolina, Georgia, Mississippi, Tennessee, Missouri, Florida, and Texas.[13] The significance of this grouping is that the breeding states tended to have a more liberal attitude towards Negroes while the buying states tended to be more hostile towards Negroes. The point to be made here is that even though the cliometricians claimed a liberal attitude towards slavery, they completely ignored this important statistic. They instead turned their attention to the profitability question.

The profitability of slavery

Fogel and Engerman believed that the profitability issue was divided into two camps: "Those scholars who attempted to ferret out those economic forces that would eventually lead to the self-strangulation of slavery" (p. 62), and "those who believed that slaveholders earned high rates of return" (pp. 62–3).[14] These scholars also saw the profitability issue revolving around three main points: First, "it was asserted that southern planters were beset by an irresistible tendency toward the overproduction of cotton;" second, "southern planters believed in the theory of natural limits." This second point is further subdivided accordingly: (1) the climate and soil set a limit to the geographic extension of the cotton culture and hence, of slave agriculture, and (2) slavery requires continuous territorial expansion in order to remain profitable. The third point used by southern planters to support their self-strangulation theory of slavery asserted an incompatibility between slavery and urban society (pp. 64–5). Fogel and Engerman saw the solution of these problems as a means of placing slavery in a sound scientific configuration. Consequently, they did not believe in the "self-strangulation" theory. They tended to believe that slavery was alive and well and that the relationship between the master and the slave helped to determine the worth of the institution. Concerning this, they wrote:

> There is too much evidence of deep personal attachments between owners and their bondsmen to deny that this was a facet of the slave system.... While we do not mean to imply that affection for slaves was purely a function of their earning capacity, we do mean to suggest that it was more usual for affection and productivity to reinforce each other than to conflict with each other. Both cruelty and affection had their place on southern plantations [pp.77–8].[15]

While there is a certain amount of romanticism in this statement, there must also be a certain amount of truth. The question that is significant to this research is: Did the slave holder have to sacrifice profit in order to be humane in his treatment of the slaves? Fogel and Engerman believed that they did not. And while even statistics and mathematics cannot measure kindness, they do seem to indicate that there was a degree of kinship between master and slave. This premise will be further examined in the final chapter; for now, let it suffice to say that this mysterious relationship between slave and master raised a sordid issue, that of slave-breeding.

Slave-breeding

Fogel and Engerman believed that in order for the "Old South" to be able to have any sizeable profit margin from slave-breeding not only would they have had to develop a specific system for breeding, there would also have to be a specific market for their product (pp. 78–88). They stated:

> Systematic breeding for the market involves two interrelated concepts: 1, interference in the normal sexual habits of slaves to maximize female fertility through such devices as mating women with especially potent men, in much the same way as exists in the breeding of livestock; 2, the raising of slaves as the main objective, in much the same way as cattle or horses are raised [p. 78].[16]

Fogel and Engerman built their case on statistical information such as the distribution of slaves according to sex, age, and ratio of males to females (pp. 39–58). This inadvertently led them to believe that "the demographic argument for the existence of slave-breeding is based on two principal observations." They listed them in this manner:

> First, the slave exporting states had fewer slaves in the age group fifteen to twenty-nine, and more at very young and old ages, than the slave importing states. Second, the fertility rate, measured as the ratio of children under one year to women aged fifteen to forty-nine, was slightly higher in the exporting than in the importing states [p. 79].

Fogel and Engerman further challenged the traditional view of slave-breeding on the following principles:

> First, that it was only in the Old South, where the land was of poor quality, that planters had an inducement to encourage fertility; while in the New South, where the yield of the soil was high, planters preferred to have "female slaves working in the field than to have them indisposed with pregnancy or occupied with children." Second, the assumption that interference with normal family life to increase fertility could have had a large and positive effect on profit. And third, the contention that it (slave-breeding) would rest on two dubious assumptions: 1, that a large increase in the fertility rate of females would result in a large increase in plantation income; 2, that there was no cost to interfering in the sexual lives of slaves [pp. 79–83].[17]

This line of investigation led them inadvertently to conclude, "No set of instructions to overseers has been uncovered which explicitly or implicitly encouraged selective breeding or promiscuity" (p. 86).

Next, Fogel and Engerman began to develop their model along the lines of their predecessors in that they chose the same subject areas for their line of investigation. These subjects are as follows:

Exploitation

To them exploitation fell into two categories: an unjust or improper use of another person for one's own profit or advantage, and utilization of the labor power of another person without a just or equivalent return (p. 107). They felt that the slave was exploited in both of these senses. They agreed with Elkins and Stampp that "little positive development of black culture or personality was possible under the unbridled exploitation of slavery" (p. 108).

Food

According to these authors, "the belief that the typical slave was poorly fed is without foundation in fact" (p. 109). It would seem that this mistake came about through a misreading or a misinterpretation of plantation records. For example, Phillips, Stampp, and Elkins tended to believe that the slaves were only fed corn and pork while Fogel and Engerman felt that there were many more staple foods plus extras such as fruits and home grown vegetables. They listed beef, pork, mutton, milk, butter, sweet potatoes, white potatoes, peas, corn, wheat, and minor grains (pp. 113–5). This account would seem to be more reasonable in light of the personal experiences cited by many ex-slaves. Furthermore, if the slave had to work some fourteen hours a day, he would have to have more to eat than corn and pork (p. 115).

Housing

Fogel and Engerman examined the census figures of 1860 and found that on an average each slave lived 5.2 persons to a single household while the average free family consisted of 5.3 persons (p. 116). This did not say that the average slave family was living better than the average free family but that the average slave had more living space than the average free family. The size and type of living quarters could not be readily determined; however, from traveler's report and scarce plantation records, it is assumed that most of these slave quarters had dirt floors, boarded windows, and were usually made of logs (p. 117). Judging from Phillips, who was proslavery, these facts agree with his.

Clothing

The cliometricians tended to agree with Phillips' account of clothing allowance, which was, "for adult males, four shirts, four pairs of pants, and one or two pairs of shoes." Adult women were issued "four dresses per year, and headkerchiefs" (p. 127). There are spotty records of issuing such items as underclothes, petticoats, socks, underwear, jackets and overcoats. Fogel and Engerman were of the opinion that some slaves earned money from outside employment and with this money they purchased some of their clothing needs. Data contained in this research project do not support this position, especially since most slave records show that most slaves were not allowed to leave the plantation. However, in the final chapter, this premise will be examined thoroughly so that a more objective conclusion may be reached.

Medical care

Fogel and Engerman wrote:
> While the quality of slave medical care was poor by modern standards, there is no evidence of exploitation in the medical care typically provided for plantation slaves [p. 117].

It should be noted here that when all four models are compared and contrasted, the views expressed here will be examined for clarity and authenticity, and a formal opinion will be reached based on the data that emerges.

The slave family

Fogel and Engerman were of the opinion that most large plantations were based on two slave organizations, fieldworkers and the family unit. Of this they wrote:
> Planters assigned three functions to the slave family. First, it was the administrative unit for the distribution of food and clothing and for the provision of shelter.... Second, the family was an important instrument for maintaining labor discipline.... Third, the family was the main instrument for promoting the increase of the slave population [p. 127].

This disclosure indicates that the slave family unit was an intrinsic part of the plantation structure and that, contrary to the views of Phillips, Stampp and Elkins, the slave's family unit was as necessary to the master as it was to the slave. In the final chapter this premise will be examined and contrasted with the other three models in order to determine if there is any evidence that will support the premise that through the slave family unit the slave was able to maintain a reasonable amount of autonomy.

Punishment, rewards and expropriation

It would seem that all four models include punishment as a means of obtaining absolute control of the slaves. Fogel and Engerman wrote:

> Whipping was probably the most common punishment metered out against errant slaves. Other forms of punishment included the deprivation of various privileges (such as visits to town), confinement in stocks, incarceration, sale, branding and the death penalty [p. 144].

It should be noted that the master had absolute control of his slaves and while it was to his advantage not to maim his property, the other models acknowledged that oftentimes very harsh forms of punishment were used, such as gelding, the cutting of limbs, burnings, the use of the thumb screw, etc. Aside from punishments as a control mechanism, most masters used rewards just as widely. Fogel and Engerman tended to believe that the master would frequently reward a female if she had the desired number of children. During her pregnancy her work load was reduced; the good and the obedient were allowed to have such rewards as a vegetable patch, chickens, visits to town, extra food and clothing — in general, most of the things that a "good parent" would give his children. Fogel and Engerman wrote:

> While whipping was an integral part of the system of punishment and rewards, it was not the totality of the system. What planters wanted was not sullen and discontented slaves who did just enough to keep from getting whipped. They wanted devoted, hard-working, responsible slaves who identified their fortunes with the fortune of their masters [p. 147].

Thus the slave was controlled not only to produce a profit for his master but controlled to the point of having no will of his own. It would seem that there is little or no evidence to dispute the claim that some expropriation did take place. The amount of expropriation and its longevity is of little consequence to this research. The concern here is that there was some expropriation.

The Economic Indictment of Slavery

Fogel and Engerman approached this side of their investigation by restating Cassius Marcellus Clay's position (pp. 148–57). Clay was the first historian to use an economic approach to the slavery question and, according to Fogel and Engerman, his pamphlet entitled, "Slavery: The Evil — The Remedy," contained two main elements:

> (1) Slavery was an inefficient form of economics because it impoverished the soil, because, in comparison with whites, slaves were "not so skillful, so energetic, and above all, have no stimulus of self-interest"; because three million slaves performed "only about one-half of the effective work

of the same number of whites in the North"; because slaves not only "produce less than freemen" but also "consume more"; slavery was "the source of indolence, and destructive of all industry"; slavery caused the "poor" to "despise Labor" by "degrading" it, while simultaneously turning the mass of "slaveholders" into "idlers." (2) Slavery retarded economic growth and development by restricting education, by diverting capital into the purchase of slaves, by discouraging the development of "mechanical" skills, and retarding the growth of manufacturing [p. 160].

This pamphlet according to Fogel and Engerman inadvertently opened the door for antislavery spokesmen to move slavery from a moral argument to an economic argument. Hinton Rowan Helper was the first to take up the challenge.

In 1857, just seventeen years after Clay's indictment, Helper wrote *The Impending Crisis of the South*. His method was to compare the growth of three pairs of states over a period between 1790 and 1850 — Virginia with New York, Massachusetts with North Carolina, and Pennsylvania with South Carolina. His conclusion was that slavery had done more harm than good in these Southern states (pp. 161–9). In his follow-up, he compared the aggregates of free and slave states and found that free states led the slave states by substantial margins in such matters as total wealth, manufacturing production, investment in railroads and canals, issues of patents on new inventions, and in the value of agriculture production (p. 162).[18] These findings at that time shocked most historians and politicians, and even more significant was the fact that these findings opened the door for Frederick L. Olmsted, an accomplished writer, who after writing twenty-five articles on slavery for the *New York Times*, incorporated them into his best known book, *The Cotton Kingdom*. It regulated Olmsted's influence. Fogel and Engerman stated:

> Among those whose conceptions of slavery were influenced by Olmsted were John Cairnes, Karl Marx, Lewis C. Gray, Charles Sydnor, E. Franklin Frazier, Avery O. Vracen, Richard Hofstadter, John Hope Franklin and Kenneth Stampp [p. 170].[19]

This indicates that Olmsted's work not only changed the focus of traditional interpretations of slavery but that it merited the respect of some of the most prestigious writers of our times. Fogel and Engerman wrote:

> Olmsted's essays dealt with all aspects of southern culture. He commented incisively on such matters as the manners, dress, housing, diet, education, religion, marriage, family, morals, literature, amusements, and health of both blacks and whites of lower as well as upper classes [p. 170].

Fogel and Engerman further quoted Olmsted as saying, "The peculiar institution kept not just slaves but virtually the entire free population in deep poverty." This was a new approach to the problem (p. 171). It gave rise to the idea that "the most serious defect of the system was that the labor of slaves was typically of a very low level of production; it degraded the entire standard of labor" (p. 172). Fogel and Engerman believed that because of the ill effects of slavery, even the free white workers became less effective. They wrote:

> White southern labor was even less efficient than slave labor, on average accomplishing only about two thirds as much as slave labor. The poor quality of all southern labor resulted in wasting resources: the natural fertility of land was rapidly undermined; tools were frequently broken; livestock was neglected; labor skills were allowed to decay; managerial skill was scorned [p. 172].

Fogel and Engerman believed that in spite of the serious indictment of the institution posited by Olmsted, he still felt that the Negro was just a victim of the system and should he be removed from his present circumstance, he would become just as efficient as any other good worker (p. 179).

It would seem that one of the significant tenets of Olmsted's essays was his refusal to accept the premise that Southern agriculture held onto slavery for its labor-profit margin. Fogel and Engerman quoted Olmsted as saying:

> What rescued the system from oblivion was the internal slave trade "which makes slaves valuable property, otherwise than for labor." For even if slave labor could not produce a surplus over that required for its own substance, slavery persisted because the increasing value of the stock of slaves made slave rearing a profitable venture [p. 174].

Elkins embraced this position also, and as previously stated, slave mongering will be examined thoroughly in the final chapter. What is significant here is that Olmsted supported this position long before the slavery question became anything but a moral issue.

John E. Cairnes was the last of the early economists to issue an economic indictment of slavery. While he was greatly influenced by Olmsted, he tended to differ with him significantly in that he "sought a reformulation of Olmsted's basic economic critique which did not involve the proposition that planters generally failed to earn profits on their investment in slaves.... [Although] slavery was beset by a tendency toward unprofitability, that tendency could be thwarted under certain circumstances" (p. 184). Fogel and Engerman quoted Cairnes as listing these circumstances:

1. There had to be a demand for crops which could be more efficiently produced on a large rather than a small scale.
2. The method of cultivation of these crops had to require large amounts of labor per unit of land.
3. Soils had to be of a high fertility and practically unlimited in extent.
4. There had to be a substantial interregional slave trade [pp. 184–5].

According to Fogel and Engerman, "these four propositions allowed

Cairnes to discard Olmsted's contention that slavery was generally unprofitable, while still maintaining that it was an inefficient system which
retarded the growth of the South" (p. 185). Since Cairnes' thesis included major portions of Clay's, Helper's and Olmsted's theses, the view
is not unreasonable that all four writers are significant to the present
research.

According to Fogel and Engerman, most of the earlier central asser-
tions of the economic indictment of slavery are no longer valid. However,
they are significant to the present research because they provide an explanation of some of the reasons for many accepted Negro stereotypes.
Fogel and Engerman's reasons for discarding these earlier indictments
of slavery are of major significance, especially since these indictments have
stood for some one hundred years. It would seem that Fogel and Engerman used an instrument for measuring and comparing the relative
efficiency of the agriculture in the North and South called "geometric
index of total factor productivity."[20] They wrote, "With this index,
efficiency is measured by the ratio of output to the average amounts of
the inputs" (p. 192). With the use of this instrument, they were able
to generate the following findings:

1. Southern agriculture as a whole was about 35 percent more efficient than
   northern agriculture in 1860.
2. Both southern farms using free labor and southern farms using slave
   labor were more efficient than northern farms.
3. There were economies of scale in southern agriculture. This means that
   a single large farm using given quantities of inputs could produce more
   output than a group of small farms which together used the same quantities of inputs.
4. Economies of scale were achieved only with slave labor.
5. There were significant differences in the relative efficiency of slave plantations within the two major subregions of the south [pp. 192–6].

The conclusion that they reached was "that southern agriculture was
more, not less, efficient than northern agriculture" (p. 196). This supplies to this research project another piece of data that will help clarify
the examination of the profitability question in the final chapter.

Fogel and Engerman summed up their position on the work of Clay,
Helper, Olmsted, Cairnes, and Phillips this way:

> The writings of these men, particularly those of Olmsted and Cairnes,
> have never been allowed to slip into the category of intellectual history.
> Continual reliance on their arguments and their evidence by modern
> writers has kept their indictment alive, has maintained their position as
> the principal antagonists on the issues of the profitability and viability
> of slavery. Their work is the core around which the traditional interpreta-
> tion of slavery has been molded [p. 190].

The Quality of Slave Labor and Racism

Up to this point, slave labor has been viewed as an inefficient system of labor because the slave was seen as lazy, shiftless, dull brained, incompetent, destructive, and in general, more trouble than he was worth. However, Fogel and Engerman tended to feel that their evidence showed that even after making certain allowances for plantation pecularities, the agricultural system of the South was a far better system than its counterpart of the North. They wrote:

> The advantage of plantations, at least that part which has been measured thus far, was due to the combination of the superior management of planters and the superior quality of black labor [p. 210].

This finding is very significant to this research because the data examined in this project tend to show that far too many Negroes believe that their slave ancestors contributed very little to the well-being of the plantation and that even in the contemporary setting of today, Negroes, in general, contribute very little to the well-being of American economy. Fogel and Engerman went on to say:

> Whatever the contribution of management, however, it should not all be assigned to white planters and overseers. For blacks—though slaves, though severely limited in the extent to which they could climb the economic ladder of antebellum society—were a vital part of the management of plantations and, in this capacity, of the economic successes of the plantations [p. 210].

This contrary conclusion by Fogel and Engerman raises a serious question: How could many scholars have been so badly misled on this issue? Fogel and Engerman seemed to think that one possible explanation is that "The views of historians regarding the nature of plantation management are based [first] on inferences from correspondence between owners and overseers" and second "on the way in which many historians have accepted the argument of the authors of the economic indictment of slavery" (p. 212). They cannot be too far from the truth because, as noted in Phillips' discourse, he used plantation letters and records as his primary resource. Other writers referred to in this research seemed to have followed Phillips' example.

The next unanswered question that arises out of this section of resource data is, how could these stereotypes regarding blacks come into being, and how could they have persisted for so long? Fogel and Engerman wrote:

> Resolution of the first issue involves consideration of the intricate ways in which variations of racist viewpoints among critics and defenders of slavery, among northern and southern whites—for with very few exceptions they were all racists—interacted with each other to create an almost indestructible image of black incompetence [p. 215].

It would seem, based on this position, that it would be almost impossible for the slave/Negro to be viewed in any positive configuration, and furthermore, as long as the Negro leaves his history to be interpreted by white scholars, very little change can be expected. Fogel and Engerman wrote:

> What bitter irony it is that the false stereotype of black labor, a stereotype which still plagues blacks today, was fashioned not by the oppressors who stove to keep their chattel wrapped in the chains of bondage, but by those most ardent opponents of slavery, by those who worked most diligently to destroy the chains of bondage [p. 215].

Finally, the cliometricians sought to discredit the traditional interpretation of slavery on five major propositions using mathematics and statistics as their primary tool. Fogel and Engerman list the following as being the components of this traditional interpretation:

1. That slavery was generally an unprofitable investment, or depended on a trade in slaves to be profitable, except on new and fertile ground.
2. That slavery was economically moribund.
3. That slave labor and agricultural production based on slave labor, was economically inefficient.
4. That slavery caused the economy of the South to stagnate.
5. That slavery provided extremely harsh material conditions of life for the typical slave [pp. 4–5].

Whether Fogel and Engerman were able to accomplish their aim will be determined in the final chapter of this research. However, in all fairness to their efforts, the following statement by Fogel and Engerman exemplifies their commitment to doing exactly what they proposed.

> While keenly aware of the torment which these false stereotypes of incompetence have helped to impose on blacks for more than a century, we are, social scientists, impressed by this exceptional demonstration of the power of ideology to obliterate reality, and we view it as an unparalleled opportunity to investigate the complex interrelationships between ideas and the material circumstances of life [p. 215].

Later in their discourse they wrote:

> *Time on the Cross* did not come to an end for blacks with the downfall of the peculiar institution. For they were held on the cross not just by the chains of slavery but also by the spikes of racism. It is one of the bitterest ironies of history that the anti-slavery critics who worked so hard to break these chains probably did as much as any other group, perhaps more, to fasten the spikes that have kept blacks in the agony of racial discrimination during their century of Freedom ... [p. 263].

Needless to say, this writer has disagreed with much that has been written in these four chapters. However, it was necessary to explore the scholarly historians' views on slavery first, because they represented the generally accepted scholarly interpretations of Negro American slavery.

Second, if there is to be a new interpretation of American Negro slavery and culture, there must first be a putting aside, through scholarly research, the old interpretations; and third, any new interpretation of slavery must begin with the slaves' views of his enslavement.

Summary of the Elements of the Model

In conclusion, this model is comprised of the following elements:

The Negro/slave was
1. A poor victim of circumstances
2. Exploited
3. Highly productive and efficient
4. Not used exclusively as a breeder
5. Profitable to masters
6. Able to build a reasonably sound family structure
7. Living on a scale that was comparable to that of the free industrial worker

The institution of slavery was
1. Destined to continue
2. Shown to provide adequate food, clothing, medical care, and sound housing
3. Able to control the slaves with a minimal of force
4. An efficient system of labor
5. Caught up in the social and economical pressures of the time (1600–1900)

Chapter VI
The Four Models Compared

In this chapter each of the four models for interpreting slavery in the United States will be compared and contrasted; the data that emerge will be presented in separate summaries.

The Progressive Model

In developing the progressive model, the following tests were used in selecting and interpreting information:

1. *Do the tenets of the progressive ideology reflect the contemporary Negro as being racially inferior?*
Phillips believed that the Negro was racially inferior, a property to be owned and used. He wrote, "Slaves were both persons and property, and as chattel they were investments" (Phillips, p.viii). He also wrote:

> The Negroes themselves show the same easygoing, amiable, serio-comic obedience and the same personal attachment to white men, as well as the same sturdy light-heartedness and the same love of laughter and of rhythm, which distinguished their forebears [pp. 342-3].
>
> At any rate a generation of freedom has brought less transformation in the bulk of the blacks than might casually be supposed [p. viii].
>
> ... and the slaves were Negroes, who for the most part were by racial quality submissive rather than defiant.... Every plantation of the standard southern type was, in fact, a school constantly training and controlling pupils ... the habits and standards of civilized life they could only acquire in the main through examples reinforced with discipline [p. ix].

In general, this model maintains that the Negro American is racially inferior to all non-African groups.

2. *Are Phillips' interpretations based on evidence, or are they a cultural tool used to justify treatment of the Negro?*
Given a knowledge of Phillips' source material there is no evidence that he intentionally ruptured his resources. Using some of the same

sources, Stampp and Elkins reached conclusions similar to those of Phillips. All three were caught up in what Myrdal called "the principle of cumulation," however, and were somewhat bound by their cultural heritage. Myrdal explained this principle in this manner: "White prejudice and discrimination keep the Negro low in standards of living, health, educaton, manners and morals. This in turn, gives support to white prejudice and Negro standards thus mutually 'cause' each other" (Myrdal, p. 75). The answer to the question is at best equivocal: the interpretation presented by Phillips is based on empirical evidence, and it is also used as a culturally-bound tool.

3. *Is there any evidence that would cause Negro Americans to internalize the views and values of the progressive ideology?*
Since there is no documented evidence that would explain the effect of prolonged enslavement on human beings, there is no way to determine whether the Negro has internalized the ideology of the progressives. However, there are strong implications that the changes which took place in the slaves' personality were of such a magnitude that there could be rudimentary effects which might influence his/her offspring. Myrdal believed that this was actually the case (Myrdal, pp. 113–137).

4. *Is there any bias evident in the source material presented by Phillips?*
Given the time and authority of Phillips' sources, it is easily assumed that there is an unequivocal bias present that, to many Americans, white and black, is offensive and untenable. However, it must be made clear that Phillips presented the facts as his culture would have him understand them, and even though most contemporary historians do consider him to be a racist, they also concede his work to be the first scholarly historical account of slavery. "Even in 1953, Phillips' *American Negro Slavery* was the only comprehensive scholarly work on the subject" (Myrdal, p. 2).

The Racial Enlightenment Model

The following questions guided the examination of the racial enlightenment model.

1. *Is the ideology of Stampp reflected in integrationist doctrine?*
David B. Davis wrote, "Stampp has also come to symbolize the unwitting arrogance of white integrationists."[1] It would seem that Stampp in his attempt to dethrone Phillips fell victim to his own ethnic bias in the same manner as Phillips. He spent a considerable amount of effort in positing Northern attitudes towards the Negro as more humane than

those of the South. Even though Stampp did not overtly consider Negroes to be racially inferior, he still saw them as a less advanced people needing much "schooling" and the means of "losing" their black skin color. This position, if not reflective of the integrationist ideology, is, to say the least, reflected in most social programs whose primary design is to "elevate the Negro masses."

Stampp explained his understanding of the Negro in this manner:

> Modern biologists, psychologists, sociologists, and anthropologists offer an impressive accumulation of evidence that Negroes and whites have approximately the same intellectual potentialities ... this is the fact that variations in the capacities and personalities of individuals within each race are as great as the variations in their physical traits [Stampp, p. 10].

This premise enabled Stampp to challenge Phillips on the grounds that the slave was not happy, childlike, carefree, etc.; and according to Davis and the research data which emerged from examining Stampp's *Peculiar Institution*, Stampp did set the tone for the integrationist ideology.

2. *What is the significance of Stampp's treatment of the conflict between the oppressed and the oppressor; between the weak and the powerful; between the innocent and the guilty?*

Stampp saw these conflicts as indications that the slave (the oppressed, weak, and innocent) wanted freedom just as much as anyone else and the slave holder (the oppressor, powerful, and guilty) needed the services of the slave for his own betterment. In support of this premise, Stampp remarked:

> Slaves showed great eagerness to get some — if they could not get all — of the advantages of freedom [Stampp, p. 10].
>
> If slaves yielded to authority most of the time, they did so because they usually saw no other practical choice [p. 91].
>
> Given the general hostility toward free Negroes in both North and South and the severe handicaps which they faced, the choice between freedom and slavery did not always seem to be an altogether clear one [p. 93].

Stampp also used these conflicts to cite the effect that each group had over the other. The data from Stampp's *Peculiar Institution* indicates that each of these oppositions helped to shape the slave's personality, as well as the personality of the slave holder.

3. *Is there any evidence to support the claim that Negro Americans have adopted Stampp's premise that Negroes are white people with black skins?*

It would appear that Stampp's assumption is that "there is no convincing evidence that there are any significant differences between the innate emotional traits and intellectual capacities of Negroes and whites" (Stampp, p. vii). He believes, "Innately Negroes are, after all, only white men with black skins" (p. viii). Whether Negroes have adopted this view depends upon the way integration is perceived. For example, if integration is perceived as a means of developing all Americans to their greatest potential, then it is assumed that, other than social and economic differences, all Americans are equally endowed by nature and can attain comparatively equal advancement in an equal and just environment. If however, integration is perceived as a means of assimilating minority ethnic groups into the dominant ethnic group, then it would have to be further assumed that the assimilated is valued less than the dominant one or that the assimilated is not as accepted as the dominant group. In either of the latter cases, Stampp's "white man in a black skin" premise could not apply. The overriding data of Stampp's *Peculiar Institution* indicates that white integrationist America is convinced that Negroes are just white men in black skins and should they be removed from their degrading environment, the negative connotations associated with skin color would soon be ignored by all America. While this assumption is generally accepted as a positive move towards easing racial tensions, James Otis asked the more provoking question, "Does it follow that, t'is right to enslave [discriminate against] a man because he is black?"[2]

The Counter-Progressive Model

The following questions were employed to examine the ideology of the counter-progressive model.

1. *What is the significance, to contemporary Negro America, of the relationship between cultural heritage and plantation agriculture?*
Both Elkins and some of his critics agree that the pressure of plantation agriculture was very influential in determining the cultural heritage of the slave.[3] He noted:

> Both the traditional legal structure of American slavery and the social character of ante-bellum plantation life did tend to produce slaves who were in fact helpless, dependent, and lacking in initiative. As isolating mechanisms, law and custom, precisely in their most genial form, functioned with an efficiency so thorough that perhaps no one could have foretold or understood the entire web of consequences [Elkins, pp. 240–241].

This statement indicates not only that the pressure of plantation agriculture controlled the slave but also that the effect of this control was possibly transferred from generation to generation. William H. Grier and Price M. Cobb, two black psychiatrists, wrote:

> The black man of today is at one end of a psychological continuum which reaches back in time to his enslaved ancestors ... observe closely

a man on a Harlem street corner and it can be seen how little his life experience differs from that of his forebearers.[4]

After describing this street corner hiring scene, Grier and Cobb wrote:

... no imagination is required to see this scene as a direct remnant of slavery ... the psychic structure of the black men being selected has altered little since slavery [Grier and Cobb, p. 25].[5]

Many of Elkins' critics believed that he did not have enough evidence to support his claim. However, many noted Negro scholars agreed with Elkins. For example, James P. Gomer stated that many problems which confront the contemporary Negro had their beginnings in slavery.

Slavery—whether pleasant and paternalistic or harsh and rejecting—reduced most of the African captives to a state of psychological childhood. The captive was rendered helpless and totally dependent on an all-powerful master by a set of overwhelming circumstances.... the master's total control enabled them to infantilize many slaves.[6]

Grier and Cobb have added:

We must concede that much of the pathology we see in black people had its genesis in slavery. The culture that was born in that experience of bondage has been passed from generation to generation [Grier and Cobb, p. 31].

Thus, the pressure of plantation agriculture directly affects the contemporary Negro, especially in how he perceives himself (Grier and Cobb, pp. 23–38).

2. *What is the significance to contemporary Negro America of the relationship between the slave's accommodation and the slave's resistance?*

Elkins believed that the few incidents of slave resistance were the exception rather than the norm. He observes:

... the revolts that actually did occur were in no instance planned by plantation laborers but rather by Negroes whose qualities of leadership were developed well outside the full coercion of the plantation authority system. Gabriel, who led the revolt of 1780, was a blacksmith.... Denmark Vessey, leading spirit of the 1812 plot at Charleston, was a freed Negro.... Nat Turner, the Virginia slave who formed the massacre of 1831, was a literate preacher.... They are, indeed, all too easily identified, thanks to the system that enabled them as individuals to be so conspicuous and so exceptional and, as members of a group, so few [Elkins, p. 139].

Elkins believed that the slaves' resistance was overshadowed by their accommodations. Significantly, Aptheker notes that out of some two hundred and fifty revolts, only four deserved mention. He suggests that because the slave expected to receive outside help and that because each revolt was inspired either through rumor or rebellion in other slave societies, their chance for success was limited.[7] Granted that all four models used in this study support this premise, they also suggest that many other factors helped determine the failure of the slave revolts. For example, the visibility of skin color, the lack of weapons, the fear of white men engendered by their severe controlling practices, and the hopeless situation produced by the institution of slavery to name a few.

Davis suggested that Negro history and slavery could be better understood if more serious attention was given to slave narratives—slaves speaking for themselves.[8]

3. *What is the significance of the findings in questions 1 and 2 above to the way in which white America perceives contemporary Negro America?*

The following may be found in Elkins' answer to the above questions:

> The crux of the matter was that the South [white America] simply could not picture the Negro as an adult, and it was this aspect of slavery that no amendment of the Constitution, even when ratified in good faith by Southern [white] conventions themselves, could do very much to alter; the South's [white America] incapacity to imagine the Negro in any role but that of a hopeless dependent would influence for years every effort of [liberal] white community to establish a new and stable relationship with its former slave [p. 240].[9]

The Cliometric Revolutional Model

The following questions guided the examination of the cliometric revolutional model.

1. *What is the relationship between the slave's humaneness and the slave's productivity?*

Fogel and Engerman did not concern themselves with those elements of slavery that could not be measured with statistics and mathematics. Therefore, they did not attempt to measure the humaneness of the slave. They depicted the slave as a worker who in spite of the limitations of slavery, compared favorably in productivity to the free industrial worker.

2. *What is the relationship between the profitability of slavery and the proslavery position?*

Fogel and Engerman were of the opinion that those people who supported the proslavery position eagerly accepted any and all postulates that would show slavery to be unprofitable.[10] Fogel and Engerman explain their positions in this manner:

> On the other hand, there is considerable evidence that slave owners were hard, calculating businessmen who priced slaves, and their other assets, with as much shrewdness as could be expected of any northern

capitalist.... Thus, the frequent contention that slaveowners preferred to work slaves to death at early ages, in order to avoid the burden of maintenance at late ages, is unfounded. Slaveowners were generally able to employ their bondsmen profitably throughout the life cycle. Planters solved the problem of old age by varying tasks according to the capacities of slaves [pp. 73–75].

Thus, for Fogel and Engerman, the proslavery position was an attempt to hide the real motive for having slaves (profit). Therefore, the relationship between the profitability posture and proslavery becomes a vital link in understanding how and why the African was selected for enslavement and why a "Christian" people could permit it to flourish for some three hundred years.[11]

3. What is the relationship between slave agriculture and the Northern system of family farming?

Part of the traditional debate over slavery centered around the proposition that the slavery system of agriculture was less profitable than the Northern system of family farming. Fogel and Engerman disagreed with this position because it was not founded on measurable evidence. They cite many historians and use a variety of sources to support their position.[12]

4. What is the relationship between the slaves' material standard of life and that of the free industrial worker?

Here again, Fogel and Engerman disagreed with the traditional view, which stated that the material standard of life of the slave was much lower than that of the average free industrial worker. They cited many sources and authors in support of this view.[13]

5. What is the significance of the relationships described in questions 1–4 above?

The data from questions one through four explain Fogel and Engerman's position against the traditional interpretation of slavery. They believe that the issues these questions examine form a solid basis for a systematic inquiry into slavery outside a moral perspective.

The traditional interpretation of slavery in the United States showed the slave to be unproductive, unskilled and for the most part having a material standard of living far below that of the average free industrial worker. Fogel and Engerman insisted instead that the slave was productive and skilled and had a material standard of life comparable to that of the free industrial worker. This position did not settle the profitability question, nor did it ease the tension between the proslavery and antislavery debators; however, it did generate some new sources and instruments for discussing the slavery issue. These questions provide a means for viewing the slavery issue within measurable limits by positing the slave as a human element in a humanly created situation.

Comparing and Contrasting the Four Models

For many years the slavery question oscillated between its moral ambiguity and its economic advantages to the slave holding class. It seems that the white world, especially white America, was caught up in this dualism to the point that guilt and shame became a permanent burden. The different models confront these issues.

Phillips, in *American Slavery*, based his premise on the racial inferiority of the Negro slave. He examined plantation records and found that the slaves were content and happy with their lot. Their behavior showed them to be incapable of self-control; and in almost every instance, the slaves readily responded to the driving forces of the institution of American slavery. Stampp, on the other hand, in *Peculiar Institutions*, used not only plantation records as his primary source, but also every available document on slavery including travelers' reports. Stampp found that the Negro slaves hated slavery and their white masters and used every available means to register this hatred. Slavery to Stampp was a cruel system of labor, exploiting and brutalizing its victims beyond human endurance.

In his *Slavery*, Elkins, like Stampp, used every available means to ensure that his research would be as unbiased as possible, and as a consequence, he also found the institution of slavery to be a cruel and dehumanizing system. Elkins further believed that the North American system of slavery was more closed than the Latin American system and, as a consequence, the North American system produced a "Sambo" type personality. While Elkins agreed with Stampp on many points, his corollary on Latin American slavery and Nazi concentration camps proved to be a major departure from both Stampp and Phillips.

Fogel and Engerman, in *Time on the Cross*, disagreed with all three others, holding instead that the traditional interpretation of slavery was unscientific in that its postulates were immeasurable. They felt that the slaves were exploited and mistreated; to them, however, slavery was first of all a highly efficient system of labor that not only used the slaves wisely but was open enough that the slaves enjoyed a standard of living that was comparable to the average free industrial worker. This indifference did not allow Fogel and Engerman to become proslavery thinkers; however, it did allow them to generate a system of measurement that changed Negro historiography.

The question then becomes, did these authors accurately interpret their source materials, or were they blinded by the influences of their culture? Many Americans have accepted the thesis of one or more of these writers. Accordingly, Negro slaves, as well as contemporary black Americans, are for the most part identified with one or more of the four models considered here. The main elements of each model will now be examined.

Racial inferiority

It would seem that in order for white America to justify the African's enslavement, some type of intellectual foundation had to be laid. Elkins remarked, "Phillips found that, in the light of what he saw as the inherent character of the Negro race, plantation slavery was by no means a cruel and inhuman system" (Elkins, p. 22). This supported Stampp's position that, "The use of slaves in southern agriculture was a deliberate choice made by men who sought greater returns than they could obtain from their own labor alone" (Stampp, p. 5). Thus, it would seem that in actuality, the racial inferiority of Negroes was a construct of white thinking and that Negro utility was the central issue. The question now becomes, did Negroes behave in such a manner that would allow Phillips to legitimately claim them racially inferior? Some data would indicate that some slaves did accommodate, act childlike, display a fondness for their masters, and in general, behave in the manner in which Phillips depicted them. However, did this behavior constitute racial inferiority, and was this behavior indicative of the whole slave population? Phillips, in attempting to establish the authenticity of this premise, quoted Monk Lewis as saying:

> The Negroes cannot be silent; they talk in spite of themselves. Every passion acts upon them with strange intensity, their anger is sudden and furious, their mirth clamorous and excessive, their curiosity audacious, and their love the sheer demand for gratification of an ardent animal desire [Phillips, p. 52].

This statement by Lewis indicated to Phillips an inferior nature in the Negro slave. It should be noted that these observers drew their conclusions from the data contained in the plantation records and generalized their findings to all Negroes, slave as well as free. This short-sighted methodology drew much criticism from Phillips' peers. For example, the *Journal of Negro History* in the late thirties and early forties featured the following articles: Harvey Wish, "American Slave Insurrections before 1861," XXIII (October, 1938), pp. 435–450; Ramond A. Bauer and Alice H. Bauer, "Day to Day Resistance to Slavery," XXVIII (October, 1942), pp. 388–419; Kenneth W. Porter, "Three Fighters for Freedom," XXVIII (January, 1943), pp. 51–72. The most outspoken critic of that time was Richard Hofstadter, who wrote:

A materially different version of the slave system would emerge if
scholars not sharing Phillips' bias were to subject the system to as intense
a study as had Phillips.... [L]et the study of the Old South be under-
taken by other scholars who have absorbed the viewpoint of modern
cultural anthropology, who have a feeling for social psychology ... who
will concentrate upon the neglected rural elements that form the great
majority of the southern population, who will not rule out the testimony
of more critical observers, and who will realize that any history of slavery
must be written in large part from the standpoint of the slave — and then
the possibility of an Old South as a field of research and historical experience will loom larger than ever.[14]

Thus, even though Phillips projected a highly visible side of Negro personality, many of his peers viewed his conclusions as racist and unsound
historically.

DuBois believed that groups, and especially the slave group, cannot be perceived in this manner because of the inability of normal man
to see the whole of any amalgamated living situation. Therefore, the
behavior that Phillips observed did not find total acceptance as an indication of Negro inferiority; instead, Phillips' premise pointed to a
weakness in early Negro historiography. For example, in order for the
Englishman to enslave the African, the Englishman had to first abolish
(within himself) the individual African and accept in his or her place
the African as a group which he could then redefine according to his
own needs.[15] Phillips' model, then, fell victim to the age-old habit of,
first, fearing the different and, secondly, creating social constructs that
would justify this fear.

It is unlikely that any contemporary Negro would deny that a few
Negroes behave in the manner as described earlier by Monk Lewis; yet
what most contemporary Negroes would resent is the implication that
all Negroes behave in this manner. This is not to say that those who act
differently are above or better than those whom Lewis observed. Blacks
for the most part have presently either become more assimilated into the
dominant culture or have, through acceptance of the concept of negritude,
matured with their culture to a more sophisticated level of behavior.

When Elkins examined the same sources as Phillips, he saw in the
Negro a childlike person who had been corrupted by the institution of
slavery. Stampp, on the other hand, saw "a white person with a black
skin." All three were looking at the same behavior, yet they each reached
different conclusions. It might be added that while each of them reached
different conclusions, they were all very ethnocentric in their views. It
should be noted that the Negro American culture is a very young culture,
having existed for a little more than three hundred years, and has existed in a configuration of subservience, devoid of the means of self-
examination (that is, unbiased means), and powerless to use what

little power that it may have had because of its internal composition.

Stampp believed that this powerlessness of the Negro slave was brought about through deliberate planning since the Southerner did not spuriously conceive the institution, nor was it an accident of nature (Stampp, p. 5). Elkins, on the other hand, believed that because the traditional institution was under fire, slavery as an institution was doomed (Elkins, pp. 27–28). He charged the inception and development of the institution of slavery to American creative genius (Elkins, pp. 37–38). The point to be made here is that each of these scholars saw the Negro problem and slavery at three different historical periods. That is to say that while each author was viewing primarily the same subject and the same material, Phillips viewed his source material around 1900, Stampp around 1950, Elkins around 1955, and Fogel and Engerman around 1970. The time differences allowed the ramifications due to social and anthropological change to influence each author's point of view.

For example, after a few years had elapsed, Phillips softened his attitude towards his "racial inferiority" thesis. Elkins, in commenting on a later book by Phillips, *Life and Labor in the Old South*, which was published some eleven years after his *Negro Slavery*, stated, "Actually, Phillips' tone throughout this work is much subdued in comparison to that of a decade before"(Elkins, p. 17). Granting that this observation by Elkins is correct, time and changing attitudes played an important role in determining how the slavery question would be perceived. As social attitudes changed, so did the perception of slavery, and as a consequence, each proceding author was able to view slavery through the same source material reaching different conclusions.

Fogel and Engerman saw Phillips' "racial inferiority" thesis as a scholarly attempt to sustain the traditional interpretation of slavery. They felt that Phillips' love for his native South clouded his mind to the significance of the facts. Stampp and Elkins too, according to Fogel and Engerman, were locked into the traditional interpretation of slavery and, while they professed to see the slaves as fully human, they unwittingly ascribed the slaves to a position somewhat below "white" mental standards. Thus, it seems that in each model, the progressive, the racial enlightenment, and the counter-progressive, slaves were viewed as racially inferior to the planter class.

In conclusion, the behavior that Phillips, Stampp, and Elkins identified as inferior was perhaps the beginning of a new culture. If the accounts of these authors are authentic, then the behavior of the slaves clearly indicates that when compared to the behavior of free Americans, slaves exhibited an undeveloped cultural system. The term "racial inferiority" is a misnomer because all humans are racially equal but socially different. In the case of the African, this social difference allowed non–Africans to delineate African behavior as primitive, beastly, savage, and in a word, "nonwhite." Jordan believed that these differences caused the early English to not only fear the African but resent the many similarities to their own past behavior (*White Over Black*, pp. 3–43).

Most western historians and social scientists readily agree that "all men are created equal," and that in the case of Negro Americans, social deprivation is usually identified as racial inferiority. A better approach may be that the so-called "social deprivation" is the first sign of a beginning culture. Thus, the sin, shame, and guilt inherent in the institution of Negro American slavery not only caused many contemporary white Americans to become ashamed of their institution but forced Negroes to share in their shame. Therefore, in order to understand better the slaves' behavior, which is directly related to their confinement in the institution of plantation slavery, that institution needs examination.

The plantation system

Phillips regarded the plantation system of slavery as a much needed school where the "uncivilized mass of African savagery could be trained" (Phillips, p. 43). He believed that slavery was good, not only for the slaves but also for the slave holders as well. This idea caused Elkins to regard the plantation system as a debilitated regime that could only survive through the absolute control of its inmates. Stampp, on the other hand, believed that the plantation system existed primarily because the trading in slaves was a profitable enterprise. Regardless of either position, the plantation system of slavery did exist and by so doing caused its slaves to become pawns in an intellectual shuffle. Even today the effects of that system are felt throughout all America.

Conversely to either Phillips, Stampp, or Elkins, Fogel and Engerman saw the plantation system as a highly efficient system of labor management. They felt that the slaves enjoyed a standard of living that was at least on a par with that of the average free laborer. It appears that all of these writers were so engaged with defining the institution that the main elements of the institution were overlooked. While the primary function of the institution was to bring in added wealth to its owner/operator, the social structure of slaves, who in essence made the system a workable mechanism, was almost entirely ignored.

Elkins attempted to focus on this social structure by comparing Latin American slavery to North American slavery. He succeeded in that he caused the differences between these two systems to be placed on the historian's main agenda; however, he failed in that he did not delineate these differences as constructs of contemporary American thought.

The North American plantation of slavery was without reservation a cruel, exploitive means of survival. However, the loss of life, the inhumane treatment and poor living conditions, etc., that were forced upon the slaves were of little significance to Negro Americans and Americans in general. The greatest loss experienced by all Americans was the inability of white America to perceive the slaves as fully human and their forcing of the slaves to see themselves only through the eyes of their masters.

Stampp's premise "to make them stand in fear," and Elkins' Sambo premise more than adequately defined a central element of the plantation system; however, neither premise attempted to show the relationship between the treatment of slaves and the behavior of the Negro masses of today. Both Stampp and Elkins' ideas began with observations of the structure of the slaves' family. The inability of the slaves to construct a family life-style after their foreparents and the refusal of their masters to allow them to construct an imitation of this family life style caused a kind of social deprivation that in the end produced a paradoxical social situation akin to chaos. Andrew Billingsly saw this social situation differently from each of the authors in this study.[16]

The slaves' families

Phillips saw the slave family as a social arrangement whose sole purpose was to increase the utility of the slaves. He believed that "Negroes furnished inertly obeying minds and muscles; slavery provided a police; and the plantation system contributed the machinery of direction" (Phillips, p. 339). Thus, to Phillips the slave family structure could have but one purpose, the betterment of the master. Consequently, the long respected institution of marriage, as far as the slave was concerned, had no legal sanction, no religious significance and no power to protect itself from any outside influence, except those sanctions and powers granted to it by the master.

Stampp agreed with Phillips up to a point. Where Phillips saw the African coming from a barbarous situation, Stampp saw the African as having "a regulated family life and a rigidly enforced moral code" (Stampp, p. 340). To Stampp the stripping away of the Africans' culture forced them into a situation of powerlessness where the old standards could no longer support them and the new standards found in the master's family structure were denied. Stampp believed that because the slave family had no legal status, it was viewed as a system of control in that most masters believed that a happy slave was a more productive worker. Needless to say, Stampp condemned the plantation system of slave marriage as a racist attempt to gloss over inhumane conditions that had caused this type of family to come into being.

Here again, Elkins followed the course set by Stampp in that he saw the system of North American slavery as so debilitating that the slave family structure could only reflect a feeble attempt, by the slaves, to mimic that of their masters. Elkins believed that a "father among the slaves was legally unknown, a husband without the rights of his bed, the state of marriage defined as only that of concubinage." To Elkins, "Motherhood was clothed in the scant dignity of the breeding function" (Elkins, p. 55).

Granting that Phillips, Stampp, and Elkins followed the traditional method for interpreting slavery in the United States, the slave could not have developed a family system comparable with the master's family system. However, Fogel and Engerman posited a slave family structure that fits more easily into Negro history in that it afforded the slave family a type of utility. It would not have been to the advantage of the slave holding class to allow the slaves to build any social system that did not serve their (slave holders) needs. Therefore, while the slaves' family structure was not comparable to the slave holder's family, it did allow the slaves to have some type of social family structure that met their daily needs, if only in a limited sense. Fogel and Engerman believed that the slaves' family unit served as a place for distributing slave rations, an instrument for developing pride in their work, and a preventative for runaways. They saw this unit as a social instrument that allowed a form of religion as well as a psychological release from the strains of slavery. Stampp and Elkins agreed with Fogel and Engerman on these two points; however, Stampp and Elkins believed that the system of slavery was so cruel that the family system developed by the slaves had little or no relevance to the daily routine of plantation life.

George Rawick disregarded Phillips, Stampp, Elkins, and Fogel and Engerman's models of Negro family structure where the absence of the Negro male played an important part, and expressed the notion that the previously mentioned family models did not serve the needs of the Negro slave family. Rawick wrote:

> The slave community acted like a generalized extended kinship system in which all adults looked after all children and there was little division between "my children for whom I'm responsible" and "your children for whom you're responsible." I would suggest that such a generalized extended kinship system was more functionally useful and integrative under the conditions of slavery in which both mother and father usually worked in the fields than would be one which emphasized the exclusive rights and biological parents, the parents of the nuclear family. There was always some older person who would, with relative ease, take over the role of absent parents—as is usually the case today in the black community [*The American Slave*, p. 93].

This understanding of Negro family life differed greatly from that of Stampp's, who saw the black family as in a constant state of chaos brought about by the degrading effects of slavery. Stampp believed that the slave family structure had no relevance to the everyday life of the slave because it had lost its African supports and was allowed to exist only so long as it served the needs of the master. He described it in this manner:

> In Africa the Negroes had been accustomed to a strictly regulated family life and a rigidly enforced moral code. But in America the disintegration of their social organization removed the traditional sanctions which had encouraged them to respect their old customs.... Because the slaves failed to conform to the white pattern, the master class found the explanation, as usual, in the Negro's innate racial traits [Stampp, p. 340].

The notion that the slave had no positive family structure is somewhat suspect because, as Stampp projected, the slaves could not identify with much of the "white caste's family pattern" because much of this family pattern was denied them. The point that is obvious in an examination of Phillips, Stampp and Elkins' ideology is that slaves, even though denied access to the slave holder's family structure, did create a family structure that could serve their daily needs.

Support for this type of reasoning came from such authors as E. Franklin Frazier, who for many years was the absolute authority on the American black family. However, Rawick was of the opinion that Frazier was a victim of the Americanization process and as such presented much material in his book, *The Negro Family in the United States*, that complemented Stampp, Phillips and Elkins. While Rawick did not criticize Frazier, he did point to a central weakness in his research:

> When Frazier emphasized tendencies that weakened the black family, lessening, for example, the authority of the father, his followers have concluded that the reason why the contemporary black ghetto household is often characterized by the absence of a functioning male figure stems from the supposed similar experience under slavery [Rawick, p. 92].

Rawick goes on to give his reason for citing this weakness in Frazier's research:

> I do think careful reading of the slave narratives collected in the 1930's modifies in some crucial ways Professor Frazier's conclusions. I think that there were probably more stable kinship units among the slaves than he did; and I think that the presence of a relatively strong male figure in that kinship unit was more common than he did; and I think that in general the slave family was better adapted to the conditions of the slaves, including their ability to struggle against those conditions, than he did [pp. 92–93].

Rawick believed that Frazier's source material might have been contaminated by its very nature:

> Frazier's sources were those left by slaves unique enough to have written books, and black college students in the 1930's whom Frazier

interviewed for family reminiscences. That is, his sources were people who were very likely part of that "black bourgeoisie" and their ancestors, that is, most likely to have accepted a negative assessment of the black family, from which they worked so hard to distinguish themselves [pp. 92–93].
This weakness in interpreting the slave's history has in many instances failed to reflect the slave's point of view, consequently causing many Americans to ask: Are the facts under investigation real, or have they been filtered through the ethnic considerations of the generating author? Admittedly, there is no absolute way of determining whether the facts are pure or not; nevertheless, Rawick's observation must be seriously considered.

Rawick raises a significant issue. Were slaves, as Phillips depicted them, childlike and uncaring, or as Stampp would have it, in a constant state of chaos, or, as Elkins saw them, white men in black skins, or, per Fogel and Engerman, highly efficient workers caught in an unfortunate situation? The data does not provide a concrete answer to this question; however, it supplies a reasonable amount of evidence that supports the premise that Negro Americans are a people, uniquely conceived and able to function as any other rational human beings under stress. Rawick wrote about the Negro family in this manner:

> While sociologist and social workers have been worrying that the black kinship structure and patterns do not prepare blacks for entry into middle-class American society, blacks have gone ahead rather successfully in creating ways whereby they could survive as blacks in the United States.... Indeed, the activity of the slaves in creating patterns of family life that were functionally integrative did more than merely prevent the destruction of personality that often occurs when individuals struggle unsuccessfully to attain the unattainable. It was part and parcel of the social process out of which came black pride, black identity, black culture, the black community, and black rebellion in America [Rawick, p. 93].

Because of the Negroes' inability to project their inner feelings on dominant thought, they are perceived as having no national pride, national holidays and authentic national leaders. This weakness in their perception of Negroes often causes white America to assume that the contemporary black must fit one of the four models previously described. In addition, this accepted view of the Negro is ethnocentric in nature because it is the view that most white Americans would like to believe as the true image. Myrdal believes that this condition is the byproduct of the Americanization process.

In conclusion, contemporary blacks, like their forebears, have two choices: they either model their family's structure after the white family structure, or they build a family structure that will meet their daily needs. The implication is that since each ethnic group exists within the constructs of its own ethnocentric value system, to attempt to mimic another ethnic group's values is tantamount to disavowing one's own image as it is reflected in a mirror.

Rawick observes that those Negroes who seem capable of interpreting and defining Negro history and culture are so engrossed in assimilating white culture that they usually reflect a negative configuration of Negro culture and history. This provides a central weakness in Negro historiography. The black family is usually depicted as a primitive configuration attempting to emulate the average white family. Heretofore, this weakness in family definition has caused many blacks to internalize the negative views projected by the white community and in the same instance reinforce these negative views in the white community.

For example, the television shows *Good Times*, *The Jeffersons*, and *Different Strokes* all embrace most of the negative stereotypes held by the general white community. It seems highly unlikely that these negative stereotypes will soon lose their social implications. The slave family was and is depicted as an animalistic entity whose function must be directed and controlled. Phillips believed this to be true, and Stampp and Elkins developed a thesis that explained why it is true.

Phillips, quoting Hammond, wrote, "Marriage is to be encouraged as it adds to the comfort, happiness and health of those who enter upon it, besides insuring a greater increase" (Phillips, p. 269). Elkins wrote, "That most ancient and intimate of institutional arrangements, marriage and family, had long since been destroyed by the law, and the law never showed any inclination to rehabilitate it" (Elkins, p. 53). Stampp notes that, "Since slaves, as chattels, could not make contracts, marriages between them were not legally binding" (Stampp, p. 198). Fogel and Engerman believed as did Phillips with this exception, "First and foremost, planters promoted family formation both through exhortation and through economic inducements" (Fogel and Engerman, p. 128).

These inducements usually included such things as a larger house, a lighter work load for expectant mothers, better food, and the expressed joy or pleasure of the master. So from the beginning, the black family was seen as animal husbandry where utility was the primary concern. However, Rawick believed that the slave family unit had very strong kinship ties. He wrote:

> As soon as the Civil War was over, and even in the few years before the end of the war when the discipline on the plantations was virtually destroyed, thousands of slaves went looking for and found their mothers, fathers, sisters, brothers, sons and daughters from whom they had been separated [Rawick, p. 90].

Rawick thus presents a view of the slave family that differs greatly with that of the four models under examination.

Paternalism

Paternalism and slavery cannot be examined without examining Negro identity because it seems that the two are inextricably linked. The mystical link between the Negroes' identity and their relationship to white America defies a rational explanation. It is comparable to the relationship of the Jews and their SS guards with the exception that the Jews never lost their customs and Jewish identity. Blacks, on the other hand, lost their African customs and in most instances were conditioned to accept the customs and traditions of white America as most desirable. This "urge to whiteness" allows many Negroes to understand negritude as something undesirable and degrading while accepting white values as the standard for right and wrong. Stampp and Elkins believed that slavery so conditioned Negroes that in many instances they could not separate their own identity from that of white America.

The myth that the slave holder loved his slaves and treated them as children formed one of the strong points for Phillips and his followers (Phillips, pp. 261–290, 387, 398, 410). Stampp, on the other hand, believed that the profit motive caused a psuedo-love by the master for his slaves (Stampp, pp. 76, 96, 162–163, 228–231, 313, 322–330). According to Elkins, the slaves' personality had been so drastically changed that they could not behave in any other manner (Elkins, pp. 81–88). As these three interpretations of paternalism are examined, the question is raised, did the slave holder have to sacrifice any material gain in order to be paternalistic toward his slaves? Fogel and Engerman believed that they did not, and there is an abundance of hard evidence to substantiate their claim (Fogel and Engerman, pp. 73, 77, 129).

Stampp asked three questions concerning paternalism. First, how much paternalism was there? He answered:

> Plantation paternalism, then, was in most cases merely a kind of leisure-class family indulgence of its domestics.... A planter sometimes whimsically select[ed] a slave or two for special pets. He pampered them, consulted them with mock gravity about large matters, and permitted them to be impertinent about small ones.... This kind of paternalism (Fanny Kemble likened it to "that maudlin tenderness of a fine lady for her lapdog"), which often arose from the master's genuine love for his slave, gave its recipient privileges and comforts but made him into something less than a man [Stampp, p. 327].

Second, under what circumstances did it occur?

> From such close association an owner might develop a deep affection for a slave.... On the plantations the master's intimate personal contacts were confined almost exclusively to household servants; rarely did he have more than a casual acquaintanceship with the mass of common field-hands [pp. 324–25].

Third, what was its nature?

A Mississippi planter grieved at the death of a slave child, whom his whole family had loved, as if he "had lost some dear relative." More commonly, however, his grief seemed to arise from the loss of property. "Dick died last night, curse such luck," he wrote. And again: "Mary's son, Richard, died tonight. Oh! my losses almost make me crazy." [p. 326].

Paternalism may thus be construed as an owner/pet relationship.

While Elkins did not expound greatly on the paternalistic theory, he did see the slave in generally the same configuration as Stampp with the exception that the personality of the slave was so drastically changed that his resulting personality was that of a typical "Sambo." This understanding allowed Elkins to develop his "Sambo thesis" which in actuality closely resembles Phillips' description of Negro personality development.

Elkins asked three questions about Sambo. First, is the concept real? Second, what order of existence, what rank of legitimacy, should be accorded Sambo? And third, is there a scientific way to talk about this problem? In answer to the first question, Phillips' whole discourse was in support of his (Sambo's) realness. Accordingly, what Phillips' critics cited as racism was actually to Phillips a definite Sambo-type personality. The question that arises at this point is, where does racism leave off and historical fact begin? Since there is no scientific means for answering this question, it seems only proper to regard Phillips' thesis as historical writing, rather than to dismiss it as racist propaganda. Nevertheless, Phillips tended to disregard the next two questions by simply positing the notion that the slave was inferior by nature (Phillips, pp. 52, 291-293, 339-343). Stampp, on the other hand, tended to believe that the Sambo behaviors displayed by the slaves were a disguise for their deep-seated hatred for the whole slavery system. He further believed that the slave took every opportunity to show this hatred. He wrote:

They were not reckless rebels who risked their lives for freedom; if the thought of rebellion crossed their minds, the odds against success seemed too overwhelming to attempt it. But the inevitability of their bondage made it none the more attractive. And so, when they could, they protested by shirking their duties, injuring the crops, feigning illness, and disrupting the routine. These acts were, in part, an unspectacular kind of day-to-day resistance to slavery [Stampp, pp. 108-109].

Fogel and Engerman agreed with Stampp and Elkins up to a point. They did not believe that the system was as cruel and devastating as Stampp and Elkins had supported. They were more inclined to believe that the slave holders were astute businessmen who used sound principles in managing their plantations, therefore using minimal force in accomplishing their goals. They comment:

What was crucial to the system was not cruelty but force. Force could,

and often did, lead to cruelty, but not as much cruelty as Stampp then
believed. For what most planters sought was not "perfect" submissions
but "optimal" submission.... The shrewd capitalistic businessmen who
ran the slave plantations were not usually psychological perverts who gloried
in the exercise of unlimited force for its own sake. They generally used
force for exactly the same purpose as they used positive incentives—to
achieve the largest product at the lowest cost. Like everything else, they
strove to use force not cruelly but optimally [Fogel and Engerman, p. 232].

Assuming that all of the above mentioned authors were using factual data, it is permissible to conclude that (1) there are four historical
stages for interpreting Negro personality and culture, (2) North American
slavery produced a change in the African's personality, (3) contemporary
Negro American culture had its beginning in slavery, and (4) there is
no scientific way to talk about this personality change because, as of now,
there are too many unknown elements involved.

The rank and legitimacy that should be afforded this problem should
be determined by the rank and legitimacy afforded American history
because slavery, Negro culture, and personality are all part of American
history, and irrespective of prevailing moralistic attitudes towards slavery,
the phenomenon did exist. While establishing this legitimacy may prove
to be a tedious task, some of the difficulty may be overcome by accepting the slave narratives as factual history and as authentic Negro observations. These narratives are the only concise records of slavery left by
those who bore the "marks of oppression." Furthermore, when those
Negroes born around 1900 die, the last living connection to slavery will
be lost forever. Can America afford this loss?

Genovese believed that there was a degree of attachment to the slaves
by their masters; however, he did not think that this attachment constituted paternalism. It was more of a pet/master relationship, and granting that the masters only developed a fondness for those slaves who served
as house servants, the masses of the slaves and fieldhands were usually
perceived by the masters as merely utilitarian in nature and were treated
as such.

Genovese wrote that "southern paternalism, like every other paternalism, had little to do with Ole Massa's ostensible benevolence, kindness, and good cheer. It grew out of the necessity to discipline and morally
justify a system of exploitation." Genovese agreed, in a limited sense,
with Stampp, Elkins, Fogel and Engerman when he wrote:

A paternalism accepted by both masters and slaves—but with radically
different interpretations—afforded a fragile bridge across the intolerable
contradictions that had to depend on the willing reproduction and productivity of its victims. For the slave holders paternalism represented an
attempt to overcome the fundamental contradiction in slavery: the im-
possibility of slaves ever becoming the things they were supposed to be.

Paternalism defined the involuntary labor of the slaves as legitimate return to their masters for direction and protection. But, the masters' need to see their slaves as acquiescent human beings constituted a moral victory for the slaves themselves [Genovese, pp. 4-5].

This statement by Genovese supports the notion that slavery was a system of exploitation. His position, "Where ever paternalism exists, it undermines solidarity among the oppressed by linking them as individuals to their oppressors" (Genovese, p. 5), might explain why contemporary blacks seek to develop a close relationship to whites in general. Phillips saw this "link" as the slaves being cheerful, happy, and content with their paternal masters; Stampp saw the link as white men in black skins; Elkins saw it as a Sambo personality; and Fogel and Engerman saw the link as a form of ignorance about the actuality of slavery.

As stated earlier, the different levels of the Negro's personality development are represented in each model respectively, and as a consequence, the Negro is perceived at different levels in this development. The first level is represented in Phillips' model, namely the progressive (Genesis Age), which shows the slave accepting his slave status and in most instances viewing the master as his "parent," preferring accommodation rather than struggling for freedom (Phillips, pp. 86-140).[17] This is not to contradict the previous statement, which asserted that the slave holder did not see himself as a parent, but rather to affirm that the slave perceived the slave holder as his parent.

Throughout these narratives (Rawick, *Slave's Narratives*), the slaves speak of their master whipping them "to make them good, because they need it, and because they (slaves) could not be controlled without it." In forty-one volumes of the *Slaves' Narratives*, there were few cases where the slaves said that the slave holder did not have the right to whip them; however, many of them complained about the severity of the whippings. It would seem that the slave's personality had been changed to Stampp's childlike, submissive illustration—that they were indeed "just a white man in a black skin." These same slaves were to Elkins "docile but irresponsible, loyal but lazy, humble but chronically given to lying and stealing." Elkins saw these traits as an indication of the Sambo personality.

In actuality, the narrative data show that both Stampp and Elkins projected a limited model of Negro personality—and neither qualified their model. For example, they projected their individual model as the total personality. The childlike person that they depicted was in actuality only one type of Negro personality. This child who loved his master was the first stage of Negro development; and as with most children, loving and hating are so closely related that separation is virtually impossible.[18] This slave/master relationship caused many white Americans to believe that the slave loved his situation. Stampp explained the situation in this manner:

Critics of slavery, certain white men think, err when they assume that Negroes suffered as much in bondage as white men would have suffered. One must remember, argued the critics of critics, that to Negroes slavery seemed natural; knowing no other life, they accepted it without giving the matter much thought. Not that slavery was a good thing, mind you— but still, it probably hurt the Negroes less than it did the whites. Indeed, the whites were really more enslaved by Negro slavery than were the Negro slaves [Stampp, p. 429].

In the past, minorities have not been perceived as they may actually be, but only as white America was able to perceive them; and in all probability, minorities will continue to be perceived in the same manner [Myrdal, pp. 586–589]. This weakness on the part of white America causes much suffering among many of America's ethnic groups. Jews, people of Slavic descent, Hispanics, Islanders, American Indians, etc., all fall prey to one form or another of America's racism. Charles E. Silberman wrote:

By itself, however, the fact of slavery does not begin to explain "the crushing sense of nobodiness" with which Negroes are afflicted. People of Slavic descent have no trouble holding their heads aloft, although "Slav" originally meant "slave." And the Jews, far from trying to erase the memory of slavery, have made it central to their religion: every Jew is enjoined to recall the fact that "we were slaves to Pharoah in Egypt." The pronoun "we" is used because each individual is to imagine that he himself, not just his ancestors, had been enslaved.[19]

Silberman is alluding to one of the peculiarities of the Negro's stay in America. While all minorities suffer some form of racial prejudice, Negroes seem to suffer the most. It seems that Silberman is indicating that one of the ways in which minorities can lessen the brunt of racial prejudice is through an acceptance of their history, the good as well as the evil. Silberman went on to explain the differences between the Jew's enslavement and the Negro's enslavement. He concluded the matter in this manner:

We need not labor the point. What is essential is neither to rewrite history as some liberals have done nor pretend that the by-products of a slave system are nonexistent. Instead, Negro and White need to use history for an understanding of the current "inferiorities" that do exist, and search for new identities [Silberman, p. 80].

Today with so many nations challenging America's right to world leadership, America cannot any longer afford to have within its national family any citizen who feels that America is not home for him, and much less that America does not intend to declare war on American racism. Elkins believed that one such citizen, the Negro American, is caught up in this kind of dilemma. Concerning this he wrote:

And if Sambo is uniquely an American product, then his existence, and the reasons for his character, must be recognized in order to appreciate the very scope of our slave problem and its aftermath [Elkins, p. 85]. This understanding by Elkins suggests that those forces which will or will not allow the Negro American to enjoy full citizenship had their roots in the institution of American slavery.

It seems to be an inescapable fact that the Negro experience in America has been and still is a dark one. For example, like all other Americans, Negroes must share the national responsibility for being American. However, Negroes in a real sense cannot claim the rights and privileges afforded to white Americans, and even if Negroes desired to, they cannot claim their "mother" country as their own. In a sense, Negroes are displaced persons whose very name identifies them as property. For example, a Negro names Schwartz is immediately identified as having in his lineage a master named Schwartz. Thus, Negroes are caught in a system which predetermined how their ancestors would be identified, and which consequently determines how present-day Negroes may be identified. Contemporary blacks may today find that their great-grandmother was a slave, and that their great-grandfather was a slave holder; that their grandmother was very dark complexioned; and that their children's complexion could fall anywhere between "black" and "white." This not only puts a tremendous strain on the homogeneity of their present family, but attacks the very roots for building good relationships between family members.

It is generally accepted that the family unit is the primary unit in the shaping of personality; the mother is the transmitter of culture, and the key influence in the young child's early life, especially the young male child (Rawick, pp. 91–93). If this is true, then what might have happened to a young boy's personality as he watched his mother being stripped on a public auction block, as he watched his mother being assaulted in the presence of his father, who could offer no defense, and what might have happened to his identity when he watched his father being beaten worse than an animal? Erikson spoke of this "surrendered identity" in this manner:

> As I studied Freud's address, I remembered a remark made recently by a warm-hearted and influential American Jew: "Some instinctive sense tells every Jewish mother that she must make her child study, that his intelligence is his pass to the future." Why does a Negro mother not care? Why does she not have the same instinctive sense?... I suggested that, given American Negro history, the equivalent "instinctive sense" may have told the majority of Negro mothers to keep their children and especially the gifted and questioning ones, away from futile and dangerous competition, that is, for survival's sake to keep them in their place even if that place is defined by an indifferent and hateful "compact majority" [Erikson, p. 236].[20]

This situation points to a paradox of the Negro identity problem. Stampp and Elkins believed that the institution of slavery subjected the Negroes to a type of "seasoning process" which demanded that they surrender their identity to their masters (Stampp, p. 143; Elkins, p. 82). Contemporary blacks, being the offspring of this system, are treated in somewhat the same manner as their foreparent slaves, except that today, Blacks are expected to behave as if slavery never existed; and while they are expected to ignore their history, they are judged according to the interpreted effects of their history (Frazier, p. 10). Erikson described the process in this manner:

> ... "mothers" immediately marks one of the problems we face in approaching Negro identity. The Jewish mothers he had in mind would expect to be backed by their husbands or, in fact, to act in their behalf; Negro mothers would not. Negro mothers are apt to cultivate the surrendered identity forced on Negro men for generations. This, so the literature would suggest, has reduced the Negro to a reflection of the "negative" recognition which surrounds him like an endless recess of distorting mirrors. How his positive identity has been undermined systematically—first under the unspeakable system of slavery in North America and then by the system of slavery perpetuated in the rural South and urban North—has been extensively, carefully, and devastatingly documented.[21]

That the Negro's positive identity has been undermined needs no further documentation at this time. What is needed is a re-examination of the side effects of this negative identity. Erikson seems to believe that as the individual grows, he is presented with both negative and positive images. The negative comes as a result of "rewards and punishments, parental examples, and by community's typology as revealed in wit and gossip, in tale and story" (Erikson, p. 237).

The positive arrives through warning the individual "not to become what he often had no intention of becoming so that he can learn to anticipate what he must avoid" (p. 236). It would appear that without the proper balance of these two identities, the developing human would have a tendency to be controlled by the stronger force. This might explain how the effects of slavery could be a disturbing influence for the contemporary Negro American. For example, if the negative is a result of the community's direct influence, then the slave could have a negative identity; and if the parents present more negative examples than positive, and if the evil prototypes (whippings, brandings, hangings, etc.) outweigh the good prototypes (humane treatment), then the slaves would inevitably accept a negative identity for themselves. Once this negative identity is firmly established, it becomes the foundation upon which all other social development is placed.

The plantation system was a negative environment, and as such it could only offer negative experiences to the slaves. Stampp and Elkins believed that this situation caused the slave, first, to resist and, second, to undergo a profound personality change (Stampp, p. 363; Elkins, p. 85). Erikson supported this kind of logic:

> The individual belonging to an oppressed and exploited minority, which is aware of the dominant cultural ideals but prevented from emulating them, is apt to fuse the negative images held up to him by the dominant majority with his own negative identity [Erikson, p. 237].

It would seem that because of the way in which Negro personality was formed, and who became the authority in interpreting this formation, its outstanding characteristics, such as obstinate meekness, exaggerated childlikeness, and superficial submissiveness, will continue to be viewed as defensive mechanisms against the attitudes and behaviors of the very forces that formed it.[22]

It would seem, based on the data reviewed here, that any system which oppresses falls victim to its own internal support mechanisms and usually becomes the unconscious victim of the very negative identities which it projects on the oppressed. Erikson stated it this way:

> As yet least understood, however, is the fact that the oppressor has a vested interest in the negative identity of the oppressed because that negative identity is a projection of his own unconscious negative identity—a projection which, up to a point, makes him feel superior but also, in a brittle way, whole [Erikson, p. 238].

Because of the way that the Africans were brought to this country, they had, from the very beginning, to learn to understand and to anticipate their masters; the masters never had a need to actually understand "his Negroes"; he could then as well as now rely on some form of power to produce the type of behavior he desired; whether the behavior was real or role-playing really did not matter. The question that should be asked of the dominant group is, do you know the "real" Negro? Are they really the way that you perceive them?

It seems that since the slave holders placed themselves in a paternal role, they were able to perceive themselves as paternalistic. They in turn allowed this identification to become a catch-all for all attitudes and behaviors in dealing with their slaves. Furthermore, it seems that since slaves had to depend on their masters for every necessity, the masters assumed that the slaves were happy in their slave status. It would also appear that the slave holders would not allow themselves to probe the reasons for the slaves' seeming acquiescence to slavery. Phillips, the most avid proslavery writer, admitted that many slaves were troublesome, crazy for freedom, etc., and did not seem to be able to appreciate their paternal relation to their masters. Part of the psychological conditioning that the slaves had to undergo included an acceptance of the paternalistic thesis. Paternalism then became the means through which the subjugation of the African became complete. It is interesting to note what Marden and Meyer wrote:

> The dominant group in a society is one which is able to control power, both economic and political, toward two ends: (1) to protect and advance its own group interest by restricting the opportunities of other ethno-racial groups; and (2) to perpetuate its own ideas of what is "right," "desirable," "good." Like all other peoples, dominants believe the survival of the society depends on "others," to a degree at least, coming to share their values and to behave accordingly.[23]

Marden and Meyer indicate that the dominants in a society could very easily perceive themselves as paternalistic. This being the case, white Americans then would perceive themselves as paternalistic and all the other ethno-racial groups would either adhere to the value system of the dominant group or be classified as something less than desirable by the dominant group. Marden and Meyer explain:

> Members of the dominant group share a common value system, a common language, and a common history. Dominant norms are historically derived, and their preeminence is established by custom and law. To the extent that subgroups do not fully share these assumptions, they are restricted, formally or informally, to a greater or lesser degree, from full and equal participation in the full range of the life of the society [Marden and Meyer, p. 38].

Thus, it would seem that paternalism would be viewed by the dominant group as a logical derivative of "the right to govern." As a consequence, Phillips understood slavery to be paternalistic and because it was such, the slave holders had a "natural" right to expect some profit from their investment in slaves. Thus, Phillips and the proslavery thinkers through social definition developed an esoteric system whereby the property rights of man became inherent in belonging to the dominant group. While Stampp, Elkins, Fogel and Engerman expressed the notion that they were opposed to Phillips' ideology, they also by virtue of being white enjoyed the benefits derived from the institution of American slavery.

It is of particular interest to note that the general American public did not see the need to abolish slavery until the United States could replace the slave with machinery. A further point to be noted here is that while many liberal Americans deride the paternal aspects of slavery, few, if any, deride the paternal aspects of the contemporary welfare system. It seems that while most Americans are willing to accept the end results of slavery as depicted in contemporary black behavior, few are willing to become less paternal in order that the black will become less dependent. Friere wrote that "in order for the poor to become less poor the rich must be willing to become less rich." Thus, it seems that paternalism in America has become so entrenched in the American way of life that poor people have been reduced to "money movers" whose welfare depends on how well they are able to accept the exploitation directed at and against them. Paternalism was an intricate part of the maintenance system of slavery which will be examined next.

Maintenance and control

As has been previously noted, the forerunner of the models under consideration, the progressive model, comprises six primary concerns: food, shelter, clothing, police regulations, medical care, and the innate racial inferiority of the Negro American. Since Stampp and Elkins followed basically the same categories, differing mainly in attributing the inferiority of the Negro to the conditions of slavery, and since Fogel and Engerman's treatment of these categories add little or no new data, it will serve no useful purpose to rehash these categories. Instead, a limited portion of the *Slaves' Narratives* will be examined in order to compare the way the slaves perceived the categories of Phillips, Stampp, Elkins, and Fogel and Engerman.

Slave foods

There is no absolute scale for determining the actual status of the feeding of slaves because each plantation system was different. However, there are enough comments by ex-slaves themselves to at least get an indication of what actually happened. For example, Rawick cited these accounts by ex-slaves and/or near relatives of slaves:

> Campbell Armstrong from Arkansas—They'd give you three pounds of meat and a quart of meal and molasses when they'd make it. Sometimes they would take a notion to give you something like flour. But you had to take what they give you. They give out the rations every Saturday. That was to last you a week.... George Kye, born in Virginia in 1820—"We had stew made out of pork and potatoes, and sometimes greens and pot liquor, and we had ash cake mostly, but biscuits about once a month." ... Solomon Oliver, born in Mississippi in 1859—Ration day was Saturday. Each person was given a peck of corn meal, four pounds of wheat flour, four pounds of pork meat, quart of molasses, one pound of sugar, the same of coffee and a plug of tobacco. Potatoes and vegetables came from the family garden and each family was required to cultivate a separate garden [Rawick, p. 68].

There is very little difference between what the slaves had to say about their food allowances and Phillips', Stampp's, Elkins', and Fogel and Engerman's account of the same.

Slave housing

Housing, like food, varied from plantation to plantation. Daniel Dowdyn, ex-slave, born in 1856 in Georgia, said:

> We lived in weatherboard houses. Our parents had corded-up beds with ropes and we chillun slept on the floor for the most part or in a hole bored in a log. Our houses had jest one window jest big enough to stick your head out of, and one door, and this one door faced the big house which was your master's house. This was so you couldn't git out 'less somebody seen you [Rawick, p. 71].

Slave clothing

Slave clothing was also a preference of the master. For the most part, the master bought clothing according to his economic status. However, since each plantation was controlled by a person, each plantation system was governed by the nature of that person.

Police regulations

Slaves did not know much about the external forces that governed their lives. They understood the simple plantation rules which culminated in the master who could make new rules or change the old rules to suit his immediate need. However, there was an unwritten code that demanded that each master stay within certain limits. It should be noted, however, that there was no way to force him to abide by this code. The *Slaves' Narratives* tended to show that most slaves had a deep fear of the slave patrols because the patrollers could whip them. Sallie Carder, born 1849, Tennessee stated:

> De patrollers would go about in de quarters at night to see if any of de slaves was out or slipped off. As we sleep on de dirt floor on pallets, de patrollers would walk over and on us and if we even grunt dey would whip us. De only trouble between de whites and blacks on our plantation was when de overseer tied my mother to whip her and my father untied her and de overseer shot and killed him.... Elige Davison, born a slave in Virginia—Us couldn't go nowhere without a pass. The patterrollers would git us and dey do plenty for nigger slaves. I's went to my quarters and be so tired I jest fall in de door, on de ground, and a patterroller came by and hit me several licks with a cat-o-nine-tails, to see if I's tired 'nough to not run 'way. Sometimes dem patterrollers hit us jest to hear us hollor.... Sylvester Brooks, born 1850, in Alabama—Next thing I 'member is de patterrollers, 'cause dey whip me everytime dey catches

me without my pass. Dat de way dey make us stay home at night and it made good niggers out of us 'cause we couldn't chase round and git into meanness [Rawick, p. 61].

Medical care

The procedure followed by most masters was to do only that which was necessary to keep the slaves able to work. The *Slaves' Narratives* present very much the same information that is contained in all four models. Therefore, there seems little need for an extended analysis of this element. However, for the sake of clarity, Graff Editing, a slave on Henry Toler's plantation near Lynchburg, Campbell County, Virginia, gave this account of medical procedure there:

> Befo de wah we nevah had no good times. Dey took good care of us though. As pa'taculah with slaves as with the stock — that was their money, you know. And if we claim a bein sick, they give us a dose of caster oil and tu'pentine. That was the principle medicine cullud had to take, and sometimes salt. But we nevah wisky — That was nevah allowed and if we was real sick, they had a doctor fo us [Rawick, pp. 6–100].

The above categories allowed Phillips, Stampp, and Elkins to adopt the paternal thesis — a thesis which held that the master was a parent to the slaves; that he viewed the slaves as little children who loved him and were grateful for whatever he did for them. This thesis set the pattern for all subsequent interpretations of slavery and thus undermined the authenticity of and/or usefulness of these traditional interpretations.[24]

In conclusion, the providing of food, shelter, clothing, medical care and police regulations for the slaves became the focal point in determining the moral support for the existence of slavery. Masters prided themselves in having the best kept slaves in the system. They enjoyed showing to all that would look the happy, content, and accommodating slaves. Thus, the proslavery thinker as well as the antislavery thinker was caught up in a miasma of attitudes and feelings that restricted clear thinking. Phillips and his followers saw the care provided by the masters as "fatherly love." Stampp saw this caring as a means of further exploitation. Elkins saw this caring as a force necessary for the survival of the institution, and Fogel and Engerman saw this caring as a necessity for good management practices. The significant point is that the masters had no choice but to care for their slaves if they were to reap the benefits from their labor.

A contingent aspect of the slave maintenance system was the exploitation of the female slave — exploitation in the sense that her function as a slave entailed the status of "breeder." While it seems that the general attitude of the slave holding class was anti–slave breeding, there nonetheless was an appreciable amount of slave breeding taking place during the period.

Slave breeding

While the Sambo personality and the plantation mentality exerted a sizable amount of influence on the general development of Negro personality and culture, the treatment of the female slave had a greater long range effect on the total development of the slave community. Thus, slave breeding stands out as one of the most devastating aspects of American Negro slavery. Phillips believed that there was little evidence to support the notion that slave breeding occurred on an appreciable scale.

> A planter here and there have exerted a control of mating in the interest of industrial and commercial eugenics, but it is extremely doubtful that any appreciable number of masters attempted any direct hastening of slave increase. The whole tone of the community was hostile to such a practice [Phillips, p. 362].

Stampp disagreed with Phillips and saw slave breeding as a highly profitable enterprise. He comments:

> Many masters counted the fecundity of Negro women as an economic asset and encouraged them to bear children as rapidly as possible. In the exporting states these masters knew that the resulting surpluses would be placed on the market. Though few held slaves merely to harvest the increase or overtly interfered with their normal sexual activity, it nevertheless seems proper to say that they were engaged in slave breeding [Stampp, p, 246].

Elkins agreed with Stampp; even though he did not greatly elaborate on slave breeding, he did note:

> The picturesque charge that the planters deliberately "bred" their slave women has never been substantiated, and Avery Craven's point that white women bred about as often as their black sisters is a sensible one. But with no law to prevent the separation of parents and children, and with the value of the slave being much in excess of what it cost to rear him, the temptation to think and talk about a prolific Negro woman as a "rattling 'good' breeder" was very strong [Elkins, pp. 55–56].

Fogel and Engerman believed that slave breeding was a myth. They report, "No set of instructions to overseers has been uncovered which explicitly or implicitly encouraged selective breeding or promiscuity." (Fogel and Engerman, p. 86). Thus, the primary authors used in this research were fragmented on the issue of slave breeding. In order to bring some degree of clarity to the issue, the narratives espousing the views of slaves themselves were examined. Many of the slaves interviewed believed that slave breeding was a normal part of their existence.

Elige Davison, a former slave in Virginia, reported:

> I been marry once 'fore freedom, with home weddin' massa, he bring some women to see me. He would't let me have jus' one woman. I have 'bout fifteen and I don't know how many chillen [Rawick, p. 88].

Katie Darling, born a slave in Texas in 1849, reported:

> Niggers didn't cou't then like they do now, massa pick out a po'tly man a po'tly gal and jus' put 'em together. What he want am the stock [Ibid.].

Jeptha Choice, born in 1835 in Texas, reported:

> The master was mighty careful about raisin' healthy nigger families and used us strong, healthy young bucks to stand the healthy nigger gals. When I was young they careful not to strain me and I was as handsime as a speckle pup and was in demand for breeding [Ibid.].

Participation in slave breeding was a function of slavery which some slaves believed to be a great honor.

If slave breeding did take place, as so much of the material contained in the narratives indicates, then what were the psychological effects of this breeding on the young children who grew up in a slave community? How did this adult role affect the young male? The data appear to imply that the slave children were "conditioned" to accept every aspect of slavery as right and proper for them; therefore, slave breeding was no more or no less evil than anything else. While this is the position dictated by the tone of this research, there is also information that implies that the slaves, in spite of their "conditioning," did develop a family system which allowed them to separate "the good" from "the evil" and by so doing develop a moral code which supported them after the coming of freedom (Rawick, p. 96).

Slave breeding, then, not only provided a peculiar behavior pattern for the slave to emulate, but it also showed a side of the slave holder's personality that might easily be more "beastly than that attributed to the African" (Jordan, pp. 154–163).

The Africans that were brought to this country were primarily of one complexion. However, by the time of their emancipation, the Africans had become an amalgam of many colors and blood mixtures. The implication is, since the Africans were powerless, they cannot be held responsible for this "blood mixing." Slave breeding, then, was not only profitable to the slave holders, but also an instrument in developing a class of Negroes that makes it almost impossible to identify ethnically the Negro community as a whole. The problem of miscegenation was treated by Phillips as a minor incident within the plantation system. He did not deal with the broader implication that the mulatto presence brings about. Stampp, Elkins, Fogel, and Engerman did not seem to understand this dilemma either. Maybe only those persons who look in the mirror and see an almost white image which must nevertheless be

accepted as "black" can really understand the broad implication of color. The pain of being classified as a Negro while feeling anything but
like a Negro is lost to most liberal minds; however, the mulatto existence
is real, a product of miscegenation fostered by white America. According to Joel Williamson, the mulatto has not been fully incorporated into
Negro/Caucasian history because mulattoes represent to the white mind
a physical manifestation of the sins of their forefathers.[25]

Aside from the ethnic division caused by slave breeding, slave
breeding is credited with establishing a moral laxity among the masses
of Negroes that time has not been able to erase. For example, Phillips
wrote of the "passion" of slave women. Elkins wrote of personality change
in slave women that allowed them to succumb too easily. Stampp wrote
of the naturalness of the institution that fostered a "harem" condition.
Fogel and Engerman wrote of a system of "inducements" that overpowered
the simple minds of the slave women. All four sets of postulates bring
some form of enlightenment to the slave breeding issue; however, neither
writer dared to address the possible effect that slave breeding could have
on the personality formation of Negro women in general. It seems that
it was easier for the general American public to assume that "all" Negro
women are just a "cut" above being a "whore" than to face the accusation that, "Like Negro men, Negro women are what the white man
made."[26] Slave women could not force themselves on their masters.
They did not have the time or the means to make themselves acceptable
to white men, and they dared not assume that their masters found in
them some semblance of desirability. How then did the slave women
come to have white children? They became what the white man made
of them: "A cut above being a whore."

Williamson in his *New Negro*, spoke of contractual arrangements
between the families of mulatto girls and white "gentlemen," where these
gentlemen agreed to pay a given amount of money if the family would
allow these young mulatto girls to be "kept." These arrangements usually stipulated that any children coming out of this relationship would be
taken care of by the father. It should be noted that this type of
"whore/pimp" relationship took place after the emancipation of the
Negroes. The implication is that the laxity in the moral behavior of slave
women not only allowed the female slave to have an added inducement
toward miscegenation, but it afforded the white males an opportunity
to relieve much of their inner frustration, which evolved out of their relation with the male slave (Kardiner and Ovesey, p. 45).

In conclusion, it seems that since the Africans came from a society
that had no need for slave breeding, the notion of slave breeding had
to have had its inception in the minds of the slave holders. Furthermore,
since the Atlantic slave trade had been suspended in the seventeen hundreds, the need for slaves exceeded the slave supply. The implication

generated by the fact that the South's economy remained relatively stable is that the needed slaves had to come from somewhere—and slave breeding was the answer.

The significant issue to be considered here is the psychological impact on the developing personality of the slave. For example, what are the possible side effects that a system of low moral standards could have on a new and developing culture? Kardiner and Ovesey expressed the notion that the absence of the slave father coupled with his inability to provide for and protect his family, caused the slave mother to be viewed as the central power figure within the slave family structure (pp. 44–46).

This matriarchal family then became the nexus for social cohesion in the slave community. Since the greater community, the plantation, was male-orientated, the slave family, in actuality, only served to reinforce the powerfulness of the white male. The white male, then, not only set the moral tone for the plantation but established a psychological workshop that forced the male slave to accept the sexual exploitation of his slave wife as a normal part of slave family structure. For example, the master could have sexual copulation with a slave's wife and still pronounce that wife to be highly moral and virtuous—the implication being that the male slave had no "rights to human feelings"; that as long as the female slave's sexual activity received the approval of the master, it was moral and right. The question that most slave literature overlooks is, what were the actual feelings of the male slave in matters of this kind? Were these degraded slave fathers actually able to love and respect their slave wives? Could there be any inner assurance within the male slave that the child born to his wife was actually his issue? It seems that the sexual exploitation of the female slave not only produced a false sense of worth in the female slave but it also established barriers between the male and female Negro that time has not been able to erase. Even today the Negro family is usually a mixture of colors and physical features. A Negro family's complexion can range from dark brown to almost white. The question, usually unasked, is, do these Negro fathers actually accept these mixed children as their own or do they simply show their lack of acceptance by not performing as a "rational" father should? The answers to these questions were not found in slave literature nor are they likely to be found in contemporary literature because of the ethnocentric bias of the white writer and the urge to whiteness on the part of many Negro writers. The group of Negroes most likely to be caught up in this kind of social dilemma are usually unable to overcome their deep-felt personal shame and the kaleidoscopic effects of racist oppression.

In summary, the attitudes of white America which caused slave breeding are still, in effect, producing in many contemporary blacks the belief that morality is contingent upon white approval. To these "Americans," their personal worth is determined by their proximity to white ideals. They do not seem to be able to accept morality as a "thing in itself." As a consequence, many Negroes engage in self-debasing activities believing that they have white America's approval. It would seem, however, that the majority of white America see this behavior as "the expected" and in many instances allow it to continue because they do not want to be known as "racist."

Negro personality cannot be attributed to any one influence. Slave breeding is but one of the elements; directly related to this is the Negro's relationship to power.

Power

The relationship between power and powerlessness is one of projection and acceptance. This is best exemplified in the following passage:

"When I use a word," Humpty Dumpty said in a rather scornful tone, "it means what I chose it to mean—neither more nor less."

"The question is," said Alice, "whether you can make words mean so many different things?"

"The question is," said Humpty Dumpty, "Which is to be master—that's all."[27]

This is a clear indication of who had the means for effecting change and who had to accept the change. The powerlessness of the Negro American is best demonstrated in his quest to redefine himself. In the early sixties, Stokely Carmichael coined the phrase "black power" which eventually led to the concept "black is beautiful." The question is, to whom was black beautiful? Did Negroes become beautiful in spite of their blackness, or did they become beautiful because of their blackness? Carmichael saw this "black is beautiful" concept as the ability of the Negro community to "assert their own definitions, to reclaim their history, their culture; to create their own sense of community and togetherness." (Carmichael and Hamilton, p. 37). Few, if any, blacks nowadays will disagree with these goals; however, some blacks believe that the Negro community has always sought these goals. Whether "black consciousness" or traditional "Negro pride" is viewed as the social tool for black advancement is of little consequence. The concern is that each American find his or her place in America's "Great Society."

Having power usually indicates the ability to change some external situation socially, as well as economically. Negroes have never had this type of power, and the intimation that such power is now available is to create within the Negro community a false sense of security which might cause many of the masses to cease from their struggle for equality. What the Negro masses need is the means for freeing their minds. A good example is the attitude of slaves towards slavery. It would seem that it would have been better to die than to be treated as a lower animal.

Phillips, Stampp, Elkins, Fogel and Engerman all agreed that one of the reasons that white indentured servants were not used extensively was that "white men would not be driven." This infers that slaves could be and were driven. What would have happened if the slaves had agreed not to be driven? One possible answer is that there would have had to be a new consideration for labor in colonial as well as contemporary America. The powerlessness of the slave was a necessary condition if the slave holders were to reap the profits from slave labor. The question then becomes, is there any difference in the profit motive of contemporary white America and colonial white America as far as the Negro is concerned? While there is no easy answer to this question, all four models used in this study lead to the conclusion that through the institution of racism many Negro Americans enjoy a very limited amount of power.

African history, as well as world history, shows that there always has been some type of slavery. The difference is that North American slavery is the first recorded form of slavery that reduced slaves to "chattel personal." Many historians recount a type of slavery in Africa that was little better than the American form of indentured servitude, and as a consequence, Africans could very easily identify with a master-slave relationship. However, it is simplistic to believe that the Africans were prepared for the type of slavery that they found in North America. The significance of this is that the acceptance of slave status by the African is no indication of a deprived nature. Conversely, the fact that the African survived the debilitating effects of slavery is a strong indication of a well-grounded and stable historical background.

The powerlessness of the Negro American is not due to the factors in Phillips' innate racial-inferiority theory or Stampp's harsh definition of slavery or Elkins' white-man-in-a-black-skin theory or Fogel and Engerman's attack on the traditional interpretation of slavery. The Negroes' powerlessness lies in their inability to "name their own world." Freire stated that, "Freedom is not obtained as a gift — it is gained through conquest." Without taking this to an extreme configuration, Silberman stated that, "Negroes must grapple with the universal 'who am I?'" (Silberman, p. 111). Ralph Ellison used "invisibility"; James Baldwin's metaphor was, "Nobody Knows My Name." Some Black Muslims use an "X" for a last name. The situation of powerlessness seems to have evolved into a situation of confusion. This is not to say that all is gloom and despair but simply to say that many negative elements enter the world of the average Negro American that go unnoticed by most other Americans. The Negro professors, doctors, teachers, etc., have the expertise to name their world; consequently, in many instances, these professionals feel very little of the pressures experienced by the Negro masses. Billingsly has remarked:

Most Negro families are composed of ordinary people. They do not get their names in the paper ... they do not show up on welfare roles or in crime statistics.... They are headed by men and women who work to support their families.... They are not what might be generally conceived of as "achieving families...." They are likely to be overlooked when the white community goes looking for a Negro to sit on an interracial committee.... They are likely to be overlooked by the poverty program. They are, in a word, just folks. They are the great unknown, and yet, these ordinary Negro families are often the backbone of the Negro community [Billingsly, p. 137].

The significance here is that these "average families" do very little to call attention to themselves, and as a consequence they are not usually considered, according to Billingsly, "... by white people, particularly white people who depend on books and other mass media for their knowledge of life in the most important ethnic subsociety in America." Who speaks for them? Will the powerful give up some power so that the powerless may become a little less powerless? To America's shame, these citizens are virtually out of sight, out of mind.

One question that kept arising throughout this research was, why did the slaves permit the planters to treat them in the manner in which they did? Contained within the Slaves' Narratives is overwhelming evidence that the slaves' personality was so warped that they believed that the master had the right to do according to his nature. If he was a mean man, he acted mean; if he was a good man, he acted good. The final word was always with the master. Certainly, this is not to say that slaves enjoyed harsh treatment; they hated it, but their minds were so shaped by the institution that they found it too difficult to resist. For example, a slave is born two generations into slavery; his only male models are the overseer, driver, and master; he quickly learns that everything he gets comes from one of the three; he watches as some poor "soul" who dared to think for himself is taught to leave the thinking to the "holy three"; he constantly hears and sees that he is just personal property and slowly comes to realize that if he is to survive, he can only survive as a slave. This acceptance is the will to live, even if living means to be in a constant state of dying.[28] For example, Rawick wrote about an interview with Eli Coleman, born a slave in Kentucky in 1846:

Massa whooped us slave if we got stubborn or lazy. He whooped one so hard that the slave said he'd kill him. So Massa done put a chain round his legs, so he jest hardly walk, and he has to work in the field that way. At night he put 'nother chain round his neck and fastened it to a tree. After three weeks Massa turn him loose and he the prodes' nigger in the world, and the hardes' workin' nigger Massa had after that [Rawick, p. 57].

This was just one of thousands of reports by former slaves of how the master continued the "seasoning" process. The initial seasoning process lasted for about a three-year period. This type of conditioning produced the chatter boxes, the light-hearted, and to some extent the Nat Turners and the Frederick Douglasses. Many historians see the institution of slavery's "seasoning" process producing an ethnic group of "bronze men and regal black women from whose loins sprang one out of every ten Americans."[29]

While this view may be one that most modern-day blacks can readily accept, it belies the fact that negative types were also produced. The carefree, childlike, submissive behavior that Phillips observed is but one side of Negro development, and while it is not necessarily complimentary, it did exist, and it should be accepted by all parties concerned. This does not mean that it reflects total Negro development nor does it mean that the Negro should be satisfied with or ashamed of it. The concern of all Americans should be to understand the currents of their national history and to make sure that negative influences will not continue unchallenged.

There is a peculiar relationship between blacks and whites, a relationship that defies a rational explanation; one so peculiar that former slaves themselves could not explain it. For example, Frederick Douglass, after his escape to freedom, found himself lonely for his plantation life, about which he wrote:

> I have been frequently asked, when a slave, if I had a kind master, and do not remember ever to have given a negative answer; nor did I, in pursuing this course, consider myself as uttering what was absolutely false; for I always measured the kindness of my master by the standards of kindness set up among slave holders around us. Moreover, slaves are like other people, and imbibe prejudices quite common to others. They think their own better than that of others. Many, under the influence of this prejudice, think their own masters are better than the masters of other slaves; and this, too in some cases, when the reverse was true. Indeed, it is not uncommon for slaves to even fall out and quarrel among themselves about the relative goodness of their masters.... They seem to think that the greatness of their masters was transferable to them.[30]

This would indicate that in spite of the harsh treatment received by slaves, they still found some source of their identity within their masters. Pauli Murry tells of her great-great-grandmother who was sold to a white doctor as a companion for his young daughter who was about the same age as Harriet, the great-great-grandmother. She wrote:

> These two women, the slave and the mistress, grew into the most intricate of relationships filled with all of the human drama of love, anxiety, and hate imaginable.[31]

Peter L. Berger saw this problem as being common to human beings. He understood humans as having a deep-rooted need to see in their children a form of immortality (Berger, p. 62). Elkins saw this problem as being a situation of institutions or the lack of institutions. Stampp saw this problem similarly to both Berger and Elkins; he believed that "above all, slavery was a labor system" (Stampp, p. 34). Typically, Phillips saw the identity problem as one in which the slave was cheerful and happy and the institution as being a "school" guiding and correcting its simple children (Phillips, p. 343).

The identity situation which confronted Negro slaves was one in which they were forced to think, act, and believe as slaves; and in spite of their situation, they were socially judged by a system in which they were not allowed any positive input. Erik Erikson quotes from a work by William James:

> A man's character is discernible in the mental or moral attitude in which, when it came upon him, he felt himself most deeply and intensely active and alive. At such moments there is a voice inside which speaks and says: This is the real me![32]

This statement was taken from a letter of a free white man to his white wife. Therefore, he could allude to an awakening of the inner self; to the choices which belong always to the dominant class. Slaves had no such choice because their survival depended on their being only that which their master desired. The "real me" had to be buried under fear and accommodation if the "present me" was to make any claim on life in the now. Identity for the slave began with trying to make some order out of disorder; the ability to suppress any such inner voice and avoid as much as possible the dreaded effects of "seasoning."

Elkins believed that the system of slavery allowed very little room for the slave to maneuver, and as a consequence, he was under the complete control of the "holy three." The majority of the *Slaves' Narratives* support Elkins, and as debasing as it may seem, the mind of the African was, with few exceptions, completely "brain-washed." This brainwashing, or mind control, had such a damning effect that when certain slaves were taken by their masters into free territory and given a vacation, they would, of their own volition, return to their maters at the appointed time. The institution of slavery not only limited the space of slaves, but by destroying their traditions, reduced or disallowed their own value system to have any relevance to their daily activities.

Stampp and Elkins believed that the slaves' personality under went a drastic change; however, neither developed their premise to its fullest potential. For example, even Phillips conceded that the "Negro is what the white man had him to be." Stampp and Elkins dismissed Phillips as being a racist without attempting to analyze his position. Rawick, on the other hand, seemed to believe that new cultures are tediously formed:

> Culture and personality are not like old clothes that can be taken off and thrown away. The ability of anyone to learn even the simplest thing is dependent upon utilizing the existing cultural apparatus. "New" cultures

emerge out of old cultures gradually and never lose all the traces of the old and past [Rawick, p. 6].

According to this premise, Africans, unlike emigrants, were not able to bring anything with them. They were totally cut off from everything that was familiar. Rawick wrote:

> ... as slaves, not only were they prevented from bringing material objects with them, but they also could not even bring over their older social relations or institutions [pp. 6-7].

The Negro, then, if viewed according to Rawick's premise, is in the process of developing a "new" culture. However, the task of authenticating this "new culture" will prove to be a difficult one because as Rawick states:

> The discussion of the sociology of slavery in the United States has been too often based on unexamined and unverified assumptions. These assumptions have been usually ones that fit in with the ways whereby middle class white intellectuals often handle their guilt-feelings about treatment of blacks in the United States [p. 91].

Stampp and Elkins, who saw themselves as liberal white Americans, fell prey to their own ethnocentric values as suggested by Rawick in the above quotation. Erikson believed that traditional institutions and supportive roles provide the proper atmosphere for identity building. He wrote:

> For a mature psychosocial identity presupposes a community of people whose traditional values become significant to the growing person even as his growth and his gifts assume relevance for them. "Roles" which can be "played" interchangeably are not sufficient; only an integration of roles which foster individual vitality within a vital trend in the existing or developing social order can support identities [Erikson, p. 231].

Elkins and Stampp believed that the basic personality of the slave was changed. However, based on Erikson's understanding of identity, his thesis of "specieshood" could probably be a better model for Negro identity (pp. 232-236).

Stampp believed that slaves hated slavery with a passion so intense that they sought every opportunity to register their hatred. This may have been the case; however, even Stampp admitted that slavery was so cruel that eventually the slaves had to succumb to the conditioning effects of the institution. This implies that at some point in the transition from a free African to a docile slave, the African accepted the mentality of a slave, and, contrary to what most liberal Americans wish to believe, the African, for all intents and purposes, ceased to exist (see Kardiner and Ovesey, pp. 39-41; Grier and Cobb, p. 25).

The developing Negro culture underwent many adaptative features, such as loss of self-esteem. The slaves, not being able to do any of the things that they observed free people doing, had no choice but to look upon themselves as "less than" all other people. They found some measure of relief by adopting the views and attitudes of their masters. The most damaging result from this attitude was that in accepting the status system of the master they thereby exalted the status of house servants over that of field hands; they exalted a lighter skin over that of a darker skin; and finally they accepted the female slave as an object to be exploited. The loss of cultural forms and the forced adoption of new cultural traits (see Kardiner and Ovesey, pp. 39–41) forced the slave to become just "so much clay" in the pottering hands of whites. The destruction of the family unit (see Stampp, pp. 340–349) brought about such a psychological trauma that family roles were reversed. The female became more pronounced, having all of what little authority was allotted to the family. This situation also created a double role for the female slave. She became a sex object for the white male and a "mammy" for white children. Kardiner and Ovesey believed that "these two features could only have the effect of increasing the white man's fear of the Negro male." Since the Negro male was the legitimate possessor of the Negro female, the white man's fear eventually "led to fantastic exaggerations in the white man's mind of the Negro male's sexual prowess" (Kardiner and Ovesey, p. 45). The love/hate complex caused the slaves to identify with the power display of their master while hating the white man for his inhumane use of power over them. Negro development became an amalgam of interest and feelings which, according to Brody, developed a different kind of schizophrenic behavior in the Negro male (Brody, pp. 337–345).

Finally, the Negro identity, subjectively and objectively, is directly related to the mode of power distribution in the greater society. That is to say that the amount of power that Negroes are able to use in determining their self-worth is directly proportional to the amount of positiveness their identity encompasses. Studies on majority/minority relationships indicate that minorities, especially Negroes, are restricted by the lack of power available to them and the immoral use of power by the dominant group. The implication is that because the black presence in America had its beginning in an immoral situation generated by white America, white America finds it difficult to allow blacks any identity other than that which "false generosity" generates. Thus, white America, rather than admit its responsibility in the shaping of Negro identity, prefers to highlight the negative aspects of that identity. This accomplishes two purposes: first, it confuses the issue by conditioning blacks to desire whiteness; and second, it blinds white liberals to the presence of racist ideology.

The dominant group in any society can afford to be lax in many areas of social concerns because they have the power to interpret their own actions. Minorities, on the other hand, do not have such power; and as a consequence, they must always be overly concerned about every social activity. Because the minority cannot effect change (at least they are led to believe that they cannot), they must constantly prove that all the stereotypes directed at them are false. Consequently, according to Kardiner and Ovesey, the masses of Negroes cease to struggle against seemingly impossible odds and settle down to "accepting their place." They conclude by stating that racism and prejudice become an acceptable social form for the Negro and an unconscious reaction on the part of white America.

Phillips, Stampp, Elkins, and Fogel and Engerman were all influenced by a kind of ethnocentrism that would not allow their premises to be as pure as the data demanded. This type of ethnocentrism is defined by most scholars as racism. According to William Norris, racism is "the notion that one's own ethnic stock is superior."[33]

Racism and Negro culture

Stampp believed that there were three myths that kept the Negro in bondage for some three hundred years. He listed them in this manner:

> ... the first myth that an "all-wise Creator" had designed the Negro for labor in the South, and the second myth that by intellect and temperament he was the natural slave of the white man ... the third, that Africans were barbarians who therefore needed to be subjected to rigid discipline and severe controls. Their enslavement was essential for their own good and for the preservation of white civilization [Stampp, pp. 10–11].

While Stampp disagreed with these myths, Phillips, on the other hand, accepted them as concrete evidence for the enslavement of the Negro (Phillips, pp. 341–342). Phillips' ideology subsequently became the primary method for interpreting Negro culture in the United States for 1918 to the late 1950's.

Elkins saw this racism as the "inability of the South to see the Negro as an adult"; this, in turn, allowed him to perceive slavery as a product of the South with the North being the primary antagonist against slavery. Fogel and Engerman saw racism as the primary force that permitted slavery to exist. They even contended that racism profoundly influences contemporary white America's attitudes towards contemporary Negro America (Fogel and Engerman, p. 263).

The question then becomes, what of racism? Was it then and is it now a primary cause for poor black/white relations? In answer to these questions—as racism is defined in this research—Negro and white relations have always been of such a character that the Negro was subordinated to whites. This relation created then as well as now a hostile and volatile climate. Genovese wrote:

> Slavery rested on the principle of property in man—one of man's appropriation of another's person as well as the fruits of his labor. By

> definition and in essence it was a system of class rule, in which some peo-
> ple lived off the labor of others. American slavery subordinated one race
> to another and thereby rendered its fundamental class relationships more
> complex and ambiguous.... The racism that developed from racial subor-
> dination influenced every aspect of American life and remains powerful
> [Genovese, p. 3].

Thus, to conclude that racism was and is a primary reason for poor relations between blacks and whites seems appropriate. Research further suggests that the system of labor favored by the plantation owners was not
destroyed with the signing of the Emancipation Proclamation; instead,
it shifted to the free labor market, allowing racism to replace the chains
of slavery.

Racism then became the logic used to justify the powerful's right
to exploit the weak. It allowed a system of justice to be developed wherein
skin color and/or ethnic origin established a weighted counterbalance
on the scales of justice. Greed and self-centeredness became the motive
for prosperity and advancement.

While the writers used in this research dealt with many issues arising out of racism and racial prejudice, they did not adequately address
the nature of prejudice. For the purpose of this research, racism and prejudice are interchangeable; errors of prejudgment are different from prejudice in that errors of prejudgment are those which when confronted
with new data change or cease to exist. Prejudgments become prejudice
only if they are not reversible when exposed to new knowledge. This
delineation is necessary because research indicates that there are many
instances in which the position of the writer under consideration was one
of prejudgment and not prejudice, thereby falsely raising a charge of
racism when racism was not the case. For example, the view of the plantation system, whether that of Phillips, Stampp, Elkins, or Fogel and
Engerman, was always portrayed as a racist institution unable and unwilling to change. This hard-nosed position by both pro- and antislavery
thinkers lumped all slave holders together as evil persons who could not
be converted. The facts, however, show that many slave holders once
shown their error of prejudgment were willing to consider means of
dismantling the institution of slavery. (See Elkins, pp. 206–222.) This
is not to provide an apology for the institution of slavery but rather to
expose a side of slavery that has received little attention. While it is true
that those slave holders who showed a willingness for conversion soon
lapsed back into a proslavery position, the idea that they were willing
to consider a rational solution to slavery indicates that all attitudes that
are contrarily identified as prejudice are not necessarily so.

Admittedly, the models contained in this study have portrayed many
negative aspects of early Negro American development. This is due
primarily to the nature of the subject, slavery. The institution of North

American slavery was a debilitating experience for the Negro slave. However, his plight was not ignored by the free Negro community because as early as 1700 many Negro groups were addressing their energy towards freeing the slave community. For example, in 1787 a Negro society was founded in Philadelphia; in 1787 Negroes asked for equal education in Boston; in 1788 Prince Hall presented to the Massachusetts legislature a protest against kidnapping and the slave trade; in 1791 the free Negroes of Charleston, South Carolina, presented to the legislature of that state a protest against Jim Crow laws; in 1793–94 free Negroes in South Carolina protested the unfairness of the poll tax.[34] These few incidents are included to show that even though slavery was well grounded throughout America, Negroes were not as happy with the institution as Phillips' model would lead one to believe.

Granting that racial prejudice was a strong support mechanism for the institution of slavery, it is well to be careful not to over-categorize, especially when dealing with highly sensitive issues. Allport believed that "over-categorization" allows a minimum of facts to become the total conception of the whole. For example, a few opportunistic slaves may well have conformed to the roles assigned them by their masters, thereby allowing all slaves to be categorized as accommodating. Misconception then is blown out of proportion to the point that prejudgments set into motion belief structures that destroy any hope for rational thinking and self-reevaluation. A possible result from this kind of logic is that a Christian nation did not see the necessity to eliminate the institution of slavery until machines were developed to replace the Negro slave.

Finally, racism not only affects a minority in every aspect of cultural development, it affects every child born into the dominant society. This aspect of racism's influence is best reflected by a statement by Lillian Smith who wrote:

> I do not remember how or when, but by the time I had learned that God is love, that Jesus is His Son and came to give us more abundant life, that all men are brothers with a common father, I also knew that I was better than a Negro, that all black folks have their place and must be kept in it, that sex has its place and must be kept in it, that a terrifying disaster would befall the South if I ever treated a Negro as my social equal.[35]

Racism assigns a place for everyone in a given society. It allows entities such as skin color to become a rubric for categorizing. Robert Coles has stated, "Every Negro child I know has had to take notice in some way what skin color signifies in our society."[36] Billingsly emphasizes, "To deny the history of a people is to deny their humanity.... If, on the other hand, the Negro people constitute in some important respect an ethnic subsociety with a distinct history, what are the essential elements of this history?" (Billingsly, p. 37). Racism then is anti–American.

Chapter VII
The Four Models and the Contemporary Negro

This study has shown that each model, Progressive, Racial Enlightenment, Counter-Progressive, and Cliometric Revolutional, may be seen as representing a distinct historical age in the development of Negro American culture. The Progressive Model is representative of the *Genesis Age*, the beginning of a culture; the Racial Enlightenment Model is representative of the *Nomadic Age*, which traces the movement of the African from a free state to a slave state; the Counter-Progressive Model depicts the Negro American slave as a docile "Sambo" type whose personality has been so warped that slave identity has become his only identity and thus frustration and accommodation becomes the major psychological release available to them. The *Puberty Age*, as reflected in the Cliometric Revolutional Model, measures the slave as entering the early stages of maturation. They are productive, socially oriented and moving into this new culture with some degree of sophistication and dignity.

The African became the focal point for a debate that lasted some two or three hundred years, finally ending in a bloody Civil War. It seems that in spite of that great debate, the Civil War, congressional action, demonstrations in the streets, and the Civil Rights Movement, the African presence is still a troublesome one and still remains a central issue in the Americanization of Negro Americans. Elkins cites President Johnson's address at Howard University in June, 1965 as "the first time any President had suggested that a minority group needed anything more than equal opportunity in order to take its rightful place in society at large." He quoted the President as saying that:

> ... among the experiences of all other American social and ethnic minorities, that of the Negro had been unique. Merely to end discrimination was not enough because much of the Negro community is buried under a blanket of history and circumstances and to repair the profound damage done by ancient brutality, past injustice, and present prejudice require positive action [Elkins, p. 245].

Thus, Elkins believed that "Lyndon Johnson knowingly or not entered an historical debate that has gone on since the beginning of the present century. What precisely were the sins of our fathers?" In answer to this question, Elkins wrote:

> If I were to identify the worst of our father's sins in the matter of slavery, it would not be cruelty or exploitation of even prejudice. It would be rigidity of mind, lack of inventiveness, and an almost incredible absence of social imagination.... From the earliest colonial times, a man was either Negro or white.... The single category "mulatto" served for everything in between, but it carried no special legal or social distinction [Elkins, p. 246].[1]

Therefore, it seems that the need for a president to enjoin the American people to engage in "positive action" in order that any group of Americans may be able to take their "rightful place in society at large" is a powerful indication of the social disparity in American society. Elkins believed that this disparity had its beginning in the extreme rigidity of the English colonial mind on all matters concerning slavery. Accordingly, he wrote:

> The starkness of contrast between black and white seemed to require a distinction equally stark between slave and free. For example, neither the English colonist nor their American descendants two hundred years later were ever really able to conceive a workable status for the free Negro [Elkins, p. 248].

This statement by Elkins suggests that the social conditions which permitted slavery still exert a sizable amount of influence on white America's attitude toward present-day black society. Louis Hartz saw the Negro situation in a similar manner. He wrote:

> In a bourgeois community where the Negro is either an item of property or an equal human being, a free Negro under conditions of slavery is an enormous paradox. How can an object of property be free? Or if it can be free, it must be human and hence all Negroes must be free.[2]

Therefore, only an understanding of North American slavery can be the means whereby the image of the contemporary black American may be better understood.

The Image of the Contemporary Black

Each of the models under consideration here has posited the Negro American slave in a particular configuration. Phillips' model set the level of historiography for identifying the slave by presenting the notion that the Negro slave was what the white man had made: a docile, childlike, inferior, plantation-type of individual who enjoyed his slave status. Stampp's model viewed the same source material used by Phillips and came to the conclusion that the racial inferiority of the African slave was due to the inhumanity of the institution of slavery. While this model outwardly registered disagreement with its forerunner, internally its postulates reflected the basic ideological structure of its forerunner. Elkins' model sought to annul both the progressive and the racial enlightenment models by showing that the institution of North American slavery was so debilitating that a drastic personality change took place in its victims that was represented in a basic "Sambo" type. Fogel and Engerman's model sought to display the Negro slave as a skilled, productive workman. While neither of these models clearly depicts the Negro American slave as a new people, they all suggest that the African became something that he was not. The question then becomes, who or what did the African become? To answer this question, one must find answers to several other questions.

Do black Americans have a culture that is uniquely their own?

Contemporary blacks are not Africans nor of any other ethnicity except American. Africans were stripped of their original culture and not allowed the opportunity to fully assimilate white American culture. According to Kardiner and Ovesey, the loss of culture signifies that all social support structures no longer have any significant relevance and that some new form of social support must replace the lost form (Kardiner and Ovesey, pp. 38–41). If the Africans were no longer Africans, who or what were they? Slave literature answers by declaring that a slave is a slave. Contemporary historians, on the other hand, declare that this definition is insufficient. Accordingly, historians such as Davis, Stampp, Elkins, Fogel, Engerman, Franklin, Frazier, Jordan, Olmsted, etc., have spent many long hours in delineating slavery and slave status. Most historians overwhelmingly agree that for all intents and purposes a slave, as defined in the institution of North American slavery, was a property, a thing to be owned, a person void of personhood as a slave, a chattel personal, and above all else, a product of that institution. Thus, the African slave began his stay in America as a mere utility, extending to his descendants the same negative identification. While most contemporary Americans will agree that identifying blacks with the status assigned to the slave smacks of racism, all Americans should be willing to acknowledge that a percentage of Americans still engage in activities that support this racist view. Billingsly remarks,

> The Negro people must be viewed, not as carbon copies of white people, but as a people with a distinctive history, a distinctive place in American society, a distinctive set of life changes, and a distinctive set of contributions to make to the wider society. The Negro people cannot be expected to melt or blend into the white society, except psychologically, and at great personal expense to the few individuals who manage to do so, and at some loss to the general welfare of the Negro people and the society [Billingsly, pp. 149–50].

Thus, it would seem that in America's attempt to mainstream the Negro American, many Americans feel that Negro history and Negro identity must melt or blend into white society. What is significantly overlooked is that in such a process, not only does the Negro lose, but all America loses; and in the end un–American groups such as the Ku Klux Klan are able to take advantage of civil insecurity and increase their hold on the minds of many white Americans.

The first step in determining an identification for those Africans who were brought to North America was established when they became slaves. Historically speaking, those first Africans who were brought to North America were Afro-American slaves because they embraced two cultures. This is to say that for at least two or three generations these Africans were able to maintain some recognizable link to their African past. However, after two or three generations, these Africans no longer had enough of their original traditions left to transfer to the next generation of slaves. As a consequence, somewhere within the fourth or fifth, or perhaps even the sixth, generation of colonial American slavery, the slaves reached a point where they had neither cultural system in sufficient amounts to be identifiable. They were neither completely African or completely American.[3] They became a mixture of the influences of many cultures, being identified formally as Negro Americans.

The North American slave community began, with the help of the institution of slavery, to formulate a social system that would allow them to survive. They built a system of family and marriage, religion, language, folklore, music, custom, dress, foods, and feelings. Basically, they became an identifiable people with a history.

Phillips, a proslavery enthusiast, stated that, "A Negro was what the white man made him," and again, "Ceasing to be Foulah, Cormantee, Ebo or Anglola, he became instead the American Negro," and still again, "... Negroes, though with many variants, became largely standardized into the predominant plantation type" (*American Negro Slavery*). While many historians dismissed Phillips' ideology as racist, most historians, when examining Negro slavery, consider his work historical and significant.

The probability that within the Negro slave community existed at least two types of personality development is suggested in much of the slave literature. For example, that gifted white author William Styron, in *The Confessions of Nat Turner*, has Turner, in describing Hark, one of his co-conspirators, state*:

These are not a black man's exact words of course; they are quoted because they tend to bridge the gap between the lack of sound Negro historiography and so-called Negro history.

> I realized that it wasn't the man himself who angered me so much as
> it was Hark's manner in his presence — the unspeakable bootlicking Sam-
> bo, all giggles and smirks and oily, sniveling servility [p. 65].[4]

...

> Can't you see the difference betwixt plain politeness and bootlicking
> ... you just got to learn man. You got to learn the difference. I don't
> mean you got to risk a beatin'.... I don't mean you got to be uppity and
> smart ... but they is some kind of limit. And you ain't a man when you
> act like that. You ain't a man, you is a fool [p. 66].

Thus, it would seem that even Nat Turner, the rebel, knew and
understood the "two faces of the slave": the smiling, docile Sambo and
the firm proud unwilling servant. Nat further stated:

> Though it is a painful fact that most Negroes are hopelessly docile, many
> of them are filled with fury, and the unctuous coating of flattery which
> surrounds and encases that fury is but a form of self-preservation [p. 67].

The significance here is that while many of Stampp's critics challenged
him on this assumption, Styron's Nat Turner, slave and revolutionist,
agrees with him. A word of caution should be noted here; while these
two sides of the slave's personality are shown, there is conflicting evidence
for and against protecting this slave behavior as only role play. Turner
admitted that some opportunistic slaves actually became the docile Sam-
bos they portrayed. The personality of the slave, like the transferal of
Africanisms to contemporary black Americans, is an area of research that
is in much need of scholarly investigation.

Granting that Nat Turner (considering him here only as William
Styron limns him) was not the typical slave in that he was highly learned,
possessing a fair degree of white culture. He was, however, a slave seeing
the slave community as only a slave could. Styron has him suggest that
the ability of the slave to perform as a slave might rest in how white people perceived slaves:

> White people really see nothing of a Negro in his private activity, while
> a Negro, who must walk miles out of his path to avoid seeing everything
> white people do, has often to suffer for even the most guileless part of
> his ubiquitous presence by being called a spy and a snooping black scoun-
> drel [p. 71].

Since the slave was seen as property, a thing, white people did not take
care to hide their "secret" personal activity from the slave, and as in the
case of Hark, who saw his young master engaged in a "strange" sexual
act with another white boy, the young master sought every means to make
Hark "pay." Even when the Negro has done no wrong he can be held
responsible for the shame and guilt found in the white mind.

For many years many Negroes were ashamed of slavery. They would
cringe at the very word, slave; and in most instances, they would go to
great lengths to avoid any mention of the word in an integrated

situation (Silberman, pp. 109–122). When caught in an unavoidable situation, the usual defense was to either look straight ahead as if in a trance
or to pretend that the conversation was not heard. The shame felt by
these Negroes was, for the most part, unknown to their white constituents. Therefore, the unwillingness of whites to perceive the Negro in
his private ability allows these whites to see all Negroes as the same. The
issue that springs from this type of social situation is one of self-definition.
While Negroes struggle to positively identify themselves, liberal whites
are caught between the many and varied forms of identification to which
the different Negro groups ascribe. Silberman commented:

> The debate over the group name has been bound up with the fun-
> damental questions not only of identity but of role, of the relations be-
> tween blacks and whites, of the relations of people of varying shades of
> darkness within the black community itself: the ways in which black
> Americans have related (or have tried to relate) to their African origins
> and to contemporary Africa; and most important of all, the debate has
> been bound up with the ways in which black Americans have tried to
> find a place in the white society which has so consistently and completely
> excluded them [Silberman, p. 112].

Silberman went on to say, "The symbolism which elevates white and
debases black inevitably affects the consciousness of every person." Thus,
the present struggle of Negro America to identify itself has a long history
which involves all America.

Many contemporary Negroes believe that they should be identified
as Afro-Americans or black Americans.[5] The unanswered question is,
what has happened socially between 1940, when to be referred to as black
was negative, and 1985 (or even 1965), when to be called black is viewed
as positive? Marden and Meyer believed that a group's norms, traditions,
etc., are arrived at historically and unless a group has historical continuity, these elements become meaningless debris.[6] It seems sad that today
when so many non–African Americans are willing to help Negro
Americans identify themselves, blacks themselves are divided on the identity question.

In spite of the lack of social cohesion within the Negro group, their
system of religion, family structure, folklore, music, dress, food, art, and
so on are uniquely negroid. Granting that there may be some Africanisms
found within this system, the data contained in this study do not substantiate any claim that this cultural system should be identified as solely
African. Also, some historians believe that there are enough Africanisms present within these cultural traits to identify them as African.
There is also a preponderance of evidence that supports the opposite point
of view.[7] Furthermore, many historians believe that the African influence has permeated most ethnic groups; however, this is not to say
that these African influences are identified as such but to state that the

African influence has been enmeshed with general world culture. Since none of the world cultures are identified as African even though Africanisms are present within their cultures, then why should the Negro American's culture be treated differently? While there is no absolute way to establish the authenticity of the Negro's culture, this study supports the notion that the Negro has a culture that is uniquely his own.

Are Negro Americans, or blacks, a new people?
This question deals with a consideration of concepts. If one belongs to the dominant group, then the idea of a new people could prove to be threatening because the "sins of the father" may be visited on the children. If, on the other hand, one belongs to a minority group, the idea of a new people may generate hope for better things to come. In either case, Negro Americans, by way of their entry into America, represent an ambiguous outcome of the Americanization process.

The Africans who were brought to North America as slaves were of one basic complexion and physical stature. They were, for the most part, identified as having a dark complexion, wooly hair, brown eyes and unaccustomed to western dress codes. They were non–Christians and considered to be savage in nature. As a result of their enslavement, they became a mixture of complexions and eye colors. They became Christians, of a sort, and they "lost" their so-called "savage nature." Therefore, by way of their physical change and social consternation, they became a new ethnic group—new in the sense that they had become what the white man had made. All four models contained in this study allude to this "new people" concept by either pointing to the developing of a new culture or by pointing to a major personality change.

Phillips believed that the African became a standardized plantation type. Stampp believed that they became a new people in the sense that the institution of slavery stripped away their Africanisms leaving a "white man in a black skin." Elkins believed that their personality was so changed that a basic "Sambo" type emerged, and Fogel and Engerman believed that they became a new people in that they became a productive labor force whose labor was synonymous to their being. All four models (Phillips' in a limited sense) acknowledged the creation of a mulatto class as evidence and support of the new people concept. From the data in this study it can further be inferred that in order for an ethnic group to create a new cultural system, they must become something different from what they had been. Therefore, black Americans are a new people in the sense that their cultural beginnings were primarily developed in America. That is to say, from those Americans born into slavery, after the fifth or sixth generation, came the first American citizens whose beginnings were grounded in America. Joel Williamson has written:

Negroes in the 1920's were indeed a new people. First they were a new

people physically.... Second and much more important, Negroes were
a new people culturally.... Along with cultural awareness inevitably came
self-awareness.... The Negro elite encapsulated the mood in the phrase
"the new Negro." The phrase carried the idea that the Negro was neither
African nor European, but both—and something more.[8]

The idea of newness is also expressed by Fogel and Engerman who
commented:

> U.S. slaves were not only in closer contact with European culture, they
> were also more removed from their African origins than were slaves in
> the Caribbean ... by 1860 all but one percent of U.S. slaves were native
> born, and most of them were second, third, fourth, or fifth generation
> Americans. These Americans not only had no personal experience with
> Africa but were generally cut off from contact with persons who had such
> direct experience [Fogel and Engerman, pp. 23–24].

This statement by Fogel and Engerman suggests that fifth generation
slaves were more American than their masters. This is made further evident by Fogel and Engerman when they state that by 1860 "a larger portion of blacks were American-born [than whites]." It is true that many
white organizations claim that their foreparents were the first citizens
of this country. They use as proof records of deeds, birth certificates, marriage licenses, church records, and other documents. The fact of the matter
is that in using these types of proofs, they prove that all of them can
trace their ancestry back to some formal cultural system and they can
be identified with a particular family group. This proves that they are,
even though American, a combination of different identifiable ethnic
groups. Therefore, they cannot in an historical sense be identified as solely
American. Black people, on the other hand, cannot, in most instances,
trace their ancestry back to their last slave residence; much less, back to
their African heritage. Novak wrote that in order for a group to have
historical continuity, it must be able to trace its ancestry back at least
three generations. Should most Negro Americans older than about 60
attempt to do this, they might find that three generations back from
themselves is the generation born into slavery ancestry. Furthermore, if
this three-generation model could be considered sound, what proof could
be found that a particular great-great-grandparent would have a particular
surname? History shows that most slaves were given the name of their
master and, in many instances, the male slave was known by his wife's
name. Furthermore, in a slave's lifetime his name could be changed five
or six times, depending on how often he was sold or traded or title to
him changed hands.

The selecting of the weak and powerless Africans for enslavement
in North America not only ensured a high rate of success for the institution of slavery but signaled the beginning of a negative experience for
all Negroes. They were denied any opportunity to have within their

numbers persons with the potential for rebellion. The slavers destroyed any social cohesion among the slaves by creating a confused social condition; that is, they would not let members of the same tribe be together and they restricted any form of communication between slaves. The slaves were disoriented and off-balance until death or emancipation.

While it is true that Negro culture was spawned in a negative and murky experience, the culture itself is not so. The only negative attributes of Negro culture are found in the minds of those outside the culture itself. For example, the slave holders saw Negro religion as a weaker form of their own. The historians saw Negro religion as a spy system or as a simplistic approach to mainline religion. However, the slave's religion was neither African nor Christian; it was a combination of both. The similarities to any established religion is an accident of formulation. The significant point here is that the masses of slaves (field hands) were never taught a pure form of Christianity because of its revolutionary features. The house servants were not taught a pure form of religion because it would have limited the white man's use of the female slave. The free Negroes did not adhere to a pure form of Christianity because it would have forced them to become concerned with the slave's plight.

According to Raboteau, religion, as the masses of Negroes know it, is first a catharsis relieving the tensions of the effects of their accumulated racial experience, and second a social instrument propagating ignorance for the purpose of keeping gifted religious leaders in an exalted position. Negro religion, while being a dynamic force within the structure of Negro culture, is not a negative element because it was and is a means for black survival.[9] It must be remembered that any Negro American religion is relatively few generations old and cannot be expected to function as smoothly as many other world religions having a history of some five or six hundred years, or far longer. However, it seems that responsible black leadership should be engaged in every effort that would help all people better understand its scope and purpose.

What might be called the "black experience," then, is to Negro culture as colonization was to white American culture, and while both white culture and Negro culture are separate historical entities, they did share the same historical ages. White culture shared the black experience of Negroes, and Negroes shared the colonization of white culture. Both cultures (and others) underwent and are still undergoing the black experience.

Ethnic identity, as a social issue, within the Negro community is one of passion and controversy primarily because each identifiable group within the community seems to believe that they have the "gnostic" truth when it comes to identifying the group as a whole. Nevertheless, the black consciousness ideology, even though highly controversial, has permeated American society, black, as well as white. It seems that while

each of the major groups—Negroes, blacks, Afro-Americans—claim to
be the voice for the masses of Negroes, they are all seeking basically the
same goals—a unified black community. The unanswered question is,
what effect is this struggle for identity having on the contemporary black
child?[10]

*How significant, to all America, is the proposition that black history be
assigned a positive position within American history?*
    Jordan wrote concerning the purpose of history:
        A comprehension of the past seems to have two opposite advantages
        in the present: it makes us aware of how different people have been in
        other ages and accordingly enlarges our awareness of the possibilities of
        human experience, and at the same time it impresses upon us those
        tendencies in human beings which have not changed and which accord-
        ingly are unlikely to at least in the immediate future [Jordan, p. ix].
Thus, it would seem that if history serves its purpose, it will present the
facts in as unbiased a manner as possible and afford each of its elements
as much authenticity as they merit. Negro history is no exception.
    It seems that white America was and is ashamed of the way that
Africans were inducted into America, and as a consequence they had to
find a way to justify the African presence. Consequently, by denying the
historicity of the African presence, white America was and is able to view
the African presence as something peripheral to American history. This
in turn allows white America to transfer to black America its own sense
of guilt. Jordan wrote, "White men projected their own conflicts onto
Negroes in ways which are well known though not well acknowledged
today" (Jordan, p. x).

Conclusions

    "To deny the history of a people is to deny their humanity," said
Billingsly. This study presents many elements that suggest that white
America has from the beginning applied racist measures, not only to deny
the Negro his history, but to formulate a depiction of that history that
would cause the Negro to be ashamed of it. Silberman has written:
        Understandably enough, Negroes have been unable to recall their ex-
        perience of slavery in the same light [as the Jew]. After all, the Jews, under
        Moses' leadership, freed themselves, and they went from Mount Sinai;
        slavery was followed almost immediately by a moment of spiritual glory.
        The Negroes, on the other hand, did not free themselves; they were freed
        by others, as a by-product of a political dispute between two groups of
        whites. Negroes were not even permitted to fight on the Union side until
        fairly late in the Civil War. And Emancipation was not followed by Ex-
        odus [Silberman, p. 78].

Chapter Notes

Chapter I. Introduction

1 John Hope Franklin, *From Slavery to Freedom* (New York: Knopf, 1974).
2 Robert Bone, *The Negro Novel in America* (New Haven: Yale University Press, 1958), p.3.
3 Michael Novak, *The Rise of the Unmeltable Ethnics* (New York: Macmillan, 1972), p.16.
4 David B. Davis, "Slavery and the Post-World War Historians," *Daedalus* (Spring 1974).
5 Martin L. King, Jr., *Where Do We Go from Here?* (Boston: Beacon Press, 1968), p.36.
6 Robert Coles, "It's the Same, But It's Different," eds., Talcott Parsons and Kenneth B. Clark's *The Negro American* (Boston: Houghton Mifflin, 1966), p.256.
7 Harry A. Ploski and Rosco Brown, *The Negro Almanac* (New York: Bellwether Co., 1967), pp.23–24).
8 Gunnar Myrdal, *An American Dilemma: The Negro Problem and Modern Democracy* (New York: Harper and Bros., 1944), p.xlix.
9 Parsons and Clark, p.vi.
10 Andrew M. Greeley, *Why Can't They Be More Like Us?* (New York: E.P. Dutton, 1971), cover page.
11 Abram Kardiner and Lionel Ovesey, *The Mark of Oppression: Exploration in the Personality of the Negro American* (Cleveland: World, 1962), p.41.
12 Martin Deutsch, *The Disadvantaged Child* (New York: Basic Books, 1967), p.51.
13 Stanley M. Elkins, *Slavery* (Chicago: University of Chicago Press, 1959), pp.10–11.
14 Ulrich B. Phillips, *American Negro Slavery: A Survey of the Supply, Employment and Control of Negro Labor as Determined by the Plantation Regime* (New York: D. Appleton, 1918), p.343.
15 Kenneth Stampp, *The Peculiar Institution: Slavery in the Ante-Bellum South* (New York: Alfred A. Knopf, 1956), p.vii.
16 Robert W. Fogel and Stanley L. Engerman, *Time on the Cross: The Economics of American Negro Slavery* (Boston: Little, Brown, 1974).
17 Charles E. Silberman, *Crisis in Black and White* (New York: Vantage Books, 1964), p.4.
18 William M. Pinson and Claude E. Fant, *Contemporary Christian Trends* (Waco, Texas: World Books, 1972), pp.66–67.

19 Winthrop D. Jordan, *White Over Black: American Attitudes Towards the Negro 1550–1812* (Chapel Hill: University of North Carolina Press, 1972), pp.44–48.

20 See also Thomas Pettigrew, *A Profile of Negro America* (Princeton: D. Van Nostrand, 1964); Edward Shils, "Color the Universal Intellectual Community, and the Afro-Asian Intellectuals," *Daedalus* (Spring 1967), pp.279–95; John Hope Franklin, *Color and Race* (Boston: Houghton Mifflin, 1968). This book contains several articles dealing with color and its effects on group and individual identity. See especially articles by Rodgers, Bastide, Parsons, Shils, and Franklin; Talcott Parsons, "Some Theoretical Considerations on the Nature and Trends of Change of Ethnicity," eds., Nathan Glazer and Daniel P. Moynihan, *Ethnicity* (Cambridge: Harvard University Press, 1975), pp.74–79; A Negro Female graduate student deals with the age old problem of color differences among Negroes, Adrienne M. Harrison, "Color, Class, and Consciousness," *The Black Scholar* (Fall 1973), pp.57–60.

21 The data contained here does not offer any other explanation for the cause of the African's skin color except that suggested in Jordan. Oscar Handlin, *Race and Nationality in American Life* (Garden City: Doubleday, 1957); Carelton S. Coon, *The Living Race of Man* (New York: Alfred A. Knopf, 1965); H.S. Jenning, *The Biological Basis of Human Nature* (New York: W.W. Norton, 1930); M.F. Montague, *Man's Most Dangerous Myth: The Fallacy of Race* (Cleveland: World, 1964). All address the reasons for a particular people being subjected to slavery. Supporting Jordan's premise by either pointing directly to slavery or by citing visibility as one of the causes for the African's enslavement. The "Great Chain of Being" theory formed the basic element for the African's skin color as a symbol of his heathenism. Arthur O. Lovejoy, *The Great Chain of Being: A Study of the History of an Idea* (New York: Harper Torchbook, 1960); reasons for slavery are aptly discussed in Ruth D. Wilson, "Justification of Slavery, Past and Present," *Phylon* (4th Quarter, 1958), pp.408ff.

22 Clifford Geertz, *The Interpretation of Culture* (New York: Basic Books, 1973), pp.89–90.

23 Talcott Parsons, *The Social System* (Glencoe, Ill.: Free Press, 1951), p.349.

24 See also W. Percy, "Symbol, Consciousness and Intersubjectivity," *Journal of Philosophy* 15 (1958), pp.631ff., a social, psychological, and cultural analysis of religious experience as it relates to Jordan's premise; Philip Mason, *Race Relations* (New York: n.p., 1970), Chap. 4; Wilcomb E. Washburn, *The Indian and the White Man* (Garden City, N.Y.: Doubleday, 1964) gives a detailed account of the Indian situation in America; Melville Herskovits, *The Myth of the Negro Past* (New York: Harper and Bros., 1942), deals with the Negro and the myths which surround with attention to the premise that Negro culture retains enough of its Africanisms to be identified as African.

25 See also Frederick Sontag and John K. Roth, *The American Religious Experience: Roots, Trends, and Future Theology* (New York: Harper and Row, 1972), pp.1–29; Benjamin E. Mays, *The Negro's God* (New York: Antheneum, 1968); Henry B. Mitchell, *Black Preaching* (Philadelphia: L.B. Lippencott, 1970); Joseph R. Washington, Jr., *Black and White Power Subreption* (Boston: Beacon Press, 1969); Albert B. Cleage, Jr., *The Black Messiah* (New York: Sheed and Ward, 1968).

26 Myrdal seems to believe that white America assumes that Negroes are unas-similable, partly because of the Negro's skin color. And while this is only one of the many physical characteristics of Negroes, they do not, like the Japanese and Chinese, have a politically organized nation and an accepted culture of their own outside of America. When the Negro's physical traits are compared to white physical traits, the Negro always falls short. Gunnar Myrdal, *The American Dilemma* (New York: Harper and Bros., 1944), pp.50–60, 137, 140. Many scholars tend to believe that miscegenation has caused the physical differences of ethnics to be a factor in maintaining the American caste system. See Thomas Pettigrew, *A Profile of Negro America*, p.71; Charles F. Marden and Gladys Meyer, *Minorities in American Society* (New York: D. Van Nostrand, 1973), pp.148–56; Otto Klineberg, *Characteristica of American Negro* (New York: Harper and Bros., 1944); Robert P. Stuckey, "African Ancestry of White American Population," *The Ohio Journal of Science* (May 1968), pp.155–56; Bentley Glass, *Genes and the Man* (New York: Teachers College, Columbia University Press, 1943), pp.173–74.

27 Aside from having their culture stripped, the African slaves were also sold at random, acquiring in many transactions the name of their new master and/or sometimes receiving the name of their wives. Furthermore, plantation records indicate that slave holders did not allow slaves to have any identity apart from that which they gave them. See Charles Wagley and Marvin Harris, *Minorities in the New World: Six Case Studies* (New York: Columbia University Press, 1958).

28 Most books on Negro culture usually start with a long discourse on Africa and attempt to show the humanness of the Negro American slaves by point-ing to the past greatness of Africa; or starting with Africa, attempt to show the primitive beginning of the African in order to subject the Negro slave to pre-ordained generalizations about their lowly nature. This continues to reinforce the projected worthlessness of the Negro. Until the Negro is accepted as having his beginning in America by Americans, he will remain an outsider struggling to become American.

29 Alphonso Pinkney, *Black Americans* (Englewood Cliffs, N.J.: Prentice Hall, 1969), p.5.

30 Martin L. King, Jr., *Where Do We Go from Here?* (Boston: Beacon Press, 1967), p.37.

31 Paulo Freire, *Pedagogy of the Oppressed* (New York: Seabury Press, 1968), p.29.

32 See Racial Enlightenment, Counter-Progressive, and Cliometrical Revolu-tional views.

33 Frank Tannenbaum, *Slave and Citizen* (New York: Alfred A. Knopf, 1946), p.52. See also Leon F. Litwack, *North of Slavery* (Chicago: University of Chicago Press, 1961), p.30.

34 John Trowbridge, *The Desolate South* (New York: Meredith Press, 1956), pp.84–85.

35 John Hope Franklin, *Reconstruction After the Civil War* (Chicago: Univer-sity of Chicago Press, 1961), p.83.

36 See also Litwack, p.31.

37 St. Clair Drake. "Anthropology and the Black Experience," *The Black Scholar* (Sept./Oct., 1980), pp.6ff.

38 Chancellor Williams, *The Destruction of Black Civilization: Great Issues of*

Race from 4500 BC to 2000 AD (Chicago: Third World Press, 1976), pp. 22–23.

39 See also Frank Snowden, *Blacks in Antiquity: Ethiopians in Greco-Roman Experience* (Cambridge, Mass.: Harvard University Press, 1970); Bernard Lewis, *Color and Islam* (New York: Harper Torchbook, 1971).

40 William Cobb Montague, "Physical Anthropology of the American Negro," *American Journal of Physical Anthropology*, 29 (1942), pp.15–59; Carlton Coon, Stanley M. Garn, and Joseph B. Birdsell, *Race: A Study of the Problem of Race Formation in Man* (New York: Norton, 1950), pp.63–91; E.W. Bovil, *The Golden Trades of the Moors* (London: n.p., 1958); Oliver Goldsmith, *An History of the Earth: An Animated Nature*, 8 vols. (London, n.p., 1740); Thomas Bendyshe, *The Anthropological Treaties of Johann F. Blumbach* (London, n.p., 1965).

41 Frederick Douglass, *Narratives of the Life of Frederick Douglass* (New York: New American Library, 1968), p.111. George P. Rawick, *From Sundown to Sunup: The Making of the Black Community* (Westport, Conn.: Greenwood, 1972), pp.3–11.

42 Joseph R. Washington, *The Politics of God* (Boston: Beacon Press, 1969), pp.104–7; Max Lerner, *America as a Civilization* (New York: Simon and Schuster, 1961); Franklin H. Little, *From State Church to Pluralism: A Protestant Interpretation of Religion in America* (New York: Anchor Books, 1962); E. Baltzell, *The Protestant Establishment: Aristocracy and Caste in America* (New York: Random House, 1964); Alexis de Tocqueville, *Democracy in America*; Oscar Handlin, *Fire-ball in the Night: The Crisis in Civil Rights* (Boston: Little Brown, 1964).

43 See also Ralph Linton, *The Individual and His Society* (New York: Columbia University Press, 1939); E. Franklin Frazier, *The Negro Church in the United States* (New York: Macmillan, 1949); John Dollard, *Caste, and Class in a Southern Town* (New York: Harper, 1937).

44 This position seems to agree with E. Franklin Frazier. Melville Herskovits expresses the opinion that "African survivals can be discovered in almost every phase of current Negro life." African survivals are found in every society throughout the world. Are these societies called African based? Why should the Negro America be treated any differently?

45 Many books have been written affirming this premise, however, the strength of this position rests with accounts by slaves themselves. Mungo Parks gives a striking account of his capture and journey from his hometown to a plantation in America: *The Travels of Mungo Parks* (New York: Everyman's Library, 1928). Bryan Edwards recites an account by an old Mandingo servant in *The History, Civil and Commercial Life of the British Colonies in the West Indies* (London, n.p., 1807), pp.71–79. Robert Park speaks of the manner in which slaves were collected and disbursed after capture: "The Conflict and Fusion of Cultures," *Journal of Negro History* IV (April 1920), p.117. George P. Rawick, *The American Slave: A Composite Autobiography*, 42 vols., (Westport, Conn.: Greenwood, 1972).

46 Phillip D. Curtin, "The Black Experience of Colonialism and Emperialism," *Daedalus* (Spring 1974), p.17. Curtin is addressing the same problem that Williams discussed earlier: most polemicists of Negro historiography attempt to show that the Negro American is fully human by citing the ability of African governments to win wars, develop art, have a religious system and create inventions. The weakness with this endeavor is that

contemporary black Americans cannot identify with Africanisms to the extent that self-pride is increased. This in turn causes many black Americans to feel without culture.

47 Robert Cruden, "James F. Rhodes and the Negro: A Study in the Problem of Objectivity," in Dwight W. Hoover, ed., *Understanding Negro History* (Chicago: Quadrangle Books, 1969), p.32.

48 Ruth Benedict, *Race: Science and Politics* (New York: Modern Age Books, 1940), p.153.

49 Two outstanding examples of this type of hate literature are represented in Charles Carroll, *The Negro ... a Beast or in the Image of God* (Savannah: Thunderbolt Press, 1928) and L.G. Lynch, *The Formation of the Negro* (New York: Carlton Press, 1963).

50 Leon Higgenbotham, Jr., *In the Matter of Color* (New York: Oxford University Press, 1978), p.30.

51 Samuel DuBois Cook, "A Conception of Negro History," in Dwight W. Hoover, ed., *Understanding Negro History* (Chicago: Quadrangle Books).

52 Theodore B. Wilson, *The Black Codes of the South* (Birmingham: University of Alabama Press, 1965), p.9.

53 Arthur Mann, *The Progressive Era: Liberal Renaissance or Liberal Failure* (New York: Holt, Rinehart, and Winston, 1965), p.6.

54 Henry F. May, *The End of American Innocence* (New York: Alfred A. Knopf, 1959), p.29.

55 C. Vann Woodward, *Reunion and Reaction: The Compromise of 1877 and the End of Reconstruction* (Boston: Little, Brown, 1951), p.44.

56 John Hope Franklin, *Reconstruction After the Civil War* (Chicago: University of Chicago Press, 1961), p.226.

Chapter II: The Progressive Model

1 Stanley M. Elkins, *Slavery* (Chicago: University of Chicago Press, 1959), p.10.

2 Phillips' credentials—A.B., University of Georgia, 1897; Ph.D., Columbia University, 1902; Honorary Litt. D., 1929; Honorary A.M., Yale University, 1929; Fellow and tutor in history, University of Georgia; Asst. Professor, University of Wisconsin; Author: *History of Transportation in the Eastern Cotton Belt; Life of Robert Tooms; Life and Labor in the Old South; Plantation and Frontier Documents; Florida Plantation Records;* these are but a few of his major works. See Appendix for personal data.

3 Theodore B. Wilson, *The Black Codes of the South* (Birmingham: University of Alabama Press, 1965), pp.13–14. Because there were so few Negroes in the early years of colonial life, they enjoyed a relative amount of freedom. Many received a considerable amount of respect from their local communities. John D. Russell, *The Free Negro in Virginia, 1619–1865* (Baltimore: Johns Hopkins Press, 1913), p.24. This period of freedom and prosperity was short-lived and as the free population increased so did hostile attitudes against free Negroes. The Virginia codes are best representative of these attitudinal changes not only because they were so thoroughly anti-Negro but because they were copied by so many of the other slave-holding states. See William Walter Hening, *The Statutes at Large Being a Collection of All the Laws of Virginia, 1619–1792*, 2 vols. (Richmond: n.p.,

1809–1823), III, pp.87–88; IV, p.132; XI, pp.39–40, 308. Most of the slave-holding states enacted similar laws; Mississippi enacted the most severe laws. For example, one such law was that a master could not take a slave to another state for the purpose of freeing him. See Helen Tunnicliff, *Judicial Cases Concerning American Slavery and the Negro*, 5 vols. (Washington: Carnegie Institute, 1927–1937). Arkansas law was so severe that by 1860 it had less Negroes than any other slaveholding state, *Arkansas Acts* (1850–1859), No. 151; (1859–1860), No. 99. While the slaveholding states were believed to be totally anti-Negro, many Northern states also excluded Negroes.

4 E. Franklin Frazier, *The Black Bourgeoisie* (New York: Macmillan, 1962), p.23.

5 For a comprehensive explanation of the free Negro in the South before the Civil War, see John H. Russell, *The Free Negro in Virginia, 1619–1865* (Baltimore: Johns Hopkins University Press, 1913); John Hope Franklin, *The Free Negro in North Carolina* (Chapel Hill: University of North Carolina Press, 1943); Luther P. Jackson, *Free Negro Holdings and Property Holdings in Virginia, 1830–1860* (New York: Appleton-Century-Crofts, 1942); Edward R. Turner, *The Negro in Pennsylvania* (Washington: American Historical Association, 1911); James M. Wright, *The Free Negro in Maryland, 1634–1860* (New York: Columbia University Press, 1921).

6 Carter G. Woodson, *Free Negro Heads of Families in the United States in 1830* (Washington: Assoc. for the Study of Negro Life and History, 1925).

7 See also James Curtis Ballagh, *A History of Slavery in Virginia* (Baltimore: Johns Hopkins Press, 1902).

8 William H. Grier and Price M. Cobbs, *Black Rage* (New York: Basic Books, 1968), p.61.

9 Lorenzo J. Greene, *The Negro in Colonial New England 1620–1776* (New York: Columbia University Press, 1942). This is a good analysis of America's attitudes toward female slaves.

10 For a detailed account of slave resistance see Herbert Aptheker, *American Negro Slave Revolts* (New York: Alfred A. Knopf, 1943); *idem*, "Maroons within the Present Limits of the United States," *Journal of Negro History*, XXIV (April, 1939); Joseph C. Carroll, *Slave Insurrections in the United States, 1800–1860* (Boston: Little, Brown, 1938); Nicholas Halasz, *Rattling Chains: Slave Unrest and Revolt in the Antebellum South* (New York: Harper and Bros., 1966); Raymond and Alice Bauer, "Day to Day Resistance to Slavery," *Journal of Negro History*, XXVII (October 1942); Lorenzo J. Greene, "Mutiny on the Slave Ships," *Phylon*, V (Fourth Quarter 1944); Richard Wade, "The Vesey Plot: A Reconsideration," *Journal of Southern History*, XXX (May 1964); William Styron, *The Confessions of Nat Turner* (New York: Viking Press, 1964); John Hendrik, *William Styron's Nat Turner; Ten Black Writers Respond* (Boston: Beacon Press, 1958); John B. Duff and Peter B. Mitchell, *The Nat Turner Rebellion: The Historical Event and the Modern Controversy* (New York: Alfred A. Knopf, 1971).

11 In order that special aspects of the Negro's social relationships be understood, the following books and articles are suggested readings: E. Ophelia Settle, "Slave Attitudes During the Slave Regime: Household Servants Versus Field Hands," *Publication of the Sociological Society*, XXVII (1934); Carter G. Woodson, "Beginning of Miscegenation of the Whites and Blacks,"

Journal of Negro History, III (October 1918); Avery O. Craven, "Poor Whites and Negroes in the Antebellum South," *Journal of Negro History*, XV (January 1930); Kenneth W. Porter, "Relations Between Negroes and Indians Within the Present Limits of the United States," *Journal of Negro History*, XVI (July 1932).

12 For the beginning of segregation see C. Vann Woodward, *The Strange Career of Jim Crow* (New York: Macmillan, 1965). For segregation in public schools, see John Hope Franklin, "Jim Crow Goes to School: The Genesis of Legal Segregation," *South Atlantic Quarterly*, LVIII (Spring 1965). Concerning the social and cultural development of the Negro American during the early 1900's, see W.E.B. Du Bois, *The College Bred Negro* (Atlanta: Atlanta University Press, 1900). For an analysis of the growth of Negro social institutions, see *idem*, "Some Facts in the Development of Negro Social Institutions," *American Journal of Sociology*, XXX (November 1934). The background sections for each chapter will further highlight the Negro situation as depicted by each model.

13 See also Genovese's *Roll Jordan Roll*, pp.97–112. For an explanation of the economic situation of the Negro, 1880–1940, see Horace M. Bond, "Social and Economic Forces in Alabama," *Journal of Negro History*, XXIII (July 1938); A.B. Moore, "Railroad Building in Alabama during Reconstruction," *Journal of Southern History*, I (November 1935). For the effects of the doctrine of the Negro's position on himself, see August Mier, *Negro Thought in 1800–1915* (Ann Arbor: University of Michigan Press, 1963). For the Negro's reaction to his plight, see T. Thomas Fortune, *Black and White: Land, Labor and Politics in the South* (New York: D. Appleton, 1884). For views of a Southern white man sympathetic to the Negro, see George Cable, *The Negro Question* (New York: Oxford University Press, 1958).

14 David B. Davis, "Slavery and the Post-World War II Historians," *Daedalus* (Spring 1974), p.2.

15 Ulrich B. Phillips, *American Negro Slavery: A Survey of the Supply, Employment and Control of Negro Labor as Determined by the Plantation Regime* (New York: D. Appleton, 1918), p.5. Many authors disagreed with the Phillips' school of thought and, for the most part, saw the African community as a well-balanced, time-tested social organization. For an exhaustive examination of both sides of this ideology, see William E. Foster, *The Negro People in American History* (New York: International Publishers, 1978); Albert J. Raboteau, Slave Religion: *The "Invisible" Institution in the Antebellum South* (New York: Oxford University Press, 1978), pp.4–42. W.E.B. Du Bois, *The World and Africa* (New York: Farrar and Rinehart, 1947). John Hope Franklin, *From Slavery to Freedom* (New York: Alfred A. Knopf, 1974), pp.6, 8, 16, 38.

16 For an explanation of the basis for this belief, see Michael Bandon, "Africa South of Sahara," ed., Melvin Tumin, *Comparative Perspectives on Race Relations* (Boston: Little, Brown, 1969). For an explanation of the thought pattern of the oppressor, see Eric Fromm, *The Heart of Man* (New York: D. Appleton, 1966). These accounts do not cover the subject thoroughly, they do indicate that while Phillips' premise is labeled "racist," he influenced many of his contemporaries to enter the debate.

17 David B. Davis, *The Problem of Slavery in Western Thought* (Ithaca, NY: Cornell University Press, 1966), pp.91–121.

18 Phillips, pp.49, 102, 262, 269, 270, 273, 275, 281, 284, 293, 296, 306, 308, 417, 418, 454, 459, 479, 501.
19 See also Gabriel Tarde, *The Laws of Imitation* (New York: Parsons Publications, 1903), pp.278–279.

Chapter III. The Racial Enlightenment Model

1 Kenneth M. Stampp, *The Peculiar Institution: Slavery in the Ante-Bellum South* (New York: Alfred A. Knopf, 1956), pp.141–191.
2 For a representation of the most widely circulated polemical literature, see Albert Barnes, *An Inquiry into the Scriptural Views of Slavery* (Philadelphia: Perkins and Purves, 1846); George Bourne, *A Condensed Anti-Slavery Bible Argument* (New York: S.W. Benedict, 1845); George B. Cheever, *The Guilt of Slavery and the Crime of Slaveholding* (Boston: R.F. Wallcut, 1852). For an illuminating defense of slavery, see Charles S. Sydnor, *Slavery in Mississippi* (New York: D. Appleton, 1933); Ralph B. Flanders, *Plantation Slavery in Georgia* (Chapel Hill: University of North Carolina Press, 1933); Rosser H. Taylor, *Slaveholding in North Carolina: An Economic View* (Chapel Hill: University of North Carolina Press, 1923); Charles S. Davis, *The Cotton Kingdom in Alabama* (Montgomery: Alabama State Department of Archives and History, 1939); James B. Sellers, *Slavery in Alabama* (University: University of Alabama Press, 1950). For the legal question, see Thomas R. Cobb, *An Inquiry into the Law of Negro Slavery in the United States of America* (Philadelphia: T. and J.W. Johnson, 1858).
3 David B. Davis, "Slavery and the Post World War Historians," *Daedalus* (Spring 1974), p.1.
4 The following list of books and articles will demonstrate the type of proliferation alluded to by Davis. On racial prejudice, see James B. Sellers, *Slavery in Alabama* (University: University of Alabama Press, 1957); Roger J. Williams, *Free and Unequal: The Biological Basis of Individual Liberty* (Austin: University of Texas Press, 1953); Julian H. Harris, *The Biology of the Negro* (Chicago: University of Chicago Press, 1942); Otto Klineberg, *Characteristics of the American Negro* (New York: Macmillan, 1944); Theodosius Dobzhansky, "The Genetic Nature of Differences Among Men," ed. Stow Persons, *Evolutionary Thought in America* (New Haven: Yale University Press, 1950); on Atlantic slave trade, see Elizabeth Donnan, *Documents Illustrative of the History of the Slave Trade to America* (Washington: Carnegie Institute Publications, 1930–1935); Philip D. Curtin, *The Atlantic Slave Trade: A Census* (Madison: University of Wisconsin Press, 1969); J.E. Inikori, "Measuring the Atlantic Slave Trade," *The Journal of African History*, 17 (1976):2. On the profitability of slavery, see James D. Hill, "Some Economic Aspects of Slavery, 1850–1860," *South Atlantic Quarterly*, XXVI (1927); Charles W. Ramsdell, "The Natural Limits of Slavery Expansion," *Mississippi Valley Historical Review*, XVI (1929). For efficiency see Larry Gara, "A New Englander's View of Plantation Life: Letters of Edwin Hall to Cyrus Woodman, 1837," *Journal of Southern History*, XVIII (1952); Robert R. Russel, "The General Effects of Slavery Upon Southern Economic Progress," *Journal of Southern History*, IV (1938). For African culture see Sidney W. Mintz and Richard Price,

An Anthropological Approach to the Afro-American Past (Philadelphia: Institute for the Study of Human Issues, 1976); Roger Bastide, *African Civilizations in the New World* (New York: Harper and Row, 1971); Boyd Christensen, "The Adaptive Functions of Fanti Priesthood," ed., William R. Bascom and Melville J. Herskovits, *Continuity and Change in African Cultures* (Chicago: University of Chicago Press, 1959). For religion see Charles Colock Jones, *Suggestion on the Religious Instructions of Negroes in the Southern States* (Philadelphia: Westminster Press, 1947); Luther P. Jackson, "Religious Development of the Negro in Virginia from 1760–1860)," *Journal of Negro History*, XVI (1931); Hortense Powermaker, *After Freedom* (New York: Atheneum Press, 1969); Bruce Rosenberg, *The Art of American Folk Preaching* (New York: Oxford University Press, 1970). For slave occupations see Frederick Law Olmsted, *A Journey in the Back Country* (New York: Random House, 1858); Duncan Clinch Heyward, *Seed from Madagascar* (Chapel Hill: University of North Carolina, 1937); Ulrich B. Phillips, *American Negro Slavery* (New York: D. Appleton, 1918). For general reading see Nathan Glazer and Daniel B. Moynihan, *Beyond the Melting Pot* (Cambridge: M.I.T. Press and Harvard University Press, 1963).

5 George P. Rawick, *From Sundown to Sunup: The Making of the Black Community* (Westport: Greenwood, 1972), p.xiv.

6 Paulo Freire, *Pedagogy of the Oppressed* (New York: Seabury Press, 1968), p.13. See also, George Hegel, *Phenomenology of the Mind* (New York: D. Appleton, 1967).

7 For background material see also Karl Marx and Friedrich Engels, *Selected Works* (New York: Harper and Row, 1968).

8 For an account of the beginning of the Harlem Renaissance see Rollin L. Hart, "The New Negro," *Independent* CV (January 15, 1921). For a description of the difficulties encountered by this movement, see James Weldon Johnson, "The Dilemma of the Negro Author," *American Mercury* XV (December 1928). For an exhaustive examination of this movement, see Nathan I. Huggins, *Harlem Renaissance* (New York: Grove Press, 1971). For a critical analysis of the New Negro, see Alain Locke, *The New Negro: An Interpretation* (New York: Harper and Row, 1925). For an overview of the Negro, see Robert Bone, *The Negro Novel in America* (New Haven, Conn.: Yale University Press, 1965), and J. Saunders Redding, "The Negro Writer: Shadow and Substance," *Phylon* (Fourth Quarter 1950).

9 Gunnar Myrdal, *An American Dilemma* (New York: Harper and Bros., 1944), p.xli. For a broader examination of this kind of premise, see Phillip S. Foner, *W.E.B. Du Bois Speaks: Speeches and Addresses 1890–1919* (New York: Pathfinder Press, 1970), pp.103–124, 219–224; Milton M. Gordon, "Towards a General Theory of Racial and Ethnic Relations," ed., Nathan Glazer and Daniel P. Moynihan, *Ethnicity*, pp.102–107; Karl E. Taeuber and Alma F. Taeuber, *Negroes in Cities* (Chicago: Aldine, 1965); Stanley Lieberson, "The Impact of Residential Segregation on Ethnic Assimilation," *Social Forms* 40 (October 1961): 52–57; Daniel Bell, "On Mediocrity and Equality," *The Public Interest* 29 (Fall 1972): 29–68. The idea that the Negro, whether found in antebellum society or in contemporary society, is viewed as a troublesome entity, will be further examined in the final chapter.

10 If Myrdal's idea concerning valuations is viewed in isolation, the thrust of it

will be lost. If however, his premise is viewed along with the principles of human development, then results a clearer picture. See T.W. Adorno, Else Frankel-Brunswick, Daniel J. Levinson, and Nevitt Sanford, *The Authoritarian Personality* (New York: Harper and Bros., 1950); Margaret Mead, *Childhood in Contemporary Cultures* (New York: Columbia University Press, 1958); Max Horkheimer, "Authority and the Family," ed., Bernard Stern, *The Family Past and Present* (New York: D. Appleton–Century, 1938), pp.423–45; Sheldon Stryker, "Social Structure and Prejudice," *Social Problems* (Spring 1959), pp.340–53.

11 A revealing effect of the caste system on Americans, white and Negro, is John Dollard, *Caste and Class in a Southern Town* (New Haven, Conn.: Yale University Press, 1937). For personal testimony by Negroes on the effects of conforming to racism, see Calvin H. Herton, *Sex and Racism in America* (Garden City: Doubleday, 1965), pp.53–58. For an in-depth discussion of racism on white America, see Lillian Smith, *Killers of Dreams* (New York: W.W. Norton, 1961). For an outline of the frustrations confronting Negroes as a result of caste discrimination, see Robert Morton, *Social Theory and Social Structure* (Glencoe: Free Press, 1957), pp.13–160. For an exploration of these frustrations, see Harry Bredemeier and Jackson Toby, *Social Problems in America: Cost and Casualties in an Acquisitive Society* (New York: John Wiley, 1960), chapters 7–8.

12 John Hope Franklin, *From Slavery to Freedom: A History of Negro America* (New York: Alfred A. Knopf, 1947), p.361.

13 E. Franklin Frazier, *The Negro in the United States* (New York: Dryden Press, 1948), p.295.

14 For an explanation of Negro middle class status and its meaning to the Negro masses, see Frank Louis Venable Kennedy, *The Negro Peasant Turned Cityward* (New York: Columbia University Press, 1930). For an examination of the effects of race mixture and mixed-blood among Negroes, see Edward G. Badger, *The Mulatto in the United States, 1918* (Boston: Gorham Press, 1918). For the best overview of the Negro middle class, see E. Franklin Frazier, *Black Bourgeoisie*. The premise that the Negro middle class only renders lip service to the Negro masses has not been thoroughly exposed because (1) the Negro masses do not, for the most part, possess the literary skills needed to produce a scholarly rendition, (2) those Negroes who have the needed skills are comfortably acting as "drivers" and therefore feel no immediate need to give up so much comfort, and (3) the white world is satisfied to "let sleeping dogs lie" as long as these dogs obey their "drivers." The data that emerged throughout this project continually shows a need for Frazier's thesis to be expanded.

15 See discussion of this premise in Jordan, pp.91–95.

16 Frederick L. Olmsted, *A Journey in the Back Country* (New York: D. Appleton, 1858), p.64.

17 Stampp, see detailed discussion in Chapter I of this research project.

18 See discussion of Southern attitudes on pp.30–1 above.

Chapter IV. The Counter-Progressive Model

1 Harry A. Ploski and Warren Marr, II, *The Negro Almanac: A Reference Work on the Afro-American* (New York: Bellwether Co., 1976), pp.32–33.

2 Peter L. Berger, *The Sacred Canopy: Elements of a Sociological Theory of Religion* (New York: Doubleday, 1967), p.62. For a better understanding of how Berger was able to reach the above stated conclusion, see George Herbert Mead, *Mind, Self and Society* (Chicago: University of Chicago Press, 1934). The point to be made here is that Mead's understanding of "internationalization" allows every human condition to select those elements and processes that will be taken by that particular individual. Negroes, on the other hand, having limited control over their physical and temporary America, perceive this type of immortality. As a consequence, most Negroes have not acquired the sophistication needed to understand that through their "children and their children's children they live forever." Peter Berger goes on to explain, "to destroy this immortality an emeny must eradicate every last living soul belonging to the collectivity." No doubt many contemporary Americans, white and Negro, believe that no such enemy exists—slavery literature clearly shows slave holders as the enemy. The social behavior of contemporary Negroes illustrates their success. For an explanation of how this collectivity premise influenced the individual self, see Emile Durkheim, *Elementary Forms of Religious Life* (Garden City, NY: Doubleday–Anchor, 1954).

3 Gunnar Myrdal, *An American Dilemma: The Negro Problem and Modern Democracy* (New York: Harper and Bros., 1944), pp.27–31. For an examination of the black/white birth rate and its effect on population distribution, see Reynolds Farley, *Growth of the Black Population* (Chicago: Markham Pub., 1970). For an analysis of the Negro's migration pattern from the South between 1951 and 1960, see Karl E. Taeuber and Alma F. Taeuber, "The Negro Population in the United States," ed., John Davis, *The Negro Reference Book* (Englewood Cliffs, NJ: Prentice Hall, 1966), Chapter 2. For an explanation by Negroes as to why many left the South during this period of time, see Richard Wright, *Native Son* (New York: Harper and Bros., 1940); Horace Clayton, *Long Lonely Road* (New York: Trident Press, 1965). The powerlessness of Negroes to effect any substantial social and economic change has already been documented in this project. Therefore, it would not strengthen this research to cite again those documents. However, in order that the Negro's situation be better understood, see E. Franklin Frazier, *The Negro Family in the United States* (Chicago: University of Chicago Press, 1966), pp.209–244. Frazier's treatment of the subject formed the basis for most of the discussion that dealt with the Negro family. The notion that the North was a better place for the Negro caused many Negro families to migrate North not realizing the hardship that they would encounter. And as a consequence, Frazier tended to believe that many of these families were forced to separate. He deals effectively with this aspect of the Negro family.

4 The idea that the white Southerner "knows" the Negro is only one side of the situation. Southern Negroes also claim to "know" the white man. The latter may be closer to the truth because of their oppressed state. This claim of gnostic truth is in actuality the tenets of the self-fulfilling prophecy. For an explanation of this theory, see Robert K. Merton, *Social Theory and Social Structure* (Glencoe, Ill.: Free Press, 1957), p.421–436. It appears that some theorists believe that the overall relations between dominants and minorities is aimed at the assimilation of the minority into the dominant society. For an explanation, see Robert E. Park, *Race and*

Culture (Glencoe, Ill.: Free Press, 1950). For an examination of Park's theory, see Seymour Martin Lipset, "Changing Social Status and Prejudice: The Race Theories of a Pioneering American Sociologist," *Commentary*, May 1950, pp.475–479.

5 This "know thy brother" attitude is not totally the responsibility of the white community. It springs from the house servant/field hand mentality. Frazier aptly explains this connection in his *Black Bourgeoisie*, pp.162–175. See also Austin Steward, *Twenty-Two Years a Slave, and Forty Years a Freeman* (Rochester: Allings and Cory, 1857), pp.30–32. This need of the Negro to assimilate into the white world will be examined further in the final chapter of this research.

6 Davis B. Davis, "Slavery and the Post-World War Historians," *Daedalus*, Spring 1974, p.4.

7 Stanley M. Elkins, *Slavery: A Problem in American Institutional and Intellectual Life* (Chicago: University of Chicago Press, 1959), pp.27–28.

8 It appeared that Elkins was also greatly influenced by Helen T. Catteral's *Judicial Cases Concerning American Slavery and the Negro*; Susie Ames' *Studies of the Virginia Eastern Shore*; John C. Hurd's *The Law of Freedom and Bondage in the United States*; James C. Ballagh, *History of Slavery in Virginia*; John H. Russel, *The Free Negro in Virginia*; and George Bourne, *Picture of Slavery in the United States of America*.

9 Oscar Handlin and Mary F. Handlin, "Origins of Southern Labor System," *William and Mary Quarterly*, 2nd Series VII (April 1950): pp.199–222.

10 This premise is reflected throughout Stampp's and Elkins' discourse on slavery.

11 See also Beverly B. Munford's *Virginia's Attitudes Towards Slavery and Secession*; Thomas R. Cobb's *An Inquiry into the Law of Slavery in the United States of America*.

12 R.S. Rattay, *Ashanti Law and Constitution* (Oxford, England: Clarendon Press, 1929), p.38.

13 For a detailed account of the middle passage, see Alexander Falconbridge, *An Account of the Slave Trade on the Coast of Africa* and Thomas F. Buston, *Letters on the Slave Trade to the Lord Viscount*. The Donnan Documents give a detailed account of the circumstances and conditions of intertribal slavery and its relationship to the Atlantic slave trade; Tannenbaum, *Slave and Citizen*, shows a major source for some of Elkins' data. These sources tend to strengthen Elkins' general premise that even from the time of capture, the African was doomed to a less than human status.

14 For survivor's accounts, see Bruno Bettelheim, "Individual and Mass Behavior in Extreme Situations," *Journal of Abnormal Psychology*, October 1943; Elie Cohen, *Human Behavior in the Concentration Camps* (New York: Norton, 1953); Olga Lengyel, *Five Chimneys: The Story of Auschwitz* (Chicago: Free Press, 1947); Elie Wiesel, *Night* (New York: Avon Books, 1958); Eugen Kogen, *The Theory and Practice of Hell* (New York: Farrar, Straus, 1946).

15 See also John Dollard, *Caste and Class in a Southern Town* (New York: Harper, 1949), p.255.

16 For a detailed discussion of this thesis, see pp.140–157 in Elkins' *Slavery*.

17 This position is based on the article by Eugene B. Brody, "Social Conflict and Schizophrenic Behavior in Young Adult Negro Males," *Psychiatry*, November 1961.

18 Ann J. Lane, *The Debate Over Slavery: Stanley Elkins and His Critics* (Chicago: University of Illinois Press, 1971), p.3.
19 David B. Davis, "The Continuing Contradiction of Slavery: A Comparison of British America and Latin America," in Lane, *The Debate Over Slavery,* pp.112–113.
20 Earl E. Thorpe, "Chattel Slavery and the Concentration Camp," in Lane, *The Debate Over Slavery*, p.24.
21 While Thorpe tended to believe that Elkins' thesis contained too much personal bias, it is the opinion of this researcher that since Elkins was the first historian to approach slavery in the manner that he did, Elkins should be allowed the errors of a pioneer.
22 Eugene D. Genovese, "Rebelliousness and Docility in the Negro Slave: A Critique of Elkins' Thesis," in Lane, *The Debate Over Slavery*, p.43.
23 Roy Simon Bryce-Laporte, "Slaves as Inmates, Slaves as Men," in Lane, *The Debate Over Slavery,* p.289.

Chapter V. The Cliometric Revolutional Model

1 Harry A. Ploski and Warren Marr, II, *The Negro Almanac: A Reference Work on the Afro-American* (New York: Bellwether Co., 1976), pp.32–33.
2 Ploski and Marr, II, pp.33–55.
3 Robert Fogel and Stanley L. Engerman, *Time on the Cross: The Economics of American Negro Slavery* (Boston: Little, Brown, 1974), p.8. For another cliometric view, see Alfred H. Conrad and John R. Meyer, *The Economics of Slavery* (Chicago: Aldine, 1964). For an historical approach, see David B. Davis, *The Problem of Slavery in Western Culture* (Ithaca, N.Y.: Cornell University Press, 1966).
4 For a different viewpoint of these principles, see Robert R. Russel, "Slavery and Southern Economic Progress," *Journal of Southern History*, February 1938, pp.34–54; Alfred H. Stone, "The Cotton Factorage System of the Southern States," *American Historical Review*, XX (1915), pp.557–565; W.J. Cash, *The Mind of the South* (New York: Alfred A. Knopf, 1941), pp.42–70.
5 For a discussion of the effects of Christianity on personality change, see Edwin W. Smith, *Knowing the African* (London: Lutterworth Press, 1946). For the effect of missionaries and their attitudes towards emerging cultures, see Arthur Phillips, *Survey of African Marriage and Family Life* (London: Routledge Kegan Paul, 1953); Horace M. Bond, *The Education of the Negro in the American Social Order* (New York: Prentice-Hall, 1934).
6 For a discussion of the relationship of the sugar plantation to capitalism and slavery, see Eric Williams, *Capitalism and Slavery* (Chapel Hill: University of North Carolina Press, 1944). For a discussion of the division of slave labor according to plantation types, see E. Franklin Frazier, *The Negro in the United States* (New York: Macmillan, 1949), Chap. II. For an explanation of the effect of sugar on the slave population in Brazil, see Gilberto Freyer, *The Masters and the Slaves* (New York: Alfred A. Knopf, 1946). For a discussion of the system of contingents and forced deliveries as a forerunner for the North American system of slavery, see Clive Day, *The Policy and Administration of the Dutch in Java* (New York: Macmillan, 1904), pp.62–75. For a discussion of the "culture system,"

another slavery prototype, see Fogel and Engerman, chapters VII, VIII, and IX.

7 For a graphic description of an early "free labor system," see Douglas L. Oliver, *The Pacific Islands* (Cambridge, Mass.: Harvard University Press, 1951).

8 A. Grenfell Price, *White Settlers and Native People* (Cambridge, Mass.: Harvard University Press, 1950), pp.10–15; S.J. Holmes, *The Negro's Struggle for Survival* (Berkeley: University of California Press, 1937), p.75; Frederick L. Hoffman, *Race Traits and Tendencies of the American Negro* (New York: Macmillan, 1896), pp.329–33.

9 For the origin and sources of slavery, see I. Finley, *The World of Odysseus* (New York: Meridian Paperback, 1959), p.50; William L. Westermann, *The Slave Systems of Greek and Roman Antiquity* (Philadelphia: Westminster Press, 1955), p.7; Isaac Mendelsohn, *Slavery in the Ancient Near East: A Comparative Study of Slavery in Babylonia, Asyria Syria, and Palestine, from the Middle of the Third Millennium to the End of the First Millennium* (New York: Alfred A. Knopf, 1949), pp.1–5; Melville J. Herskovits, *Dahomey: An Ancient West African Kingdom* (New York: Macmillan, 1938), I. 99; C. Martin Wilbur, *Slavery in China During the Former Han Dynasty*, 206 B.C.–A.D. 25 (Chicago: University of Chicago Press, 1943), pp.73–241; S.R. Driver, *A Critical and Exegetical Commentary on Deuteronomy* (New York: Oxford University Press, 1948). For an explanation of the premise that as the emerging forces of capitalism and democracy dissolved the European notion of social rank, one of the unhappy by-products was an unmitigated form of slavery, see Frank Tannenbaum, *Slave and Citizen: The Negro in the Americas* (New York: Harper and Bros., 1947); Carl Degler, *Out of Our Past: The Forces That Shaped Modern American Life* (New York: Macmillan, 1959), pp.26–39; Milton R. Konvitz, *A Century of Civil Rights* (New York: Alfred A. Knopf, 1957), pp.3–37.

10 For Elkins' treatment of this subject, see Elkins, pp.164–193. For an historian's analysis of the slavery question, see David B. Davis, *The Problem of Slavery in Western Culture* (Ithaca: Cornell University Press, 1966), pp.125–164.

11 Conrad and Meyer tended to agree with Fogel and Engerman. However, they did not credit the slave holder with as much diversification. See Conrad and Meyer, pp.80–82.

12 Conrad and Meyer, p.82. For a different view, see U.B. Phillips, *Life and Labor in the Old South* (Boston: Little, Brown, 1935), pp.174–75; *idem*, "The Economic Cost of Slaveholding in the Cotton-Belt," *Political Science Quarterly*, XX (1905), pp.257–75. It seems that all of these writers are either attempting to justify a need for slave-breeding or they are trying to prove that slavery was so profitable that there was no need to breed slaves — none of them addressed themselves to "how the slaves perceived the issue."

13 W.H. Collins, *The Domestic Slave Trade of the Southern States* (New York: Alfred A. Knopf, 1904), Chap. III. See also Frederick Bancroft, *Slave Trading in the Old South* (Baltimore: J.H. Furst Co., 1931), Chap. 18.

14 For a discussion of the allocation of slave labor, see J.S. Douesenberry, "Some Aspects of the Theory of Economic Development," *Exploration in Entrepreneurial History*, III (1950), p.9.

15 For an exploration of white-black relationships, see Melville J. Herskovits, *The American Negro* (New York: Alfred A. Knopf, 1928); John H. Burma,

"The Measurement of Negro's Passing," *American Journal of Sociology*, July 1946, pp.18–22; E.W. Eckard, "How Many Negroes Pass," *American Journal of Sociology*, May 1947, pp.498–500; W.E.B. Du Bois, *The World and Africa* (New York: Viking Press, 1947), pp.7–20, 226; E. Franklin Frazier, *The Black Bourgeoisie* (New York: Free Press, 1968), pp.60–65.

16 For a discussion of the life expectancy of male slaves, see Charles Sydnor, "Life Span of Mississippi Slaves," *American Historical Review*, April 1930, pp.556–574; L.I. Dubin, A.J. Lotka, and M. Spiegelman, *Length of Life* (New York: Ronald Press, 1949), p.51. There seems to be no accurate way of determining whether or not slave-breeding actually took place because as these sources indicate, (1) most Southern slave holders were ashamed to be known as a slave-breeder, (2) each investigator saw and recorded the facts as his culture would have him see it, and (3) the slaves have not been afforded the opportunity to speak for themselves. George Rawick seems to be of the opinion that his slave narratives are a humble beginning. For another opinion of slave-breeding, see Conrad and Meyer, pp.61–65, 80–82.

17 Many historians seemed to believe that there was a definite relationship between slave-breeding and miscegenation. For a discussion on the social effects and miscegenation, see Joel Williamson, *New People: Miscegenation and Mulattoes in the United States* (New York: Free Press, 1980), pp.5–60; John Blassingame, *Black New Orleans, 1860–1880* (Chicago: University of Chicago Press, 1973), pp.17–21.

18 For an explanation of the premise that slave economies are constantly threatened by decline because they cannot maintain the proper number of slaves, see W.A. Lewis, *Theory of Economic Growth* (Homewood, Ill.: Richard D. Irwin, 1955), pp.111–113.

19 See also Frederick L. Olmsted, *The Cotton Kingdom* (New York: Bobbs-Merrill, 1971).

20 For an in-depth explanation of this instrument, see Appendix B of *Time on the Cross* by Fogel and Engerman.

Chapter VI. The Four Models Compared

1 David B. Davis, "Slavery and the Post-World War Historians," p.2.

2 James Otis, "The Rights of the British Colonies Asserted and Proved" in *Bailyn Pamphlets*, Vol. 1, p.437.

3 Lane, p.14.

4 William H. Grier and Price M. Cobb, *Black Rage* (New York: Basic Books, 1968), p.24.

5 These authors also stated, "The practice of slavery stopped over a hundred years ago, but the minds of our [black] citizens have never been freed" (p.26).

6 James P. Gomer, "Individual Development and Black Rebellion: Some Parallels," *Midway*, January 1968, pp.33–48.

7 Herbert Aptheker, *American Negro Slave Revolts* (New York: International Publishers, 1943), pp.79–114.

8 Davis, p.7.

9 This premise is supported by Myrdal, Jordan, Rawick, and Genovese, to name a few; it gets to the heart of the Negro problem. Negroes are seen as less than human because many of them do not behave as fully human;

many are ashamed of the Negro National Anthem; Negro History Week is meaningless; everything that would support ethnic pride is integrated in order to have any value at all.

10 Robert Fogel and Stanley Engerman, *Time on the Cross: The Economics of American Negro Slavery* (Boston: Little, Brown, 1974), pp.67–72.

11 For an in-depth discussion see chapters 1 to 3 of Jordan's *White Over Black*. Jordan believed that social attitudes which were developed over many years permitted slavery to be established in the New World.

12 E.g., on pp.192, 204–207, 217–219, 221, 228, 231, 241, and 262.

13 See pp.127, 152, 202–209, 211, 229, and 262.

14 Richard Hofstadter, "U.B. Phillips and the Plantation Legend," *Journal of Negro History*, XXIX (April, 1944), pp.109–124.

15 For a detailed discussion see Jordan's *White Over Black*, Chapter 1; Foner's *W.E.B. Du Bois Speaks*, pp.102–111.

16 *Andrew Billingsly, Black Families in White America* (Englewood Cliffs, N.J.: Prentice-Hall, Inc., 1968), p.150.

17 Slave literature does not deal with accommodation and resistance in a manner that would allow them to be seen as a realistic configuration. For example, Stampp saw the slave as a troublesome property who sought every means to show disapproval of his condition. Elkins saw the slave as a helpless victim of a peculiar circumstance, and Fogel and Engerman saw the slave as a victim of racism who managed to survive rather handsomely in spite of his situation. Phillips saw the slave as childlike, loving his situation. Even slave literature (such as Herbert Aptheker, *American Negro Slave Revolts*; Joseph C. Carrol, *Slave Insurrections in the United States, 1800–1860*; Raymond and Alice Bauer, "Day to Day Resistance to Slavery," *Journal of Negro History*; Lorenzo J. Green, "Mutiny on the Slave Ships," *Phylon*, V [Fourth Quarter, 1944]; Richard Wade, "The Vessey Plot: A Reconsideration," *Journal of Southern History*, XXX [May, 1964], to name a few), presents the slave either as a superman or a docile "Sambo." This is not to say that this researcher doubts the authenticity of these works, but that they reflect either the bias of the liberal white mind or the bias of one seeking to cross "color lines." The point developed very weakly is that from the beginning the slaves had a choice; they could either succumb to slavery or resist to the "death." Slave literature points to many cases where the slaves preferred death to slavery; this mentality has not been dealt with effectively.

18 Foner, pp.20–21. While love may be too strong in describing the relationship between the slave and the master, the relationship between them is one so peculiar that not even the slave or the master could clearly define it. See also Rawick's account of this relationship in his *From Sundown to Sunup*. This kind of attachment is also explored in Bruno Bettelheim's "Individual and Mass Behavior in Extreme Situations," *Journal of Abnormal Psychology*, XXXVII (October, 1943); Elie Cohen, *Human Behavior in the Concentration Camp* (New York: Norton Press, 1953).

19 Charles E. Silberman, *Crisis in Black and White* (New York: Vintage Books, 1964), p.78.

20 This is an interesting observation because it tends to deny the responsibility of the Negro mother by implying that because she is the offspring of slaves, she must devalue the role of education for her child. Erikson explained a Negro situation through the postulates of a white mind. For

example, Rawick writes of Professor Bernard trying to explain the meaning-lessness of slave marriages by pointing to the legality of marriage denied to the slave under plantation law. He wrote, "The fact that the slaves were not legally married is no more significant than the fact that the Sioux Indian in 1850 had children born of parents not legally married by the laws of the United States." This continued attempt by white America to dilute the effects of slavery by applying double standards to the ex-slave is one of the primary reasons for so much hostility between Negroes and whites. The Negro mother, in this case, may well have been trying to protect her child from "an indifferent and hateful compact majority"; however, she must have realized that eventually the child would have to go out into this hateful world. Experience shows that when the Negro mother becomes indifferent to educating her child, there is something more than fear and the desire to protect at the bottom of her action. She usually has had so many negative experiences with the educational system that she no longer believes it can help her child, or she has been so conditioned by the Americanization process that education is no longer a viable means for obtaining the better things of life. Perhaps she has been so conditioned by the social services system that she believes that she and her child will be taken care of forever. In any case, her "instinctive sense" would have long been sensitized to respond in just the manner in which she did. As a religious leader and teacher, I teach our young people that immoral be-havior is not acceptable to the American way. The American way teaches these same young people that immoral behavior brings monetary rewards. Work is an honorable way to get the niceties of life; welfare teaches that every American has a right to these niceties simply because they are Americans. The point to be made here is that while slavery did infantilize the Negro, it did at the time teach him how to survive, and, based on his history prior to the "great thrust for integration," this survival technique produced such people as Turner, Washington, and King.

21 Erikson, p.236. This view by Erikson is interesting because he cites a situation taking place in an open and free society. His position would have been much stronger if he had followed Elkins' "concentration camp analogy." This is not to say that Erikson's premise is without value; it strengthens this researcher's position concerning the paradox of the Negro identity problem. The Negro mothers cited by Erikson do opt for the surrendered identity which the Negro male experiences; however, the Negro female has a separate identity apart from the Negro male, and to imply that the Negro female's identity is dependent upon the identity of the Negro male is to place her in a nonperson category. While it is true that both the Negro male and the Negro female underwent the damning effects of slavery, each, however, had their individual and separate roles. Jordan believed that the female slave had a much harder and longer work day; she not only had to perform her assigned task in the field, but care for her own children as well as take care of her family chores. Her duties also included being a sex object for her master and his friends. Therefore, it would seem that the Negro female's surrendered identity was more complete, if that is possible, than the Negro male's. This is not to say that the Negro male had an easier time than the Negro female; slavery demanded of both a complete surren-der. However, even in the very process of "seasoning," the female was more of a victim. The fact that the Negro female could not expect the Negro male

to come to her aid caused her to develop new methods of self-defense which, in all likelihood, is seen by many as a lack of care for her children. Note that this "noncaring" posture is suggested by white scholars who could not understand what it means to be a slave.

22 In Myrdal's *American Dilemma* the notion that the Negro American's behavior supports white racism and white racism supports Negro behavior is by far the best approach to solving America's race problem. If this idea is followed to its logical conclusion, then America would use its vast resources to help develop programs that would preserve and promote negritude. This would mean that the Negro would be encouraged to see black history as an historical record rather than a series of moralistic events. The Negro would be taught to accept his history and himself as an equal American. Elkins stated that, "The institution was formed on the spot by Englishmen." This implies that the English had certain attitudes which allowed them to perceive the African in a slave category. These attitudes were not formed overnight, nor were they conceived in hatred. They came as a result of many social developments which Jordan and Myrdal make clear.

23 Charles F. Marden and Gladys Meyer, *Minorities in American Society* (New York: D. Van Nostrand, 1973), p.37.

24 These six elements formed the primary concerns for the traditional interpretation of slavery and thereby restricted the depth of the investigation. While it must be admitted that these elements had a significant role in the development of the slave's personality, their usefulness was usurped by the significance accredited to their value. Since the nature of the institution was such that the master had absolute control of the slaves, he had no choice but to supply their daily necessities if he were to take advantage of their labor. Therefore, instead of these authors arguing about the quality or lack of quality of basic needs, they would have accomplished more and advanced the cause of better race relations if they had used their energy in explaining the reasons for these needs. The slaves were helpless individuals who could not provide for themselves, not because of an inferior nature, but because they were owned as property. One of the requirements imposed by North American slavery was that the slaves not only had to submit their bodies to the rule of the masters but they had to convince him that their minds were also surrendered. Since the slaves were forced into this kind of situation, how could they be held responsible for succumbing to it? The answer, of course, points to the weakness in human nature. When humans develop and become involved in a social situation that exposes their inner nature, they usually try to project this nature on the weaker member of the social organization.

25 For a contemporary in depth discussion see Joel Williamson's *New People: Miscegenation and Mulattoes in the United States* (New York: Free Press, 1980).

26 An adaptation of the premise as set forth by Genovese, *Roll, Jordan, Roll,* pp.413–431.

27 Stokely Carmichael and Charles V. Hamilton, *Black Power: The Politics of Liberation in America* (New York: Alfred A. Knopf, 1967), p.36.

28 Throughout the resource material authors such as Jordan, Stampp, Elkins, Rawick, and Genovese cite this type of behavior as indicative of the conditioning effect of slavery on the Negro slave. Phillips and the progressives saw this behavior as germane to the African nature.

29 Lerone Bennett, Jr., *Before the Mayflower: A History of the Negro in America 1619–1964* (New York: Penguin Books, 1962), p.3. This book presents a positive image of the Negro American from slavery to 1964.

30 Frederick Douglass, *Narrative of the Life of Frederick Douglass, An American Slave* (New York: Doubleday, Dolphin Books, 1845), pp.20–21.

31 Pauli Murry, *Proud Shoes: The Story of An American Family* (New York: Harper and Row, 1956), pp.38–48.

32 Erik Erikson, "The Concept of Identity" in Talcott Parsons and Kenneth B. Clark's *The Negro American* (Boston: Houghton Mifflin, 1966), p.229.

33 *The American Heritage Dictionary*, rev. ed. (1973), s.v. "Racism."

34 Herbert Aptheker, *A Documentary History of Negro People in the United States* (Secaucus, N.J.: Citadel Press, 1951), pp.1–17.

35 Lillian Smith, *Killers of Dreams* (New York: W.W. Norton, 1949), p.18.

36 Robert Coles, *Children of Crisis* (Boston: Little, Brown, 1964), p.62.

Chapter VII. The Four Models and the Contemporary Negro

1 For a detailed discussion of the mulatto question, see Winthrop Jordan, "American Chiaroscuro: The Status and Definition of the Mulattoes in the British Colonies," *William and Mary Quarterly* XXIX (April 1962); Williamson, *New People*.

2 Louis Hartz, *The Founding of New Societies* (New York: Harcourt, Brace and World, 1964), p.55.

3 This is a highly controversial point divided basically into two schools of thought. The first follows E. Franklin Frazier's ideology, which is outlined in such books as *The Negro Church in America* and *The Negro People in the United States*. See also Andrew Billingsly, *Black Families in White America*. The second follows the basic ideology of Melville J. Herskovits, *The Myth of the Negro Past*. While these ideological structures oppose each other, currently, there seems to be a softening of their basic principles. For an example of this, see Lorenzo D. Turner, *Africanisms in the Gullah Dialect* (Chicago: University of Chicago Press, 1949).

4 William Styron, *The Confessions of Nat Turner* (New York: Random House, 1967), p.65. For other accounts see Henry I. Tragle, *The Southampton Slave Revolt of 1831*; T.R. Gray, *The Confession, Trial and Execution of Nat Turner*; Herbert Aptheker, *Nat Turner's Slave Rebellion*.

5 Harold Isaac, *The New World of Negro Americans* (New York: John Day, 1963), gives a detailed background of the African influence on the Negro identity problem.

6 Marden and Meyer, pp.20–24. See also Melvin Tumin, *Comparative Perspectives on Race Relations* (Boston: Little, Brown, 1969; Charles Wagley and Marvin Harris, *Minorities in the New World: Six Case Studies* (New York: Columbia University Press, 1958); Robert M. McIver and Charles H. Page, *Society* (New York: Rhinehart, 1937).

7 See, e.g., Herskovits, *The Myth of the Negro Past*.

8 Williamson, *New People*, p.3.

9 Raboteau, pp.42–92. For a full understanding see also Geertz, *Interpreting of Culture*, Chapter 4.

10 For examples of studies of the effect of color on the self-image of young Negro children, see S. Asher and V. Allen, "Racial Preference and Social

Comparison Processes," *Journal of Social Issues*, 1969, pp.157–65; L. Bennett, *Confrontation: Black and White* (Baltimore: Penguin Books, 1968); James Banks, *Black Self Concept: Implications for Education and Social Science* (New York: McGraw Hill, 1972); G. Allport, *The Nature of Prejudice* (New York: Doubleday, 1954); K. Clark, *Prejudice and Your Child* (Boston: Beacon Press, 1967); *Idem*, "Racial Identification and Racial Preference in Negro Children," ed. Newcomb and Hartly, *Readings in Social Psychology* (New York: Holt, 1947); S. Cooper Smith, "Self Concept, Race and Education," ed. Gajenda and Bagley, *Race and Education Across Cultures* (London: Heinemann Educational Books, 1975); J. Hraba and G. Grant, "Black Is Beautiful: A Reexamination of Racial Preference and Identification," *Journal of Psychology*, 1970, pp.388–402; J. Williams and J. Morland, *Race, Color, and the Young Child* (Chapel Hill: University of North Carolina Press, 1976); A. Pouissant, "Building A Strong Self-Image in the Black Child," in *Readings in Early Childhood Education* (New Haven, Conn.: Duskin Pub. Co., 1977).

Appendix
Biographical Information

Elkins, Stanley M., 1930–

Born May 11, 1930, in New York, New York. Education: A.B., University of Illinois, 1952, M.A., 1953, Ph.D., 1961. Religion: Jewish. Office: Department of English, Washington University, St. Louis, Missouri, 63130.

Washington University, St. Louis, Missouri instructor, 1960–62, assistant professor, 1962–66, associate professor, 1966–69, professor of English, 1969– . Visiting professor, Smith College, 1964–65. Military Service: U.S. Army, 1955–57.

Modern Language Association of America, Awards, Honors: Longview Foundation award, 1962; Paris Review humor prize, 1964; Guggenheim Fellow, 1966–67; Rockefeller Foundation grant, 1968–69; National Endowment for the Arts and Humanitites grant, 1972.

Boswell (novel), Random House, 1964; *Criers and Kibitzers, Kibitzers and Criers* (stories), Random House, 1966; *A Bad Man* (novel), Random House, 1967; *The Dick Gibson Show* (novel), Random House, 1970; (editor) *Stories from the Sixties*, Doubleday, 1971; *The Making of Ashenden* (novella), Covent Garden Press, 1972; *Searches and Seizures: Three Short Novels*, Random House, 1973. Author of film scenario "The Six-year-old Man" (published in *Esquire*, December, 1968). Contributor to *Epoch*, *Views*, *Accent*, *Perspective*, *Chicago Review*, *Journal of English and Germanic Philology*, *Southwest Review*, *Esquire*, *Paris Review*, *Harper's*, *Oui*, and *Saturday Evening Post*. Stories appear in *Best American Short Stories*, 1962, 1963, and 1965.

Engerman, Stanley L., 1936–

Born March 14, 1936, in New York. Education: B.S., New York University, 1956, M.B.A., 1958; Ph.D., John Hopkins University, 1962.

Office: Department of Economics, University of Rochester, Rochester, New York, 14627.

Yale University, New Haven, Connecticut, assistant professor of economics, 1962–63; University of Rochester, Rochester, New York, assistant professor of economics, 1963–67, associate professor, 1967–71, professor of economics and history, 1971– . Member: American Economics Association, American Historical Association, Economic History Association.

(With Fogel) *The Reinterpretation of American Economic History*, Harper, 1971; *Time on the Cross*, Little, Brown, 1974; (with Genovese) *Race and Slavery in the Western Hemisphere*, Princeton University Press, 1974.

Fogel, Robert W., 1926–

Born July 1, 1926, in New York, New York. Education: A.B., Cornell University, 1948; A.M., Columbia University, 1960; Ph.D., Johns Hopkins University, 1963. Office: Department of Economics and History, Harvard University, 1737 Cambridge St., Cambridge, Massachusetts, 02138.

Johns Hopkins University, Baltimore, Maryland, instructor in economics, 1958–59; University of Rochester, Rochester, New York, assistant professor of economics, 1960–64; University of Chicago, Chicago, Illinois, associate professor, 1964–65; professor of economics and history, 1965–75; Harvard University, Cambridge, Massachusetts, professor of economics and history, 1975– , Taussig Research Professor, 1973–74. Ford Foundation visiting research professor at University of Chicago, 1963–64; professor of economics and history at University of Rochester, autumns, 1968–75; Pitt Professor of American History and Institutions at Cambridge University, 1975–76; centennial professor at Texas A & M University, 1976; Lecturer at dozens of schools in the United States, Australia, Belgium, Canada, France, Germany, England, Japan, Norway, Sweden, Scotland, the Soviet Union, Israel, Ireland, Denmark, and the Netherlands. Member of Mathematical Social Science Board, 1965–72.

American Academy of Arts and Sciences (fellow), National Academy of Sciences, American Association for the Advancement of Science (fellow), Econometric Society (fellow), Economic History Association (member of board of trustees, 1972– ; president, 1977–78), Royal Historical Society (fellow), Economic History Society (Glasgow; honorary vice-president, 1967), Columbia University Seminar in Economics and History (associate), Phi Beta Kappa. Awards, Honors: Social Science Research Council grant, 1966; grant from Mathematical Social Science Board, 1966; National Science Foundation grants, 1967, 1970, 1972, 1974,

1976, 1978; Fulbright grant, 1968; Arthur H. Cole Prize from Economic History Association, 1968; Ford Foundation fellowship, 1970; Schumpeter Prize from Harvard University, 1971; Bancroft Prize in American History from Columbia University, 1975.

The Union Pacific Railroad: A Case in Premature Enterprise, Johns Hopkins Press, 1960; *Railroads and American Economic Growth: Essays in Econometric History*, Johns Hopkins Press, 1964; (editor with S.L. Engerman, and contributor) *The Reinterpretation of American Economic History*, Harper, 1971; (editor with W.O. Aydelotte and A.G. Bogue, and contributor) *The Dimensions of Quantitative Research in History*, Princeton University Press, 1972; (with Engerman) *Time on the Cross: The Economics of American Negro Slavery*, Little, Brown, 1974. Also author of a Japanese book (title means "Ten Lectures on the New Economic History"), *Nan-un-do*, 1977.

Phillips, Ulrich Bonnell, 1877–1934

Born November 4, 1877, in LaGrange, Georgia. Education: A.B., University of Georgia, 1897, M.A., 1899; Ph.D., Columbia University, 1902, hon. Litt.D., 1929; hon. M.A., Yale University, 1929.

University of Georgia, fellow and tutor in history, 1897–1900; Columbia University, fellow, 1900–02; University of Wisconsin, instructor of history, 1902–07, assistant professor, 1907–08; Tulane University, professor of history and political science, 1908–11; University of Michigan, professor of American history, 1911–29; Yale University, professor of American history, 1929– . Albert Kahn fellow, toured around world and to central Africa, 1929–30. University of California, lecturer in American history, 1924. Camp Gordon, Georgia, educational director, Y.M.C.A., 1917–18; Captain, U.S.A., Military Intelligence, 1918–19.

Georgia and State Rights, 1902 (awarded Justin Winsor prize, American History Association, 1901); *History of Transportation in the Eastern Cotton Belt*, 1908; *Life of Robert Toombs*, 1913; *American Negro Slavery*, 1918; *Life and Labor in the Old South*, 1929 (awarded Little, Brown & Co. prize for best unpublished work on American history). Editor: *Plantation and Frontier Documents*, 1909; *The Correspondence of Robert Toombs, Alexander H. Stephens and Howell Cobb*, 1913; *Florida Plantation Records* (with James David Glunt), 1927.

Stampp, Kenneth M., 1912–

Born July 12, 1912, in Milwaukee, Wisconsin. Education: B.S., University of Wisconsin, 1935, M.A., 1937, Ph.D., 1942.

University of Arkansas, Fayetteville, instructor in history, 1941–42; University of Maryland, College Park, assistant professor, 1942–45, associate professor of history, 1945–46; University of California, Berkeley, assistant professor, 1946–49, associate professor, 1949–51, professor of history, 1951–57, Morrison Professor of American History, 1957– , research professor in humanities, 1965, Harvard University, visiting professor, 1955; University of Munich, Fulbright lecturer at Amerika-Institut, 1957; University of London, Commonwealth Fund lecturer in American History, 1960; Oxford University, Harmsworth Professor of American History, 1961–62. Summer lecturer at University of Wisconsin and University of Colorado. Thomas Y. Crowell Company (publishers), American history editor, 1960–70.

Membership in the American Historical Association, Society of American Historians, American Civil Liberties Union (member of board of directors, Berkeley chapter), National Association for the Advancement of Colored People, Mississippi Valley Historical Association, Southern Historical Association, Phi Beta Kappa, Awards, Honors; Guggenheim Fellow, 1952–53.

Indiana Politics During the Civil War, Indiana Historical Bureau, 1949; *And the War Came*, Louisiana State University Press, 1950; (contributor) *Problems in American History*, Prentice-Hall, 1952; *The Peculiar Institution*, Knopf, 1956; (editor) *The Causes of the Civil War*, Prentice-Hall, 1959; revised edition, 1974; (coauthor) *The National Experience*, Harcourt, 1963; revised edition, 1968; (editor) *The McGraw-Hill Illustrated World History*, McGraw, 1964; *The Era of Reconstruction*, 1865–1877, Knopf, 1965; (editor with Leon P. Litwack) *Reconstruction: An Anthology of Revisionist Writings*, Louisiana State University Press, 1969; contributor of articles to historical journals.

Bibliography

Aberbach, Joel D., and Walker, L. Jack. *Race in the City*. Boston: Little, Brown, 1973.

Ackerman, N.W. "Social Role and Total Personality." *American Journal of Orthopsychiatrics* 21 (January 1951): 1–17.

Adams, John E., and Kim Hyung. "A Fresh Look at Inter-country Adoptions." *Children*, 18 vols. September, 1971, Vol. 6.

Adorno, T.W.; Franket, Else; Levinson, Daniel J.; and Sanford, Nevitt. *The Authoritarian Personality*. New York: Harper and Bros., 1950.

Allen, James E. *The Negro in New York*. New York: Exposition Press, 1964.

Allen, William F. *Slave Songs of the United States*. New York: Simpson and Co., 1867.

Allport, Gordon W. *The Nature of Prejudice*. New York: Dover Publications, 1970.

Ames, Susie. *Studies of Virginia's Eastern Shore*. Richmond, Va.: Dietz Co., 1940.

Amory, Cleveland. *Who Killed Society?* New York: Harper and Row, 1960.

Anderson, David C. *Children of Special Value: Interracial Adoption in America*. New York: St. Martins Press, 1971.

Andrew, C.M. *The Colonial Period of American History*. New Haven, Conn.: Yale University Press, 1934–38.

Aptheker, Herbert. *American Negro Slave Revolts*. New York: Alfred A. Knopf, 1943.

_____. *American Negro Slave Revolts*. 2nd ed. New York: International Publishing Co., 1969.

_____. "Maroons Within the Present Limits of the United States." *Journal of Negro History* XXIV (April 1939): 217–223.

_____. *The Negro People in the United States*. New York: Citadel Press, 1975.

Arkansas Acts (1858–1859); (1859–1860) 99.

Asher, S., and Allen, V. "Racial Preference and Social Comparison Processes." *Journal of Social Issues* (January 1969): 157–165.

Badger, Edward C. *The Mulatto in the United States*, 1918. Boston: Gorham Press, 1918.

Bailey, Kenneth. *Southern White Protestantism in the Twentieth Century*. New York: Harper and Row, 1967.

Bailyn, Bernard. *The Ideological Origins of the American Revolution*. Cambridge, Mass.: Belknap Press of Harvard University Press, 1971.

Baker, Ray S. *Following the Color Line*. New York: Alfred A. Knopf, 1908.

Ball, Charles. *Fifty Years in Chains*. New York: Dover Publications, 1970.

Ballagh, James Curtis. *A History of Slavery in Virginia*. Baltimore: Johns Hopkins University Press, 1902.

Baltzell, E. *The Protestant Establishment: Aristocracy and Caste in America*. New York: Random House, 1964.

Bancroll, Frederick. *Slave Trading in the Old South*. Baltimore: J.H. Furst Co., 1937.

Bandon, Michael. "Africa South of Sahara." In *Comparative Perspectives on Race Relations*, edited by Melvin Tumin. Boston: Little, Brown, 1969.

Banks, James. *Black Self Concept: Implication for Education and Social Science*. New York: McGraw-Hill, 1972.

Banks, William L. *The Black Church in the United States*. Chicago: Moody Press, 1971.

Barber, Bernard. *Social Stratification*. New York: Harcourt, Brace and World, 1957.

Barnes, Albert. *An Inquiry into the Scriptural Views of Slavery*. Philadelphia: Perkins and Purves, 1847.

Barnet, Ida Wells. "Our Country's Lynch Record." *Survey* XXIV (January 1913): 220–231.

Barraclough, Geoffrey. *An Introduction to Contemporary History*. New York: Basic Books, 1964.

Barry, Mary Frances. *Black Resistance/White Law*. Englewood Cliffs, N.J.: Prentice-Hall, 1971.

Bassett, John Spenser. *Slavery and Servitude in the Colony of North Carolina*. Baltimore: Johns Hopkins University Press, 1896.

Bastide, Roger. *African Civilizations in the New World*. New York: Harper and Row, 1971.

Bauer, Raymond and Alice. "Day to Day Resistance to Slavery." *Journal of Negro History* XXVII (October 1942): 388–419.

Bell, Daniel. "On Mediocrity and Equality." *The Public Interest* 29 (Fall 1972): 29–68.

Bell, Derrick A. *Race, Racism and American Law*. Boston: Little, Brown, 1973.

Belluski, Jewel, and David, M. Stephen. *Race and Politics in New York City*. New York: Praeger, 1971.

Bendyshe, Thomas. *The Anthropological Treatise of John Fredrich Blumbac*. London: Routledge & Kegan Paul, 1965.

Benedict, Ruth. *Race Science and Politics*. New York: Modern Age Books, 1940.

Bennett, Lerone, Jr. *Before the Mayflower: A History of Negro America 1619–1964*. New York: Penguin, 1962.

_____. *Confrontation: Black and White*. Baltimore: Penguin, 1968.

Berger, Peter L. *The Sacred Canopy: Elements of a Sociological Theory of Religion*. New York: Doubleday, 1969.

Bergman, Peter M. *The Chronological History of the Negro in America*. New York: Harper and Row, 1969.

Berlin, Ira. *Slaves Without Masters: The Free Negro in the Antebellum South*. New York: Pantheon Press, 1975.

Berlyne, D.E. *Conflict, Arousal and Curiosity*. New York: McGraw-Hill, 1960.

Bettelheim, Bruno. "Individual and Mass Behavior in Extreme Situations." *Journal of Abnormal Psychology* XXXVIII (October 1943): 424–439.

Billingsley, Andrew. "Black Children in White Families." *Social Work*, 13 vols. (October 1968), Vol. 4.

_____. *Black Families in White America*. Englewood Cliffs, N.J.: Prentice-Hall, 1968.

Blassingame, John W. *Black New Orleans, 1860–1880*. Chicago: University of Chicago Press, 1980.

_____. *The Slave Community in New York*. New York: Oxford University Press, 1972.

Blaunor, Robert. "'Black Culture' Myth or Reality?" In *Afro-American Anthropology: Contemporary Perspectives on Theory and Research*, edited by Norman Whitten, Jr. and John Szwed. New York: Free Press, 1970.

Bloch, Herbert A. *Disorganization*. New York: Alfred A. Knopf, 1952.

Bond, Horace M. *The Education of the Negro in the American Social Order*. New York: Prentice-Hall, 1934.

_____. "Social and Economic Forces in Alabama." *Journal of Negro History* I (November 1938): 103–112.

Bore, Robert A. *The Negro Novel in America*. New Haven, Conn.: Yale University Press, 1965.

Bossard, James H.S., and Ball, S. Eleanor. *Ritual in Family Living*. Philadelphia: University of Pennsylvania Press, 1950.

Bourne, George. *A Condensed Anti-Slavery Bible Argument*. New York: S.W. and Co., 1845.

_____. *Picture of Slavery in the United States of America*. Middletown, Conn.: Edwin Hunt, 1834.

Bovill, E.W. *The Golden Trades of the Moors*, 2nd ed. London: Oxford University Press, 1970.

Bredemier, Harry, and Toby, Jackson. *Social Problems in America: Cost and Casualties in an Inquisitive Society*. New York: Wiley, 1960.

Brody, Eugene B. "Social Conflict and Schizophrenic Behavior in Young Adult Negro Males." *Psychiatry*, November 1961, pp. 337–345.

Brown, John. *Slave Life in Georgia: A Narrative of the Life, Sufferings, and Escape of John Brown, a Fugitive Slave, Now Living in England*. London: Routledge & Kegan Paul, 1965.

Brown, Sterling. "Negro Character as Seen Through White Authors." *Journal of Negro Education* (April 1933): 200–211.

Burma, John H. "The Measurement of Negro's Passing." *American Journal of Sociology* LII (July 1946): 18–22.

Cable, George. *The Negro Question*. New York: Oxford University Press, 1955.

Cantril, H. *Tensions That Cause Wars*. Urbana: University of Illinois Press, 1950.

Carmichael, Stokely, and Hamilton, Charles V. *Black Power: The Politics of Liberation in America*. New York: Random House, 1967.

Carrol, Charles. *The Negro ... A Beast or in the Image of God*. Savannah: Thunderbolt Press, 1938.

Carroll, Joseph C. *Slave Insurrections in the United States 1800–1860*. Boston: Little, Brown, 1966.

Cash, W.J. *The Mind of the South*. New York: Alfred A. Knopf, 1941.

Catteral, Helen T. *Judicial Cases Concerning American Slavery and the Negro*. New York: Negro Universities Press, 1968.

Cheever, George B. *The Guilt of Slavery and the Crime of Slaveholding*. Boston: R.F. Wallcut, 1952.

Christian, Boyd. "The Adaptive Functions of Ashanti Priesthood." In *Continuity and Change in African Culture*, edited by William R. Bascom and Melville J. Herskovits. Chicago: University of Chicago Press, 1959.

Clark, Kenneth B. *Dark Ghetto*. New York: Harper and Row, 1967.

_____. *Prejudice and Your Child*. Boston: Beacon Press, 1967.

Clarkson, Thomas. *History of the Rise and Progress and Accomplishment of the Abolition of the African Slave by the British Parliament*. Philadelphia: James P. Parke, 1808.

Clayton, Horace. *Long Lonely Road*. New York: Trident Press, 1965.

Cleage, Albert B., Jr. *The Black Messiah*. New York: Shead and Ward, 1968.

Cleaver, Eldridge. *Soul on Ice*. New York: Dell Delta Books, 1968.

Cobb, Thomas R.R. *An Inquiry into the Laws of Negro Slavery in the United States of America*. Philadelphia: T. and J.W. Johnson, 1958.

Cohen, Elie. *Human Behavior in the Concentration Camp*. New York: W.W. Norton, 1953.

Coles, Robert. *Children of Crisis*. Boston: Little, Brown, 1964.

_____. "It's the Same but It's Different." In *The Negro American*, edited by Talcott Parsons and Kenneth B. Clark. Boston: Houghton Mifflin, 1966.

Collins, W.H. *The Domestic Slave Trade of the Southern States*. New York: Alfred A. Knopf, 1904.

Conrad, Alfred H. and Meyer, R. John. *The Economics of Slavery and Other Studies*. Chicago: Aldine Press, 1964.

Coon, Carlton. *The Living Race of Man*. New York: Alfred A. Knopf, 1965.

_____; Carn, Stanley M.; and Birdsell, Joseph B. *Race: A Study of the Problem of Race Formation in Man*. New York: W.W. Norton, 1950.

Cox, Harvey. *The Secular City*. New York: Macmillan, 1965.

Craven, Avery O. "Poor Whites and Negroes in the Antebellum South." *Journal of Negro History* XV (January 1930): 17–18.

Cronnon, Edmund D. *Black Moses*. Madison: University of Wisconsin Press, 1955.

Cruden, Robert. "James F. Rhodes and the Negro: A Study in the Problem of Objectivity." In *Understanding Negro History*, edited by Dwight W. Hover. Chicago: Quadrangle Books, 1969.

Cruse, Harold. *The Crisis of the Negro Intellectuals*. New York: Morrow, 1967.

Curtin, Phillip D. *The Atlantic Slave Trade*. Madison: University of Wisconsin Press, 1969.

_____. "The Black Experience and Imperialism." *Daedalus* (Spring 1974): 17–28.

Dahrendorf, Ralf. *Class and Class Conflict in Industrial Society*. Stanford, Calif.: Stanford University Press, 1966.

Davis, Arthur P., and Sanders, Redding. *Cavalcade: Negro American Writers from 1760 to the Present*. New York: Houghton Mifflin, 1971.

Davis, Charles. *The Cotton Kingdom in Alabama*. Montgomery: Alabama State Department of Archives and History, 1939.

Davis, David B. *The Problem of Slavery in the Age of Revolution*. Ithaca, N.Y.: Cornell University Press, 1975.

_____. *The Problem of Slavery in Western Thought*. Ithaca, N.Y.: Cornell University Press, 1969.

_____. "Slavery and the Post-War Historian." *Daedalus* (Spring 1974): 4–9.

Davis, John. *The Negro Reference Book*. Englewood Cliffs, N.J.: Prentice-Hall, 1966.

Day, Clive. *The Policy and Administration of the Dutch in Java*. New York: Macmillan, 1904.

Degler, Carl. *Neither Black Nor White*. New York: Macmillan, 1971.

_____. *Out of Our Past: The Forces That Shaped Modern American Life*. New York: Macmillan, 1959.

Deutsch, Martin. *The Disadvantaged Child*. New York: Basic Books, 1967.

Dobzhansky, Theodosius. "The Genetic Nature of Differences Among Men." In *Evolutionary Thought in America*, edited by Stow Parsons. New Haven, Conn.: Yale University Press, 1950.

Dollar, John. *Caste and Class in a Southern Town*. New York: Harper, 1937.

Donnan, Elizabeth. *Documents Illustrative of the History of the Slave Trade to America*. Washington, D.C.: Carnegie Institute Publications N 409, 1930–1935.

Donovan, John C. *The Politics of Poverty*. New York: Pegasus Publications, 1967.

Douglass, Frederick. *Narrative of the Life of Frederick Douglass: An American Slave, 1945*. New York: New American Library, 1968.

Dousenberry, J.S. "Some Aspects of the Theory of Economic Development." *Exploration in Entrepreneural History* III (1850): 9–12.

Drake, St. Clair. "Anthropology and the Black Experience." *The Black Scholar*, September/October 1980, pp. 6–17.

_____, and Clayton, Horace. *Black Metropolis*. Vol. 1: *A Study of Negro Life in a Northern City*. New York: Harcourt, Brace and World, 1945.

Driver, S.R. *A Critical and Exegetical Commentary on Deuteronomy*. New York: Oxford University Press, 1948.

Dubin, L.E.; Lotka, A.J.; and Spiegelman, M. *Length of Life*. New York: Ronald Co., 1949.

Du Bois, W.E.B. *The College Bred Negro*. Atlanta: University of Atlanta Press, 1900.

_____. *The Philadelphia Negro*. New York: Schocken Books, 1976.

_____. *Slavery in the Construction of American Politics*. New York: New American Library, 1969.

_____. "Some Facts in the Development of Negro Social Institutions." *American Journal of Sociology* (July 1938): 403–413.

_____. *The World and Africa*. New York: Farrar and Rinehart, 1942.

_____, and Washington, Booker T. *The Negro in the South*. Northbrook, Ill.: Metro Books, 1972.

Duff, John B., and Mitchell, Peter B. *The Nat Turner Rebellion: The Historical Event and the Modern Controversy*. New York: Alfred A. Knopf, 1971.

Duhl, Leonard J. *The Urban Condition*. New York: Basic Books, 1963.

Durkheim, Emile. *Elementary Forms of Religious Life*. Garden City, N.Y.: Doubleday Anchor, 1954.

Dye, Thomas R. *The Politics of Equality*. Indianapolis: Bobbs-Merrill, 1971.

Eckard, E.W. "How Many Negroes Pass." *American Journal of Sociology* LII (May 1947): 498–500.

Edwards, Bryan. *The History, Civil and Commercial of the British Colonies in the West Indies*. (1819). New York: AMS.

Elkins, Stanley M. *Slavery: A Problem in American Institutional and Intellectual Life*. Chicago: University of Chicago Press, 1968.

Erikson, Erik H. *Identity and the Life Cycle*. New York: W.W. Norton, 1980.

Falconbridge, Alexander. *An Account of the Slave Trade on the Coast of Africa*. London: J. Phillips, 1929.

Fanon, Frantz. *The Wretched of the Earth*. New York: Grove Press, 1963.

Farley, Reynolds. *Growth of the Black Population*. Chicago: Markham, 1970.

Fenichel, O. *The Psychoanalytic Theory of Neurosis*. New York: W.W. Norton, 1945.

Finley, I. *The World of Odysseus*. New York: Meridian Paperback, 1959.

Fisk Collection. *Unwritten History of Slavery: Autobiographical Accounts of Negro Ex-slaves*. Nashville, Tenn.: Social Science Institute, Fisk University, 1945.

Flanders, Ralph B. *Plantation Slavery in Georgia*. Chapel Hill: University of North Carolina Press, 1933.

Fogel, Robert, and Engleman, Stanley. *Time on the Cross: The Economics of American Negro Slavery*. Boston: Little, Brown, 1974.

Foner, Phillips S. *W.E.B. Du Bois Speaks*. New York: Pathfinder Press, 1970.

Fortune, Thomas T. *Black and White: Land, Labor, and Politics in the South*. D. Appleton, 1884.

Foster, William E. *The Negro Problem in American History*. New York: International Publishers, 1978.

Franklin, John Hope. *Color and Race*. Boston: Houghton Mifflin, 1968.

_____. *The Free Negro in North Carolina*. Chapel Hill: University of North Carolina Press, 1943.

_____. *From Slavery to Freedom: A History of Negro America*. New York: Alfred A. Knopf, 1974.

_____. "Jim Crow Goes to School: The Genesis of Legal Segregation." Atlanta: *South Atlantic Quarterly* LVIII (Spring 1965): 403–411.

_____. *Reconstruction After the Civil War*. Chicago: University of Chicago Press, 1961.

Frazier, E. Franklin. *Black Bourgeoisie*. New York: Macmillan, 1968.

_____. *The Negro Church in America*. New York: Schocken Books, 1973.

_____. *The Negro Family in the United States*. Chicago: University of Chicago Press, 1967.

Frederickson, G. *The Black Image in the White Mind*. New York: Harper and Row, 1971.

Freire, Paulo. *Pedagogy of the Oppressed*. New York: Seabury Press, 1968.

Freud, Sigmund. *Moses and Monotheism*. New York: Alfred A. Knopf, 1939.

_____. *The Psychopathology of Everyday Life*. New York: Macmillan, 1914.

Freyer, Gilberto. *The Masters and the Slaves*. New York: Alfred A. Knopf, 1946.

Fromm, Erich. *The Heart of Man*. New York: D. Appleton, 1966.

Gara, Larry. "A New Englander's View of Plantation Life: Letters of Edwin Hall to Cyrus Woodman, 1837." *Journal of Southern History* XVIII (1952): 471–9.

Garrison, William L. *Selections from the Writings and Speeches of William L. Garrison*. New York: New American Library, 1969.

Garvey, Marcus. *Philosophy and Opinions of Marcus Garvey*. New York: Atheneum Press, 1974.

Genovese, Eugene D. *Roll, Jordan, Roll*. New York: Pantheon Books, 1974.

_____. *The World the Slaveholders Made: Two Essays in Interpretation*. New York: Pantheon Books, 1969.

Geschwender, James A. *Racial Stratification in America*. Dubuque, Iowa: William C. Brown, 1978.

Gipson, Lawrence H. "Crime and Its Punishment in Provincial Pennsylvania: A

Phase of Social History of the Commonwealth." *Pennsylvania History* 2 (1935): 3–16.

Glass, Bentley. *Genes and the Man*. New York: Columbia University Press, 1943.

Glazer, Nathan, and Moynihan, Daniel P. *Beyond the Melting Pot*. Cambridge, Mass.: Harvard University Press, 1963.

Glazer, Nathan, and Moynihan, Daniel P., eds. *Ethnicity: Theory and Experience*. Cambridge, Mass.: Harvard University Press, 1975.

Goffman, Irving. *Behavior in Public Places*. New York: Free Press, 1963.

Gomer, James P. "Individual Development and Black Rebellion: Some Parallels." *Midway* (January 1968): 33–48.

Goodell, William. *The American Slave Code in Theory and Practice*. New York: New American Library, 1969.

Gordon, Milton M. *Assimilation in American Life*. New York: Oxford University Press, 1964.

_____. "Towards a General Theory of Racial and Ethnic Relations." In *Ethnicity: Theory and Experience*, edited by Nathan Glazer and Daniel P. Moynihan. Cambridge, Mass.: Harvard University Press, 1975.

Grant, Loanne R. *Citizens in a Race with Time*. New York: Fawcett, 1968.

Greeley, Andrew M. *Why Can't They Be Like Us?* New York: E.P. Dutton, 1971.

Greenberg, Jack. *Race Relations and American Law*. New York: Columbia University Press, 1959.

Greene, Lorenzo J. "Mutiny on the Slave Ships." *Phylon* V Fourth Quarter (1944): 71–83.

_____. *The Negro in Colonial New England 1620–1776*. New York; Columbia University Press, 1942.

Grinker, Roy R., and Spiegel, P. John. *Men Under Stress*. New York: McGraw-Hill, 1945.

Guild, June Purcell. *Black Laws of Virginia*. New York: Negro Universities Press, 1969.

Halasz, Nicholas. *Rattling Chains: Slave Unrest and Revolts in the Antebellum South*. New York: Harper and Bros., 1966.

Handlin, Oscar, and Handlin, F. Mary. "Origins of Southern Labor System." *William and Mary Quarterly* 2nd Series VII (April 1950): 199–222.

Handlin, Oscar. *Fire Balls in the Night: The Crisis in Civil Rights*. Boston: Little, Brown, 1964.

_____. *Race and Nationality in American Life*. Garden City, N.Y.: Doubleday, 1957.

Harris, Julian H. *The Biology of the Negro*. Chicago: University of Chicago Press, 1942.

Harrison, Andrienne M. "Color, Class and Consciousness." *The Black Scholar*, Fall 1973, pp. 57–60.

Hart, Collin L. "The New Negro." *Independent*, January 1921, pp. 19–24.

Hay, M. *The Foot of Pride*. Boston: Beacon Press, 1950.

Haywood, Duncan Clinch. *Seed from Madagascar*. Chapel Hill: University of North Carolina Press, 1937.

Hendrik, John. *William Styron's Nat Turner: Ten Black Writers Respond*. Boston: Beacon Press, 1958.

Hening, William Walter. *The Statutes at Large; Being a Collection of All the Laws of Virginia 1619–1792*. 13 vols. Richmond: n.p., 1809–1823.

Henry, Jules. *Culture Against Man*. New York: Vintage Books, 1963.

Herskovitz, Melville J. *The American Negro*. New York: Alfred A. Knopf, 1928.

_____. *Dahomey: An Ancient West African Kingdom*. New York: Macmillan, 1938.

_____. *The Myth of the Negro Past*. Boston: Beacon Press, 1967.

Herton, Calvin H. *Sex and Racism in America*. Garden City, N.Y.: Doubleday, 1956.

Higginbotham, Leon, Jr. *In the Matter of Color: Race and the Legal Process, the Colonial Period*. New York: Oxford University Press, 1978.

_____. "A Tragic Conception of Negro History." In *Understanding Negro History*, edited by Dwight W. Hoover. Chicago: Quadrangle Books, 1968.

Hill, James D. "Some Economic Aspects of Slavery, 1850–1860." *South Atlantic Quarterly* XXVI (1929): 161–177.

Hoffman, Frederick L. *Race Traits and Tendencies of the American Negro*. New York: Macmillan, 1896.

Hofstadter, Richard. *The Progressive Historian*. New York: Alfred A. Knopf, 1968.

_____. "U.B. Phillips and the Plantation Legend." *Journal of Negro History* XXIX (April 1941): 109–124.

Holmes, S.J. *The Negro's Struggle for Survival*. Berkeley: University of California Press, 1937.

Horkheimer, Max. "Authority and the Family." In *The Family Past and Present*, edited by Bernard Stern. New York: D. Appleton-Century, 1938.

Hraba, J., and Grant, G. "Black Is Beautiful: A Re-examination of Racial Preference and Identification." *Journal of Psychology* (January 1977): 388–402.

Huggins, Matthew I. *Harlem Renaissance*. New York: Grove Press, 1971.

Hughes, Lanston; Meltzer, Milton; and Lincoln, Eric C. *A Pictorial History of Black America*. New York: Crown, 1975.

Hurd, John C. *The Law of Freedom and Bondage in the United States*. Boston: Little, Brown, 1858.

Inikori, J.E. "Measuring the Atlantic Slave Trade." *Journal of African History* 17 (1976): 192–223.

Isaac, Harold. *The New World of Negro Americans*. New York: John Day, 1963.

Jackson, Luther R. *Free Negro Holdings and Property Holdings in Virginia 1830–1860*. New York: D. Appleton-Century-Crofts, 1942.

_____. "Religious Development of the Negro in Virginia from 1760–1860." *Journal of Negro History* XVI (1931): 206.

Jenning, H.S. *The Biological Basis of Human Nature*. New York: W.W. Norton, 1930.

Johnson, Charles F. *The Shadow of the Plantation*. Chicago: University of Chicago Press, 1934.

Johnson, James Weldon. "The Dilemma of the Negro Author." *American Mercury*, December 1928, pp. 14–21.

Jones, Charles Colock. *Suggestions on the Religious Instruction of Negroes in the Southern States*. Philadelphia: Westminster Press, 1847.

Jones, Reginald J. *Black Psychology*. New York: Harper and Row, 1980.

Jordan, Winthrop. "American Chiaroscuro: The Status and Definition of the Mulatto in the British Colonies." *William and Mary Quarterly* XXIX (April 1962): 201–238.

_____. *White Over Black: American Attitudes Towards the Negro 1550–1812*. Chapel Hill: University of North Carolina Press, 1968.

Kardiner, Abram. *The Individual and His Society*. New York: Columbia University Press, 1939.

_____, and Ovesey, Lionel. *The Mark of Oppression: Explorations in the Personality of the American Negro*. Cleveland: World, 1951.

Katz, William L. *Eyewitness: The Negro in American History*. New York: Pitman, 1967.

Kelsey, George D. *Racism and the Christian Understanding of Man*. New York: Scribner, 1965.

Kennedy, Frank Louis Venable. *The Negro Peasant Turned Cityward*. New York: Columbia University Press, 1930.

Keth, Thomas J. "The Double Standard." *Journal of the History of Ideas* (1959): 302–311.

Kind, Woodie, and Lilner, Ron. *Black Drama: An Anthology*. New York: New American Library, 1971.

King, Martin Luther, Jr. *Where Do We Go from Here?* Boston: Beacon Press, 1968.

Klineberg, Otto. *Characteristics of the American Negro*. New York: Harper and Bros., 1944.

Kogen, Eugene. *The Theory and Practice of Hell*. New York: Farrar, Straus, 1946.

Konvitz, Milton R. *A Century of Civil Rights*. New York: Alfred A. Knopf, 1951.

Lander, Joyce A. *Mixed Families: Adopting Across Racial Boundaries*. Garden City, N.Y.: Anchor Books, 1978.

Lane, Ann J. *The Debate Over Slavery: Stanley Elkins and His Critics*. Urbana: University of Illinois Press, 1971.

Langness, L.L. *The Study of Culture*. San Francisco: Chandler and Sharp, 1974.

Lengyel, Olga. *Five Chimneys: The Story of Auschwitz*. Chicago: Free Press, 1947.

Lerner, Max. *America as a Civilization*. New York: Simon & Schuster, 1961.

Levine, Lawrence W. *Black Culture and Black Consciousness*. New York: Oxford University Press, 1977.

Lewis, W.A. *Theory of Economic Growth*. Homewood, Ill.: Irwin, 1958.

Lieberson, Stanley. "The Impact of Residential Segregation on Ethnic Assimilation." *Social Form*, October 1961, pp. 52–57.

Liebow, Elliot. *Talley's Corner: A Study of Negro Street Corner Men*. Boston: Little, Brown, 1967.

Lincoln, C. Eric. *The Black Church Since Frazier*. New York: Schocken Books, 1974.

Linton, Ralph. *The Individual and His Society*. New York: Columbia University Press, 1939.

Lipset, Seymour Martin. "Changing Social Status and Prejudice: The Race Theories of a Pioneering American Sociologist." *Commentary*, May 1950, pp. 475–479.

Little, Franklin H. *From State Church to Pluralism: A Protestant Interpretation of Religion in America*. New York: Anchor Books, 1962.

Litwak, John T. *The Desolate South*. New York: Meredith Press, 1956.

Locke, Alain. *The New Negro Writer: An Interpretation*. New York: Harper and Row, 1925.

Lovejoy, Arthur O. *The Great Chain of Being: A Study of the History of Ideas*. New York: Harper Torchbook, 1960.

Lowe, Jeanne. *Cities in a Race with Time*. New York: Random House, 1967.

Lynch, L.G. *The Formation of the Negro*. New York: Carlton Press, 1963.

McLoughlin, William, and Jordan, Winthrop D. "Baptists Face the Barbarities of Slavery in 1710." *Journal of Southern History* 29 (1963): 495–501.

McManus, Edgar. *Black Bondage in the North*. Syracuse, N.Y.: Syracuse University Press, 1970.

Malcolm X. *Autobiography of Malcolm X*. New York: Grove Press, 1965.

Mann, Arthur. *The Progressive Era: Liberal Renaissance or Liberal Failure*. New York: Holt, Rinehart and Winston, 1965.

Marden, Charles, and Meyer, Gladys. *Minorities in American Society*. New York: D. Van Nostrand Co., 1973.

Maritaini, J. *A Christian Look at the Jewish Question*. New York: Longman, Green, 1939.

Mason, Phillip. *Race Relations*. New York: Oxford University Press, 1970.

May, Henry F. *The End of American Innocence*. New York: Alfred A. Knopf, 1959.

Mays, Benjamin E. *The Negro's God as Reflected in His Literature*. New York: Atheneum, 1968.

Mead, George Herbert. *Mind, Self and Society*. Chicago: University of Chicago Press, 1934.

Mead, Margaret. *Childhood in Contemporary Cultures*. New York: Columbia University Press, 1950.

Meltzer, Milton. *In Their Own Words: A History of the Negro American, 1619–1865*. New York: Thomas Y. Crowell, 1964.

_____. *In Their Own Words: A History of the Negro American, 1865–1919*. New York: Thomas Y. Crowell, 1965.

_____. *In Their Own Words: A History of the Negro American, 1919–1965*. New York: Thomas Y. Crowell, 1967.

Mendelsohn, Isaac. *Slavery in the Ancient Near East: A Comparative Study of Slavery in Babylonia, Assyria, Syria, and Palestine from the Middle of the Third Millennium to the End of the First Millennium*. New York: Alfred A. Knopf, 1949.

Mier, August. *Negro Thought in 1880–1896*. Ann Arbor: University of Michigan Press, 1963.

Mintz, Sidney W., and Price, Richard. *An Anthropological Approach to the Afro-American Past*. Philadelpia: Institute for the Study of Human Issues, 1976.

Montague, William Cobb. "Physical Anthropology of the American Negro." *American Journal of Physical Anthropology* 29 (1942): 158–169.

Montague, M.F. Ashley. *Man's Most Dangerous Myth: The Fallacy of Race*. Cleveland: World, 1964.

Moor, A.B. "Railroad Building in Alabama during Reconstruction." *Journal of Southern History* I (November 1930): 311–319.

Moore, George H. *Notes on Slavery in Massachusetts*. New York: Negro University Press, 1968.

Moore, Wilbert E. *Social Change*. Englewood Cliffs, N.J.: Prentice-Hall, 1964.

Morgan, Edmond S. *American Slavery, American Freedom: The Ordeal of Colonial Virginia*. New York: W.W. Norton, 1975.

Morton, Robert. *Social Theory and Social Structure*. Glencoe, Ill.: Free Press, 1957.

Moynihan, Daniel P. *Feasible Misunderstanding*. New York: Free Press, 1969.

Munford, Beverly B. *Virginia Attitudes Towards Slavery and Secession*. New York: Longman, Green, 1834.

Murry, Lauli. *Proud Shoes: The Story of an American Family*. New York: Harper and Row, 1956.

Myrdal, Gunnar. *An American Dilemma: The Negro and Modern Democracy*. New York: Harper and Bros., 1944.

Newby, I.A. *Jim's Crow's Defense: Anti-Negro Thought in America 1900–1913*. Baton Rouge: University of Louisiana Press, 1913.

New Jersey Acts (1704): 18–20.

North Carolina Statutes (1750) XXIII, 506–509.

Novak, Michael. *The Rise of the Unmeltable Ethnics*. New York: Macmillan, 1972.

Ogburn, William F. *On Culture and Social Change: Selected Papers*. Chicago: University of Chicago Press, 1964.

Oliver, Douglas L. *The Pacific Islands*. Cambridge, Mass.: Harvard University Press, 1951.

Olmsted, Frederick Law. *The Cotton Kingdom*. 2 vols. New York: Random House, 1961.

_____. *A Journey in the Back Country* (1860). New York: Schocken, 1970.

Otis, James. "The Rights of the British Colonies Asserted and Proved." *Bailyn's Pamphlets*, Vol. 1, p. 437.

Otley, Roy, and Weatherby, J. William. *The Negro in New York*. New York: New York Public Library, 1967.

Packard, Vance. *The Status Seekers*. New York: David McKay, 1959.

Parks, Mungo. *The Travels of Mungo Parks*. New York: Everyman's Library, 1928.

Parks, Robert E. "The Conflict and Fusion of Cultures." *Journal of Negro History* IV (April 1920): 117–120.

_____. *Race and Culture*. Glencoe, Ill.: Free Press, 1950.

Parsons, Talcott. *The Social System*. Glencoe, Ill.: Free Press, 1951.

_____, and Clark, Kenneth. *The Negro American*. Boston: Houghton Mifflin, 1966.

Pennington, James W.C. *The Fugitive Blacksmith: Or Events in the History of James W.C. Pennington, Pastor of a Presbyterian Church, Formerly a Slave in the State of Maryland*. Westport, Conn.: Negro Universities Press, 1971.

Pennsylvania Statutes (1700) II, 79.

Percy, W. "Symbol, Consciousness and Intersubjectivity." *Journal of Philosophy* (1958): 631–632.

Pettigrew, Thomas. *A Profile of Negro America*. Princeton, N.J.: D. Van Nostrand, 1964.

Phillips, Arthur. *Survey of African Marriage and Family Life*. London: Routledge & Kegan Paul, 1953.

Phillips, Ulrich B. *American Negro Slavery: A Survey of the Supply, Employment, and Control of Negro Labor as Determined by the Plantation Regime*. New York: D. Appleton, 1918.

_____. "The Economic Cost of Slaveholding in the Cotton Belt." *Political Science Quarterly* XX (1950): 257–275.

_____. *Life and Labor in the Old South*. Boston: Little, Brown, 1935.

Pinkney, Alphonso. *Black Americans*. Englewood Cliffs, N.J.: Prentice-Hall, 1969.

Pinson, William, and Fant, Claude. *Contemporary Christian Trends*. Waco, Texas: Word Books, 1972.

Poloski, Harry A., and Marr II, Warren. *The Negro Almanac: A Reference Work on the Afro-American*. New York: Bellwether Co., 1976.

Porter, Kenneth W. "Relations Between Negroes and Indians Within the Present Limits of the United States." *Journal of Negro History* XVII (July 1921): 287–367.

Pouissant, A. "Building a Strong Self-Image in the Black Child." In *Readings in Early Childhood Education*. New Haven, Conn.: Duskin Publishers, 1977.

Powermaker, Hortense. *After Freedom*. New York: Atheneum Press, 1969.

Price, Grenfell A. *White Settlers and Native People*. Cambridge, Mass.: Harvard University Press, 1950.

Quarles, Benjamin. *The Negro in the American Revolution*. New York: W.W. Norton, 1973.

————. *The Negro in the Making of America*. New York: Collier-Macmillan, 1969.

Quillen, Frank U. *The Color Line in Ohio*. Ann Arbor: University of Michigan Press, 1913.

Raboteau, Albert J. *Slave Religion: The Invisible Institution in the Antebellum South*. New York: Oxford University Press, 1978.

Ramsdell, Charles W. "The Material Limits of Slavery Expansion." *Mississippi Valley Historical Review* XVI (1929): 151–171.

Raper, Auther. *The Tragedy of Lynching*. Chapel Hill: University of North Carolina Press, 1933.

Rattay, R.S. *Ashanti Law and Constitution*. Oxford: Clarendon Press, 1929.

Rawick, George P. *The American Slave: A Composite Autobiography*. 41 vols. Westport, Conn.: Greenwood, 1972.

Redding, J. Saunders. "The Negro Writer: Shadow and Substance." *Phylon* (Fourth Quarter 1950): 11–18.

Robinson, Donald L. *Slavery in the Structure of American Politics, 1765–1820*. New York: Harcourt Brace Jovanovich, 1971.

Rogers, Carl R. *On Becoming a Person*. Boston: Houghton Mifflin, 1961.

Rosenberg, Bruce. *The Art of American Folk Preaching*. New York: Oxford University Press, 1970.

Ruether, Rosemary. *Liberation Theology*. New York: Paulist Press, 1972.

Russel, John H. *The Free Negro in Virginia*. Baltimore: Johns Hopkins University Press, 1913.

Russel, Robert R. "The General Effects of Slavery Upon Southern Economic Progress." *Journal of Southern History* IV (February 1933): 34–54.

Saenger, G. *The Social Psychology of Prejudice: Achieving Intercultural Understanding and Cooperation in a Democracy*. New York: Harper, 1953.

Sargent, William. *Battle for the Mind*. London: Pan Books, 1963.

Sellers, James B. *Slavery in Alabama*. University: University of Alabama Press, 1956.

Settle, E. Ophelia. "Slave Attitudes During the Slave Regime: Household Servants Versus Field Hands." *Publications of the Sociological Society* XXVII (1934).

Shank, Allen. *Political Power and the Urban Crisis*. Boston: Holbrook Press, 1969.

Shepperson, George. "Notes on Negro American Influence on the Emergence of African Nationalism." *Journal of African History* No. 2 (1960): 489–503.

Shils, Edward. "Color and the Universal Intellectual Community, and the Afro-Asian Intellectuals." *Daedalus* (Spring 1967): 279–295.

Silberman, Charles E. *Crisis in Black and White*. New York: Random House, 1964.

Smith, Cooper S. "Self-Concept, Race and Education." In *Race and Education Across Cultures*, edited by Gajenda and Bayley. London: Heinemann Educational Books, 1975.

Smith, Edwin W. *Knowing the African*. London: Lutterworth Press, 1947.

Smith, Lillian. *Killers of Dreams*. New York: W.W. Norton, 1961.

Sontag, Frederick, and Roth, John K. *The American Religious Experience: Roots, Trends, and Future of Theology*. New York: Harper and Row, 1972.

Sorokin, P.A. *Forms and Techniques of Altruistic and Spiritual Growth*. Boston: Beacon Press, 1954.

South Carolina Statutes (1969) VII, 360.

Stampp, Kenneth M. *The Peculiar Institution: Slavery in the Ante-Bellum South.* New York: Alfred A. Knopf, 1956.

Steward, Austin. *Twenty-Two Years a Slave, and Forty Years a Freeman.* Rochester, N.Y.: Allings and Cory, 1857.

Stone, Alfred H. "The Cotton Factorage System of the Southern States." *American Historical Review* XX (1915): 557–565.

Stryker, Sheldon. "Social Structure and Prejudice." *Social Problems* (Spring 1959): 340–353.

Stuckey, Robert P. "African Ancestry of White American Population." *Ohio Journal of Science* (May 1958): 155–156.

Styron, William. *The Confessions of Nat Turner.* New York: Viking Press, 1964.

Sydnor, Charles. "Life Span of Mississippi Slaves." *American Historical Review* XXXV (April 1930): 556–574.

————. *Slavery in Mississippi.* New York: D. Appleton, 1933.

Taeuber, Karl E., and Taeuber, Alma F. *Negroes in Cities.* Chicago: Aldine, 1965.

Tannenbaum, Frank. *Slave and Citizen.* New York: Alfred A. Knopf, 1946.

Tarde, Gabriel. *The Laws of Imitation.* New York: Parsons Publications, 1803.

Taylor, Rosser H. *Slaveholding in North Carolina: An Economic View.* Chapel Hill: University of North Carolina Press, 1923.

Thomas, Keth J. "The Double Standard." *Journal of the History of Ideas* 20 (1959): 195–216.

de Tocqueville, Alex. *Democracy in America.* New York: Schocken Books, 1964.

Toffler, Alvin. *Future Shock.* New York: Random House, 1970.

Turner, Edward R. *The Negro in Pennsylvania.* Washington, D.C.: American Historical Association, 1910.

Turner, Lorenzo. *Africanisms in Gullah Dialect.* Chicago: University of Chicago Press, 1949.

Turnicliff, Edward. *Judicial Cases Concerning American Slavery and the Negro.* 5 vols. Washington, D.C.: Carnegie Institute, 1927–1937.

Vann Gennep, Arnold. *The Rites of Passage.* Chicago: University of Chicago Press, 1960.

Virginia Statutes III (1705), 461.

Wade, Richard. "The Vesey Plot: A Reconstruction." *Journal of Southern History* XXX (May 1964): 143–61.

Wagley, Charles, and Harris, Marvin. *Minorities in the New World: Six Case Studies.* New York: Columbia University Press, 1958.

Washburn, Wilcomb E. *The Indian and the White Man.* Garden City, N.Y.: Doubleday, 1964.

Washington, Booker T. *Up from Slavery.* New York: Doubleday, 1901.

Washington, Joseph R. *Black and White Power Subreption.* Boston: Beacon Press, 1969.

————. *The Politics of God.* New York: Beacon Press, 1969.

Westermann, William L. *The Slave System of Greek and Roman Antiquity.* Philadelphia: Westminster Press, 1955.

Webber, Thomas. *Deep Like a River: Education in the Community 1831–1865.* New York: W.W. Norton, 1978.

Wilbur, Martin. *Slavery in China During the Former Han Dynasty, 106 B.C. – A.D. 25.* Chicago: University of Chicago Press, 1943.

Williams, Chancellor. *The Destruction of Black Civilization.* Chicago: Third World Press, 1976.

Williams, Eric. *Capitalism and Slavery*. Chapel Hill: University of North Carolina Press, 1944.

Williams, L., and Morland, J. *Race, Color and the Young Child*. Chapel Hill: University of North Carolina Press, 1976.

Williams, R.M., Jr. *The Reduction of Inter-Group Tension*. New York: Social Science Research Council Bulletin 57–59, 1947.

Williams, Roger. *Free and Unequal: The Biological Basis of Individual Liberty*. Austin: University of Texas Press, 1953.

Williamson, Joel. *New People: Miscegenation and Mulattoes in the United States*. New York: Free Press, 1980.

Wilson, James Q. *Negro Politics*. New York: Free Press, 1960.

Wilson, Ruth D. "Justification of Slavery, Past and Present." *Phylon*, Fourth Quarter 1958, pp. 408–409.

Wilson, Theodore B. *The Black Codes of the South*. University: University of Alabama Press, 1965.

Wise, Gene. *American Historical Explanations: A Strategy for Sounder Inquiry*. Homewood, Ill.: Dorsey Press, 1973.

Woodson, Carter G. "Beginning of Miscegenation of Whites and Blacks." *Journal of Negro History* XV (January 1930): 217–228.

_____. *Free Negro Heads of Families in the United States in 1830*. Washington, D.C.: Association for the Study of Negro Life and History, 1925.

Woodward, C. Vann. *American Counter-Point: Slavery and Racism*. Boston: Little, Brown, 1971.

_____. *Reunion and the Reaction: The Compromise of 1877 and the End of Reconstruction*. Boston: Little, Brown, 1951.

_____. *The Strange Career of Jim Crow*. New York: Macmillan, 1965.

Woodward, W.E. *A New American History*. New York: Farrar and Rinehart, 1936.

Wright, James M. *The Free Negro in Maryland, 1634–1800*. New York: Columbia University Press, 1921.

Wright, Richard. *Native Son*. New York: Harper and Bros., 1946.

Index